The BEST of Reader's Digest

Reader's Digest

New York / Montreal

CONTENTS

INTRODUCTION

Reader's Digest has long provided a record of the ideas and attitudes of the day. For almost 100 years, the magazine has curated and published stories that uplift, inspire, entertain, and educate. The magazine has included the most engaging writers of the day and showcased funny and heartwarming reader-generated anecdotes along with stories of ordinary people in extraordinary circumstances.

We created this volume of *The Best of Reader's Digest* with the intention of finding more of the stories that readers enjoy most—timeless stories that stick with us or pull at our heartstrings; stories that make us feel connected; stories that are as powerful today as they were when they first appeared, whether that was 50 years ago or just last month.

We pored through the archives to find the stories that make your hearts sing; that make you marvel at the wonder of nature and the strength of the human spirit; and that make you feel connected to people who may live thousands of miles away from you but could easily be your neighbor or your family member. We think you'll be filled with hope as you read about how a newlywed couple in their 70s inspired friends and strangers alike; we hope you'll be in awe of the 9/11 widow who lost her husband but carried his memory and values with her to raise their daughter; and we're sure you'll nod in agreement as you read the words a father writes to his daughter about the responsibility of owning her first car. In addition, we've included memorable and award-winning photographs and laugh-out-loud jokes, readers' true stories, and some bonus material never published in the magazine itself.

Enjoy this volume in the spirit that it is intended—as a collection of uplifting stories that speak to the things that bring us together and give us hope in a chaotic world.

—The Editors of *Reader's Digest*

Lost in the Arctic

by Robert Gauchie

A trusted magazine helps a downed pilot hold on to hope.

When my single engine Beaver aircraft was blown off course and forced down in the winter wilds of northern Canada on February 3, 1967, I had no doubt that one of my fellow bush pilots would soon have me out and winging safely homeward. But then my radio and homing beacons failed, and I had to face the hard truth: I was lost in a blizzard-ridden land, with temperatures to 60 degrees below zero, where searchers would never even think to look.

My first concerns were food and warmth, and though these were far from abundant, I did have enough emergency gear to fend off starvation or death by exposure. But as the endless days dragged into weeks, a more menacing threat overtook me: the dark loneliness that impairs a man's judgment. For I had nothing to do but sit shivering in that derelict of a plane, listening for rescue craft that never came. I began to think that perhaps I should abandon the Beaver—the only shelter and landmark on that whole icy landscape—and wander off in a last desperate effort to find help. Or maybe I should quit fighting altogether and simply close my eyes and die.

I think now that I would have surrendered to the hopelessness of those empty hours had I not unexpectedly come upon a valued friend: a

1

copy of the *Reader's Digest* left behind by some long-forgotten passenger. I read it from front to back, and then I read it again. And I found in it the inspiration, the stimulation, to keep trying. For between those covers was a taste of the sweet world I longed to get back to: its ideas, its faith, its laughter. Through the long days, I read and reread a stirring denial that our God was dead. In the sleepless nights, I remembered touching stories of family life, and suddenly my wife and daughters were very close to me. And so I stayed alive.

And on the 59th day, having survived longer than any other man ever lost in the Arctic, I was found. A passing aircraft spotted me, entirely by chance, and I flew home at last, carrying my few belongings in an old suitcase.

But I carried that copy of the *Reader's Digest* in my hand.

Originally published in the January 1970 issue of *Reader's Digest* magazine.

THE POWER OF A MOTHER'S LOVE

It was the 70s and Women's Lib said I could have it all. Marriage and motherhood could wait. After college, I worked; traveled; learned to fly, scuba dive, and white-water raft. I was 48, however, when I finally married. Too late for that last "bucket list" wish, motherhood. Or so I thought.

My son, Jeff, arrived when I was 60. My hubby Ken's son was 38, six feet tall, and unable to manage his own life anymore due to Huntington's disease. Jeff unknowingly received this incurable genetic neurological disease from his biological mother. From me, he would receive the benefits of a nursing education as well as a mother's love. This sweet, uncomplaining man-child is now in diapers, can't speak, and is spoon-fed. It's never too late to experience the joy and heartache of motherhood in whatever form it takes. Excuse me now. My baby needs me.

—Nan McNamara, *Sun City Center, Florida*

WITH EACH BREATH

There was a first breath, and a smile, to find there is love. I was born to a religion of yoga, where breath is life. I became inspired to sing, where breath is song. I wrote words to challenge those things that don't seem right, where breath is thought. I then took to the stage, where breath is focus. I hear the words of others, where breath is knowledge. I have found passion in the touch of another, where breath is pleasure. I've felt pain and fear and have struggled, where breath is freedom. I have found freedom in friendship and solidarity, where breath is love. My life is made up of these breaths.

—Leah Chandra *Los Angeles, California*

The Cellist of Sarajevo

by Paul Sullivan, from *Hope*

Through his music, he defied the death and destruction that surrounded him.

As a pianist, I was invited to perform with cellist Eugene Friesen at the International Cello Festival in Manchester, England. Every two years, a group of the world's greatest cellists and others devoted to that unassuming instrument—bow makers, collectors, historians–gather for a week of workshops, master classes, seminars, recitals, and parties. Each evening, the 600 or so participants assemble for a concert.

The opening-night performance at the Royal Northern College of Music consisted of works for unaccompanied cello. There on the stage in the magnificent concert hall was a solitary chair. No piano, no music stand, no conductor's podium. This was to be cello music in its purest, most intense form. The atmosphere was supercharged with anticipation and concentration.

The world-famous cellist Yo-Yo Ma was one of the performers that April night in 1994, and there was a moving story behind the musical composition he would play:

On May 27, 1992, in Sarajevo, one of the few bakeries that still had

Sarajevo Opera cellist, Vedran Smailovic

a supply of flour was making and distributing bread to the starving, war-shattered people. At 4 p.m., a long line stretched into the street. Suddenly, a mortar shell fell directly into the middle of the line, killing 22 people and splattering flesh, blood, bone, and rubble.

Not far away lived a 35-year-old musician named Vedran Smailovic. Before the war, he had been a cellist with the Sarajevo Opera, a distinguished career to which he patiently longed to return. But when he saw the carnage from the massacre outside his window, he was pushed past his capacity to absorb and endure any more. Anguished, he resolved to do the thing he did best: make music. Public music, daring music, music on a battlefield.

For each of the next 22 days, at 4 p.m., Smailovic put on his full, formal concert attire, took up his cello, and walked out of his apartment into the midst of the battle raging around him. Placing a plastic chair beside the crater that the shell had made, he played in memory of the dead Albinoni's Adagio in G Minor, one of the most mournful and haunting pieces in the classical repertoire. He played to the abandoned streets, smashed trucks, and burning buildings, and to the terrified people who hid in the cellars while the bombs dropped and bullets flew. With masonry exploding around him, he made his unimaginably courageous stand for human dignity, for those lost to war, for civilization, for compassion, and for peace. Though the shellings went on, he was never hurt.

After newspapers picked up the story of this extraordinary man, an English composer, David Wilde, was so moved that he, too, decided to make music. He wrote a composition for unaccompanied cello, "The Cellist of Sarajevo," into which he poured his own feelings of outrage, love, and brotherhood with Vedran Smailovic.

It was "The Cellist of Sarajevo" that Yo-Yo Ma was to play that evening.

* * *

Ma came out on stage, bowed to the audience, and sat down quietly on the chair. The music began, stealing out into the hushed hall and creating a shadowy, empty universe, ominous and haunting. Slowly it grew into an agonized, screaming, slashing furor, gripping us all before subsiding at last into a hollow death rattle and, finally, back to silence.

When he had finished, Ma remained bent over his cello, his bow resting on the strings. No one in the hall moved or made a sound for a long time. It was as though we had just witnessed that horrifying massacre ourselves.

Finally, Ma looked out across the audience and stretched out his hand, beckoning someone to come to the stage. An indescribable electric shock swept over us as we realized who it was: Vedran Smailovic, the cellist of Sarajevo! Smailovic rose from his seat and walked down the aisle as Ma left the stage to meet him. They flung their arms around each other in an exuberant embrace. Everyone in the hall erupted in a chaotic, emotional frenzy—clapping, shouting, and cheering.

And in the center of it all stood these two men, hugging and crying unashamedly. Yo-Yo Ma, a suave, elegant prince of classical music, flawless in appearance and performance; and Vedran Smailovic, dressed in a stained and tattered leather motorcycle suit. His wild long hair and huge mustache framed a face that looked old beyond his years, soaked with tears and creased with pain.

We were all stripped down to our starkest, deepest humanity at encountering this man who shook his cello in the face of bombs, death, and ruin, defying them all. It was the sword of Joan of Arc—the mightiest weapon of them all.

*   *   *

Back in Maine a week later, I sat one evening playing the piano for the residents of a local nursing home. I couldn't help contrasting this concert with the splendors I had witnessed at the festival. Then I was struck by the profound similarities. With his music, the cellist of Sarajevo had defied death and despair and celebrated love and life. And here we were, a chorus of croaking voices accompanied by a shopworn piano, doing the same thing. There were no bombs and bullets, but there was real pain—dimming sight, crushing loneliness, all the scars we accumulate in our lives—and only cherished memories for comfort. Yet still we sang and clapped.

It was then I realized that music is a gift we all share equally. Whether we create it or simply listen, it's a gift that can soothe, inspire, and unite us, often when we need it most and expect it least.

Originally published in the November 1996 issue of *Reader's Digest* magazine.

Humor Hall of Fame

"It's the shower drain again."

E. LIAN

We Uber drivers never know whom we're going to end up with as a passenger. One day, I was driving over a bridge, the design of which was very confusing.

Completely confounded, I muttered, "I'd love to meet the genius who designed this mess." With that, my passenger extended his hand in my direction and said, "Well, today is your lucky day. My name is Mike, I work for the county engineer's office, and I'm the genius who designed this." Surprisingly, he still gave me a tip.

—PATRICK GRILLIOT
BOWLING GREEN, OHIO

Random thoughts from office drones counting the hours till the weekend.
• Today is the one-year anniversary of this six-week project.
• I keep hoping they'll put the two perfectionists on the same project and they'll correct each other to infinity and stay out of everyone else's way.
• Just once I'd like to spend more time discussing the project on a conference call than we spend asking "Who just joined?"

—MEETINGBOY.COM

Feathered Flight Attendants

We've been sharing the sky with its native aviators since the Wright brothers took off in 1903. Mostly, we come in peace: Roaring engines keep the majority of birds at bay, and pilots do their best to avoid wildlife. When bird strikes do happen—there are about 11,000 in the United States each year—they rarely imperil the plane. (If you're curious, the FAA keeps track of every strike at wildlife.faa.gov.) Astonishingly, even this Delta flight touched down without incident at Reagan National Airport in Washington, DC. Fortunately, the birds were safe that day, too.

Photograph by Andrew Caballero-Reynolds

A Shepherd's Healing Power

by Jo Coudert

Through unconditional love, a unique dog heals a sick teenager, a grieving mother, and troubled kids.

Lana Crawford sat numbly at the kitchen table. Her life in Klamath Falls, Oregon, once so happy, now lay in ruins. Her marriage was over. The two-story yellow house surrounded by lilacs and roses was about to be sold.

A glance at the German shepherd sprawled out on the floor brought fresh tears to Lana's eyes. She thought about what this wondrous animal had meant to her son, Jeremy, in the final days of his life. "Oh, Grizzly," she said softly, "what are we going to do?"

Two years earlier, the unimaginable had happened: Jeremy was found to have a bone cancer called Ewing's sarcoma. Once the teenager had been muscular and tan, filled with energy, a football player. Now he was pale and thin, fighting for life.

Lana gave up her job as a music teacher to devote more time to him. His grownup sister, Susanne, made frequent trips from Seattle to cheer him up. Still, Jeremy's physical pain and fatigue at times overwhelmed their best efforts.

Determined to bring her son some happiness, Lana drove Jeremy to visit Ella Brown, a dog breeder, at a local kennel.

"He's so beautiful," the boy said, taking one German shepherd puppy in his arms. "But why is he whimpering? Doesn't he like me?"

"That's his way of talking," Brown explained. "Once in a while there is a special dog who is a talker. He should belong to a special boy."

Named Grizzly, the dog quickly became attuned to Jeremy's voice, face, and gestures. On the good days, Jeremy threw a football across the yard, and Grizzly would race to intercept it. On the bad days, Jeremy slept fitfully with Grizzly standing guard. If Jeremy invited him, the dog would lie beside him on the bed.

Grizzly sensed when Jeremy was in pain and when he was discouraged. If it was the latter, Grizzly would nose Jeremy's hand and woof deep in his throat until Jeremy laughed. The boy would confide his feelings to Grizzly, who sat happily beside him. Just as Lana had hoped, the dog's unconditional love reinforced Jeremy's inner strength.

For two years, Jeremy seemed to be winning his war against cancer. Then, after he turned 17, tumors were discovered in both lungs. Jeremy's breathing grew labored. The stress of his illness was causing Lana's own health to decline and placing an enormous strain on her marriage.

As Jeremy's condition worsened, Lana began sleeping on the floor beside his bed. The only place for Grizzly to lie in the crowded room was in the curve of Lana's body, and there they dozed through the long nights.

Near the end, Jeremy asked for pen and paper to make his will. "I want you to have Grizzly," he said to his mother. "Maybe there'll be some way you and he can help other kids." Lana nodded, fighting back tears.

On May 17, 1989, Jeremy died in his mother's arms.

*　*　*

In the days following Jeremy's death, Lana lay in bed, unable to face a future without her son. But one afternoon, she heard Grizzly nose open the closet door, grasp something in his mouth, and place it on her pillow. It was her running shoe. He fetched its mate and began woofing.

"I can't, Grizzly," Lana told him. The dog took her sleeve in his mouth and gently tugged, finally drawing her outside. At first, Lana could only bear to go for a block or two, but as Grizzly led her farther and farther, she grew stronger, and she started to heal.

One fall day, they came upon a park where boys were playing football. Lana's heart skipped a beat when she saw one boy, tall and blond like Jeremy. Then she remembered his last request.

Gradually, a plan formed in her mind. At age 38, she decided to enroll at the University of Utah, where she took classes in psychology. Volunteer fieldwork was part of the course load, so Lana proposed taking Grizzly to the pediatric floor at University of Utah Health Sciences Center.

"I want to do more than just visit," Lana told one of her teachers. "He's just an ordinary pet, not trained to do anything special, but I want to use him as part of therapy."

The first day, Lana was nervous as a pediatric nurse led them to the room of a boy with cystic fibrosis. He was crying as a technician drew blood and hooked him up to an IV. The nurse stuck her head into the room and said, "Would you like to meet Grizzly?"

The boy's eyes widened. "A dog! Come here, Grizzly!" He forgot the needles as he tugged at the dog's ears and talked to him. Grizzly responded with his soft, muffled woofs. "He's answering me!" the boy exclaimed. "Can I take him for a walk?"

With the nurse pushing the IV pole and Lana holding the leash, the child started down the hall with Grizzly.

Lana went home that day emotionally exhausted but satisfied as well. Soon Lana and Grizzly were going for weekly visits.

Lana was at a loss to account for how Grizzly seemed to know exactly how to respond to the children, but she reflected that Grizzly grew up loving Jeremy, who had been ill. *That's why he responds to hurt and need. He knows his purpose in life,* she thought.

One day they went to the oncology unit to visit a 17-year-old boy who was losing his vision and muscular control and was severely depressed. Lana caught her breath. The boy looked devastatingly like Jeremy.

"This is Grizzly, the good shepherd," Lana explained, choking back tears. *If I can do this, I can do anything,* she thought.

"Could he lie down here beside me?" the boy asked.

The nurse nodded and moved tubes out of the way and laid a draw-sheet over the bed. Then the 95-pound dog inched himself over until he lay beside the boy, where he stayed, unmoving, until the boy relaxed and fell asleep.

Lana saw that the need for this type of therapy was too great to handle alone and soon formed a nonprofit organization, the Good Shepherd Association, to train handlers and their animals to work in therapeutic settings. The animals were taught to lie still when children climbed on them, to pull wheelchairs, to respond to commands, to remain calm in every situation.

One day Lana took the dog to a center for emotionally troubled children where they met Tammy,* an unkempt 11-year-old girl who had been in and out of 14 homes and centers, had extreme mood swings, and fought with the other children.

Tammy refused to speak to anyone or play with the dog. Midway through the hour, Grizzly stood up, walked into a hallway off the therapy room, and began his gentle "woofing talk."

"What's he doing?" Tammy demanded, anxiously.

"Maybe he's asking you to come over and see him," Lana said.

The girl shook her head violently, picked up a doll, and began twisting its arms and legs. But as Grizzly continued to talk, curiosity got the better of her, and she sidled into the hall. At first, Lana worried that she might hit or kick Grizzly, but once Tammy was alone with him, her voice softened, and she began to confide in the dog. "I'm scared," she said. I'm lonely. Nobody wants me."

Over the next two years, Lana and Grizzly visited the troubled girl every other week. When she was rough, he moved away with quiet dignity. When she was sad, he lay beside her and woofed encouragingly. Often Tammy would not tell her therapist what was troubling her, but she would let him overhear her talking to Grizzly.

"She used to throw tantrums around the other kids," Tammy's

therapist told Lana one day. "But never with Grizzly; his love seems to calm her. For the first time, she's able to trust, and slowly her behavior with the other kids is improving."

One day the training coordinator remarked that Grizzly's eyes did not look quite right, so Lana took him to a veterinarian. He said that Grizzly had been blind for years.

"How is it that he still seems to know what to do?" Lana asked Ella Brown.

"Grizzly is special," Brown replied. "He sees with his heart, not his eyes."

Being blind has not curbed Grizzly's effectiveness. With the physically handicapped or the emotionally troubled, he continues to bring the healing touch of unconditional acceptance.

*   *   *

Recently, Lana and Grizzly attended a dinner to honor volunteers at the center for emotionally troubled children. As the kids' sweet voices soared in song, an attractive girl came out on stage. Tammy, the once scared, unkempt youth who had been reluctant to speak, thanked Lana and Grizzly for all they had done.

Lana, with tears in her eyes, rose to speak. "Once there was a special boy named Jeremy," she told the crowd. "He had to leave us, but he asked Grizzly and me to try to find a way to help other children. Jeremy would be pleased tonight to know that Grizzly, his good shepherd, is your special dog, too."

Lana caught Tammy's warm gaze and held it, thinking how many children Grizzly had loved and helped. She looked at the sightless animal standing beside the child he had helped heal. *You've helped me heal, too, Grizzly.*

Originally published in the December 1996 issue of *Reader's Digest* magazine.

M 1383 9
CLEVELAND
19. 5'6: 134
MAY 27 1975
Cleveland Police

Exonerated!

by Kyle Swenson, from *Cleveland Scene*

After a crime, a lie, and life sentences came vindication, ending the longest wrongful incarceration in American history.

Before they threw him in chains, he was a gutsy kid with wandering feet.

The Cleveland Museum of Art was a favorite. He'd go alone, even though he was only six. Entry was free, and Ricky Jackson's shoes would squeak down the marble hallways hung with Dutch masters and Monets. He always stopped in the Armor Court to look at the polished knights; here was a world as strange as the places on *Star Trek*, the show his stepfather watched on TV.

He kicked around the streets, too. He'd jump on the bus and go as far as his change took him. His family—mom, stepdad, two brothers, and a sister—moved as well, from house to house, and eventually they ended up on Arthur Avenue. One house down was a family with a son around Ricky's age. Ronnie was a kid so tiny that everyone called him Bitzie, as in itsy-bitsy. Bitzie's older brother, Wiley, was known as Buddy. As teens, the trio became inseparable, playing chess and tooling around in Buddy's Sebring.

By the mid-1970s, Ricky was punching in regularly at a restaurant. Bitzie was doing shifts as a porter, and he'd completed training in welding. Wiley was in the National Guard and working at a clothing store. They were good kids easing into that age when they were starting to figure it all out.

That life came to a close in the fall of 1975, when Ricky Jackson along with Bitzie and Buddy—Ronnie and Wiley Bridgeman—were sentenced to death. A white salesman had been robbed at a corner store, shot, and killed. The police said Ronnie and Ricky beat the man before Ricky pulled the trigger and Wiley drove them away. No physical evidence linked them to the crime, but a witness, 12-year-old Edward Vernon, told police he'd seen it all.

Ricky, Ronnie, and Wiley were 18, 17, and 20 years old, respectively. They were innocent—but it would take nearly 40 years to prove it.

*　*　*

In November 2001, the past hit Edward Vernon like a falling anvil. He was at the desk at the City Mission, checking the IDs of the homeless men shuffling in. He overheard a stranger explaining he'd just paroled out after 25 years for a 1975 murder he didn't commit. When the man showed his ID, Vernon stared at the name: Wiley Bridgeman.

By 2001, Vernon's life was straightening out. His adult years had been clouded by cocaine and marijuana; he did jail time after a drug bust. But that was behind him. Now here was Wiley, one of the three he'd sent to prison, in front of him a quarter century later.

The next day, Vernon approached Wiley in a group therapy session, blubbering. The men talked. Wiley told Vernon they should go to a TV station with the truth. Vernon wasn't so sure. He kept his distance, and Wiley moved into an apartment. After an argument with his parole officer in 2002, Wiley went back to prison. As far as Vernon was concerned, the door had swung shut on the past again.

*　*　*

Home was the last place Ronnie Bridgeman wanted to go when he paroled out in 2003. (Because he was identified as the shooter, Ricky had difficulty getting parole.) "Cleveland was no longer my town," Ronnie said recently. "It represented everything that was ugly and hurtful. It had nothing to do with the people I knew per se, but it was the people who were supposed to protect and serve. They ruined it for me."

Inside, he'd converted to Islam and changed his name to Kwame Ajamu. "I decided Ronnie Bridgeman should be left there in prison," he says. Returning home made that hard. "Every day of my life, it seemed like I would run into someone from my past, someone who knew Ronnie Bridgeman but who didn't know Kwame Ajamu."

He put together a life. He married a woman named LaShawn in 2004; he found work at the County Board of Elections. Things were good, but the past kept tugging at

I expected anger from someone who'd been wrongly put away, but Kwame had learned to metabolize the injustice.

him. "For a long time, I just felt like I had abandoned those guys because they had let me out," Kwame said. "It was killing me, man. That motivated me every day."

He called people from the old neighborhood, asking if they remembered anything about the 1975 incident, and contacted lawyers about mounting a challenge to the convictions. Lawyers, however, cost money, which Kwame didn't have. I was a writer at *Cleveland Scene,* the city's alternative newsweekly, when a lawyer told me about Kwame. I went to meet him one day at a coffee shop. He was sitting with thousands of pages of court documents in a neat stack.

I expected anger from someone who'd been wrongly put away, but Kwame had learned to metabolize the injustice. He was remarkably empathic, even about Edward Vernon. "He was just a kid then," he said.

As Kwame explained it, the testimony that led to their convictions went as follows: On May 19, 1975, Vernon claimed he'd left school early and boarded a city bus home. When he arrived, he saw Ricky and Ronnie struggling with Harold Franks outside the Fairmount Cut-Rate store. They splashed the man with acid and beat him before Ricky shot him twice. The two sped off in a green car, which Vernon said he'd seen Wiley driving earlier.

All lies, Kwame said. On the day of the crime, he and Ricky played basketball in a park in the morning before heading to the Bridgeman house. Kwame and Ricky spent the afternoon at the chessboard until they heard there was trouble at the corner store. Wiley was washing his car outside. The boys went to see what was going on.

I did six months of reporting, which backed up Kwame's account. I found witnesses who said they were with Vernon when he was supposedly witnessing the crime. Others remembered being with the Bridgemans and Ricky at the time they were allegedly robbing the store and murdering Franks. None of them was approached by the police during the investigation nor had any of them come forward with their information.

My reporting showed that the men's convictions were based on Vernon's improbable, inconsistent testimony. Vernon, however, did not want to talk. "As far as I'm concerned, it's a done deal," he said in 2011 after I finally tracked him down.

Months of work built up to June 8, 2011, the day of my story's publication. Then, nothing. Ricky and Wiley were still inside. "It actually crushed me," Kwame said.

Cleveland's Emmanuel Christian Center is one of the steady pulses of life in an area of gutted blocks. Vernon has bowed his head there on Sundays for the past six years. Pastor Anthony Singleton, a lanky, dapper man of God, likes to park himself in the lives of his 200 or so parishioners. As soon as Vernon began attending, Singleton struck up a relationship. Drink, smoke, and vulgarity never passed Vernon's lips, and he knew his Scriptures and ministered to the sick. Still, "there was always this black cloud over him," Singleton said.

Bad luck dogged the man. "In a two-year period, he lost, like, two cars and three jobs," the pastor said. "I'm just saying to myself, 'This is not making any sense.'" Then there was the crying. Vernon often burst into tears at services. During the year, Singleton held shut-ins for the congregation's men, all-nighters of spiritual searching, where Vernon wept dusk to dawn.

One day Singleton answered the phone in his office. I was asking to speak to Vernon. Singleton said he'd relay my message, and he was curious about why I was calling. He asked Vernon and got the brush-off.

After my story appeared, Singleton read it. When he tried to nudge Vernon into talking, Vernon refused. Singleton knew he couldn't push it with his parishioner. But he also couldn't leave it alone.

In early 2013, Vernon was hit with skyscraping blood pressure that put him in the hospital. During the same period, an attorney from the Ohio Innocence Project called Singleton, asking to speak with Vernon about the 1975 case. One Sunday after church, Singleton trekked to the hospital and found Vernon alone. "I have something to talk to you about," the pastor said. "I've been praying about it and watching you." He explained to Vernon that he'd read my *Cleveland Scene* story. "I want to know if you're ready to talk about it."

Vernon was out of the bed like someone had cracked a starter's pistol. Arms wrapped around Singleton, he wept. The words tumbled out. Vernon confessed to Singleton. And in April 2013, in a sworn affidavit taken by the Ohio Innocence Project, he admitted he'd not only lied about witnessing the murder, but he also claimed he had been forced to do so by the police.

Vernon told the lawyers that he'd gone home on May 19, 1975, on his school bus, not earlier as he'd testified. While the bus was pulling up to his stop, Vernon heard gunshots ringing from the Cut-Rate. By the time he rushed over, Franks was gasping his last breaths. He and a friend, Tommy Hall,

Months of work built up to June 8, 2011, the day of my story's publication. Then, nothing.

walked home. Hall told Vernon he knew who did it: "Ricky, Bitzie, and Buddy."

Vernon returned to the scene later, and when an officer asked if anyone had information, Vernon offered the boys' names. "I don't exactly know why I went up to the police at first," he said later. "I think I just wanted to be helpful. You have to understand, I was 12 years old at the time. I thought I was doing the right thing."

According to Vernon, when detectives spoke with him in the days after the murder, they gave him details gleaned from other witnesses—the number of assailants, the weapons used, the make and model of the car. After police arrested Ronnie, Wiley, and Ricky, Vernon went to the station to look at a lineup.

He failed to make an ID, and a detective took him into a back room. "He got really loud and angry and started yelling at me and called me a liar," Vernon stated in his affidavit. "He was slamming his hands on the table and pushing things around, calling me this and that. I was frightened and crying. The detective said that I was too young to go to jail but that he would arrest my parents for perjury because I was backing out. My mom was sick at that time, and that really scared me."

The police wrote a statement, which Vernon signed. After the first trial, he was given a copy of his testimony to study for subsequent hearings. This testimony was all that pinned the murder to Ronnie, Wiley, and Ricky. What's troubling is how much other evidence pointed elsewhere.

The day after the murder, the FBI contacted Cleveland detectives with names from an informant. The list included brothers Arthur and Willie King, who had been tied to earlier stickups. The police also traced a green car matching the description of the getaway vehicle to 23-year-old Ishmael Hixon. A woman from the neighborhood told police she believed her 16-year-old son, Paul Gardenshire, was involved. Witnesses didn't come through with an ID. But in June 1975, after the arrests, another resident fingered Gardenshire. He claimed that the teen had a .38, the caliber of gun used in the murder, and drove a green car, but he was never charged.

* * *

Mad doesn't begin to touch it, nor does angry. Despair doesn't suffice. Use as many synonyms as you want, but words can't cage the feeling: One moment, you're a young man, life stretching ahead. Then you're in a cell. For no reason. When Jackson and the Bridgemans went to prison, each coped in his own way.

Wiley poured himself into his legal case. He won a retrial in 1977 but was again given the same sentence. At one point, he was 20 days away from execution before his sentence was commuted to life in prison. His mental state deteriorated until he was diagnosed with schizophrenia. In a way, Wiley's breakdown helped save his brother. Ronnie focused on his older sibling, worrying about his state and keeping it together for him.

Vernon's testimony was all that pinned the crime to the boys, even though evidence pointed elsewhere.

As for Ricky, "I dealt with it badly," he said. "I was acting out, showing aggression, having this I-don't-care attitude." He was racked with anxiety, his blood pressure geysered high, and a pain chewed at his stomach. It went on for years. What turned him around was the company he was keeping. He saw lifers who had let bitterness burn away everything else. He realized he couldn't let rage sit in the driver's seat. "It was a gradual thing," he told me. "It just didn't hurt as bad. But the truth is, the anger doesn't disappear."

He read all the time. Science fiction was a favorite; it went back to watching *Star Trek* with his stepdad. "As bleak as my reality was, I could always fantasize about the future or pick up a book and be on another planet or be in another time." Ricky also enrolled in classes, and he found a passion for gardening. He liked the whole process—seed to flower, the care and attention and detail—and grew poinsettias for the annual prison sale.

And he maintained his innocence. Five times, he was up for parole. Each time, he'd be considered for release if he admitted what he'd done and expressed remorse. Each time, he'd say he didn't do it. Over the decades, Ricky wrote to organizations that dealt with wrongful incarceration, including the Ohio Innocence Project.

The Ohio Innocence Project operates out of the University of Cincinnati's law school, and it had a file open on Ricky's case for years. Although the law students felt the inmate was innocent, the case lacked a sturdy legal basis. Vernon, however, was a game changer.

Last March, the Ohio Innocence Project filed a motion for new trial with the Cuyahoga County Common Pleas Court on behalf of Ricky

Jackson. It argued that Vernon's recantation was evidence that would have changed the original trial. The attorneys also filed a motion for post-conviction relief on the basis that Jackson's constitutional rights had been violated in 1975 because the defense didn't know about the pressure placed on Vernon to cooperate.

In a letter Ricky sent me in the following months, his response to the news was gut-wrenching. "Honestly, though, I doubt this will ever be over entirely. How do you shake off something that has been a part of your life for so long?" he wrote from prison. "As much as I might long for some semblance of a 'normal life,' there are certain realities that I have experienced throughout this whole ordeal that have so profoundly changed the way I look at everything and everybody, I simply have to accept the fact that I will never be happy or completely whole again. They broke something inside of me."

He also knew the odds were against him. Exoneration in wrongful conviction cases is rare: In 2013, 87 people nationwide were cleared of crimes. Ohio has an incentive to fight claims since it compensates wrongfully imprisoned individuals some $40,000 a year, as well as pays their court costs and lost wages; the state is also open to legal action by exonerees.

* * *

Ironically, Ricky's case landed in the courtroom of Richard McMonagle. His father, George McMonagle, had presided over the original 1975 trial. As Judge McMonagle's courtroom filled for Jackson's trial on the morning of November 17, 2014, Vernon—a shrunken man in his 50s—entered. At the defendant's table, Ricky, 57, his hands and feet in chains, watched the witness cross the room to take the stand.

The defense attorney took Vernon through the day of the crime and his encounters with the police. He admitted that he had not seen the crime and had not picked Ricky and Wiley out of a lineup. After that, he testified, he'd been threatened. "[The detective] said, 'We'll fix it,'" Vernon said, words trickling out between tears. "After that, they took a statement from me that I was scared, that's why I didn't pick them out of the lineup. But

"The English language doesn't have the words to express how I'm feeling right now," said Ricky Jackson, here with his lawyers on November 21, the day of his release.

I wasn't scared. I didn't pick them out because I knew they didn't do it."

Ricky's attorney, Brian Howe, asked Vernon whether he had seen Ronnie Bridgeman, Wiley Bridgeman, or Ricky Jackson tussling with Franks. No, no, no, answered Vernon.

"How did you feel about testifying about something that you knew wasn't true?" Howe asked.

"I felt really bad about it. Guilty about what I was lying about. I carried all of that," Vernon said.

Ricky's hands were clasped to his face with his eyes shut tight, as the truth was spoken. *Finally,* he thought.

Vernon's stint on the stand ended the next day, and the courtroom was largely empty as the clock swung around to 2:15 that Tuesday afternoon. Suddenly, several lawyers from the state marched in with Cuyahoga county prosecutor Tim McGinty bringing up the rear.

"We are waiving final argument on the issue," McGinty began. "The state, in light of the evidence produced by the defense at this hearing, and the total recantation of the key witness, hereby drops our opposition for a motion for a new trial.

"The state concedes the obvious; it is no longer in a position to retry the case. And as all key witnesses that might produce any collateral evidence are no longer living, we do so fully recognizing that the result will be the eventual release of Mr. Jackson and the other codefendant. If the court does grant their motion, which we no longer oppose, we will move for a dismissal today."

There was a pause as the words slid into place: Ricky was getting out.

"All right," McMonagle announced. "Mr. Jackson, we're going to get you back here on Friday, just so that all the paperwork is done."

"Thank you, sir. Thank you. Thank you," Ricky cried, before burying a sobbing head in his hands. When he came up for air, he shook hands with his legal team. Someone pulled out a phone, asking Ricky who he wanted to call. From memory, he recited Kwame's number. "Hello ... Who is this? ... This is Ricky ... Hey, it's over, man ... It's over, bro, I'm coming home ... Friday, man. Friday. Friday ... Be here to get me. Please ... Let everybody know ... I love you."

On Friday, Kwame worked the pedal with a heavy foot as he and his wife, LaShawn, drove to Ricky's 9 a.m. hearing. He hadn't slept in three days. His brother, Wiley, had been brought to Cleveland on the judge's order, so he might get out as well.

Inside the courtroom, the guards led in Ricky Jackson. His prison jumper was gone, and he was wearing dress slacks and a zip-up argyle sweater. A smile spread across his face, revealing perfect white teeth. "Life is full of small victories," Judge McMonagle said before closing Ricky's legal case. "This is a big one."

An hour later, Wiley Bridgeman walked free as well.

Ricky paced the holding cell as paperwork was stamped. More waiting in a lifetime of waiting. He didn't know it, but 16 floors below, cameras and reporters clogged the hall where he'd soon take his first free steps. According to the National Registry of Exonerations, Jackson's 39 years is the longest wrongful incarceration term to end in release in American history.

The three boys from Arthur Avenue met at a nearby hotel, all together for the first time in 39 years. Now men, they embraced. Kwame's wife, LaShawn, stepped forward. "Hey there, brother," she said before hugging Ricky.

Lunch was at Red Lobster. Ricky, Kwame, and Wiley bulldozed their feasts. Someone ordered a glass of champagne for Ricky. "Tastes like manna from heaven," he announced.

That night, although they were all exhausted, they drove around the city until 2 a.m. They rolled through their old neighborhood, including Arthur Avenue, abandoned now and drowned in shadow. For Ricky, it was like sci-fi, like getting off one of those ships in *Star Trek*, confronting a strange new world.

Originally published in the May 2015 issue of *Reader's Digest* magazine.

All three men were awarded $18 million in a 2020 settlement agreement. Jackson started a business that refurbishes buildings around Cleveland and speaks publicly about his time in prison. Ajamu also speaks, calling for the abolishment of the death penalty. Bridgeman has continued to run into legal troubles; in 2019 he was charged for a fatal hit and run.

FACES OF AMERICA

The Lucky Couple

"People often ask me when I first knew I was in love with Maureen," says Lucky Cole of Ochopee, Florida. "I tell them I've always been in love with Maureen—it just took me over 30 years to find her."

Photograph by Glenn Glasser

The Picture-Perfect Family

"[We met at a] tragic Hollywood party by a pool at the Roosevelt Hotel," says Channon Roe, in Ojai, California. "She was talking to a palm tree. I told her she was absolutely gorgeous."

"You've got to learn to fight well," notes Bianca. "We're the best of friends; we have exactly the same interests but completely different strengths. Then you get the glue, and his name is Marlon."

Photograph by Glenn Glasser

90-DAY WONDER

My life pivots around a form letter I received in the mail in 1980. The letter was addressed to "Recent College Graduate" and held out the opportunity to attend the Air Force's Officer Training School. If I completed the training, I would receive my commission and become what was known as a 90-Day Wonder.

I don't know how they got my name and address, I don't know why I just didn't toss the letter, and I don't know why I followed through to become an officer. My family was astounded by my decision. Though I felt a sense of calling, it was easier for me to tell them I wanted to see the world.

After more than 30 years, my mother still hasn't forgiven me for leaving home. But she still takes pleasure in reminding me about my first exotic assignment, to Rapid City, South Dakota.

—Daniel Campion *APO, AP*

MEDIATOR'S MASTERPIECE

My dad loved his 1940s Emerson Electric fan that stood almost three feet tall. My mom was on a mission to get rid of it. She would wait for my father to leave. As soon as his car turned the corner, she would carry the fan out to the curb. But after my mother left for work, my father would drive back and return the fan to his workroom. To bring peace, I channeled my inner Jackson Pollock. I splattered paint all over the fan's thick metal blades. The final product was a masterpiece, at least in my mother's eyes.

—Amanda Furr *San Antonio, Texas*

The Newlyweds

by Martha Weinman Lear

Everyone loves the sweet, hope-filled
optimism of second-time-around love.

Lately, we've been bringing joy to total strangers.

How? Easy. We got married.

It began like this: One icy day last winter, we headed down to the bureau of licenses in lower Manhattan. There was a security guard at the door, a big, beefy fellow, and Albert asked him where to go for a license.

"What kind of license?" the guard said.

"Marriage," Albert said.

Marriage! The guard stared at our faces, which clearly belonged (still do) to a pair of septuagenarians. And then he went totally gaga.

"You folks are getting married? Fan-tastic!" Pulled off his cap and waved it in the frigid air. Took off a glove, grabbed Albert's hand in his massive paw.

"You've made my day! Hey, Mike, come over here. Get this! These folks are getting married!" Mike also went gaga.

We went to buy a wedding band. The saleswoman looked at Albert, looked at me, and looked uncertain. "For ... your daughter?" she asked cautiously.

"For us," Albert said.

"For you? Oooh-ooh! I just love it. Helen! Stacy! Listen!" Helen, who was maybe 40, and Stacy, who looked like a high-schooler, loved it too.

It kept happening. The florist, the wine merchant, the cake-maker for our small family wedding... strangers all. At first we couldn't figure it out. Why were people going bananas about the marriage of a pair of total strangers?

*　　*　　*

Soon after the ceremony, we went to a party where we were introduced to a woman as newlyweds, and she said, "Oh, my goodness!" Hands clasped to bosom, dreamy smile. "You've made me so happy. I could cry." And, in fact, her eyes brimmed over.

Now we got it. How could we not? It had nothing to do with us, really (oh, sure, with the way we looked; but beyond that, nothing). It was all about themselves. Somehow, this marriage made them feel good about themselves—about their own hopes that might not yet have been fulfilled and that perhaps they had begun to think might never be fulfilled. Especially in the department of love.

I checked out our theory with our longtime friend, Dr. Ethel Person, the noted Manhattan psychiatrist and psychoanalyst. "Oh, no," she said. "You're exactly right. Exactly. There is such a powerful bias in this country toward believing that over a certain age, unless you're with someone, you'll never be with anyone. For people to see a pair like you opens up new possibilities for themselves. You become a wordless message that there can be new beginnings, second chances all through the life cycle."

But it is not just about love. We are also talking about work, friends, family connections, new ambitions, new adventures—as Dr. Person says, "renewal in every way."

It is sweet stuff, renewal—especially when unexpected. And I certainly did not expect it.

I had been widowed for many years when Albert came along. To tell the truth, there had been other men in those years. Fine men, worthy of loving, but never, as it happened, any I did love or wanted to share the rest of my life with. Which was okay. I had those pleasant romances, I had my work, my cherished friends, I could have gone on like that and been just fine. But face it: Love is more. Love is bigger. Love is other.

Then I went one evening to the home of friends for dinner. Table set for six (my favorite dinner-party number, the coziest, absolutely the best for conversation), and the sixth was the proverbial tall, handsome stranger—lanky, cute gray Vandyke beard, somewhat austere.

It was not a fix-up. He was a recent widower, "a basket case," my hosts told me sotto voce. They hoped to draw him out.

At the table, someone asked how long ago his wife had died. Eight months, he said. And suddenly, with no warning whatsoever, I found myself catapulted back through time to when I had been just eight months widowed, to precisely how that had felt, and I lost it. I began to cry, not decorously but loudly, pungently, the for-heaven's-sake-go-blow-your-nose kind of crying, and I mumbled my apologies and ran to another room.

He followed me. It stunned me then, and stuns me still, that this man who bore such grief of his own should come to comfort me. He was no longer austere. He sat down beside me, gave me his handkerchief, peered into my face, and said, "I know, I know."

It made a powerful, instant connection. It enabled us to bypass the usual getting-to-know-you stuff, because people who've had the experience of losing a beloved one already do know one another in a special, intimate way—a way those who've never mourned really can't understand.

He called the next week to invite me to dinner. It was an awkward call. ("Remember," he said later, "I hadn't asked a woman for a date in 40 years. What if you'd said no?" As for myself, all through that long week, I had been thinking: *Damn it, why doesn't he call? Doesn't he want that handkerchief back?*) But from the first evening together, it was a total comfort zone.

We became An Item, which seemed to please our families and friends. ("My grandpa has a girlfriend," his six-year-old granddaughter told her neighbors.) After a year—ah, impetuous youth!–we combined households. My closest friends gave a party for us in the apartment I was leaving. Swell party, warm toasts. But it was this past winter, when we decided to marry—well, that's when everyone got really twinkly. Including the butcher, the baker, the candlestick-maker. Everyone.

I have been thinking about this a lot. We all love love, of course. But I suspect that what everyone loves even more is second-time-around love. It seems to speak to each observer in a more personal way. I look into the pleasure-glazed eyes of strangers and I think, *This makes you feel good, does it? Terrific. Be my guest.*

Originally published in the February 2005 issue of *Reader's Digest* magazine.

Martha and Albert still call New York City home. She has continued writing, including for national publications such as Reader's Digest. *She is the author of* Heartsounds *and* Echoes of Heartsounds.

Speared Alive

by Chris Bohjalian

*Had John White survived the fall
only to face a slower, more terrifying death?*

From his perch high on a steel girder, Tim Marlow gazed at the construction pit below. It was a little past one o'clock on October 1, 1990, and the weather was warm, even for Charleston, South Carolina. That morning, the crew had finished sinking rows of one-inch-thick, six-foot-high steel spikes—called "rebars"—into the hole to serve as the skeleton of the future office building's parking garage.

Marlow watched his brother-in-law, John White, approach the pit. The two men were part of a construction crew from Georgia working this site. Not only was Marlow married to White's sister, but the men were good friends. However, while Marlow's marriage was happy, his friend's was troubled. John and Betty had been separated for four months. That wasn't surprising, Marlow thought. They had married in their teens and, at 25, John still envied the carefree life of his single friends. The father of two boys, with a third child on the way, he hadn't been taking his responsibilities as a family man seriously enough. Marlow believed the Whites still cared for each other, but lately he had begun to fear they'd never reconcile.

He now saw White, at the edge of the 20-foot-deep pit, toss a box of chalk down to crew superintendent Clifford Brown. As White turned away from the edge, he slipped on the sandy embankment. His hands groped for something to hold on to.

Horrified, Marlow watched as White fell headfirst toward the rebars below. The muffled thud of his body slamming into the poles sounded like a watermelon falling off the back of a truck.

He's dead! Marlow thought to himself. *Oh, God, he's dead!* Marlow prayed for a miracle as he rapidly shinnied down the scaffolding to the pit floor.

Clifford Brown was no more than a yard away when he saw John White hit the rebars. The rods pierced the young man's body and held him, impaled, four feet off the ground. Brown instinctively turned away, afraid to see a dead body. He had barely taken a step toward the construction trailer to phone for help when he was jolted by a voice behind him: "Don't leave me here! Help me down!"

Brown turned in amazement. John White was alive and conscious.

"I can't get you down, John. The rods ... the rods have run through you," he said haltingly.

White's eyes widened. "No! Oh, please, no!" he cried in disbelief, grasping the rebar in his chest. Incredibly, he felt no pain. Brown went to him and extended his arms under White's body to hold him up.

Tim Marlow ran up, shouting at the workers who were beginning to gather. "Somebody call 911!" Then he locked arms with Brown to form a cradle under White.

Marlow could now see his brother-in-law's wounds from close up. White hung sideways on three separate rebar spikes. One speared his right thigh; another ran through his left leg near the groin and came out his lower back; the third entered the side of his neck just above the collarbone and pierced his chest. There was little bleeding. Marlow wondered if the rebars themselves were sealing the wounds.

As the two men held White in their arms, he said to them, "Tell my mother I love her. Tell Betty and the boys they're the last people I thought of before I died."

Marlow swallowed hard. "You're not going to die," he assured his friend. "Tell them you love them yourself." He tightened his grip on Brown's elbows.

The wail of sirens came from the street above, and Marlow saw firefighters racing toward them across the construction pit. "Help's coming," he said, trying to sound confident. But the astonishment on the rescuers' faces told him they, too, thought White's chances were slim.

"I'm going to die here, aren't I?" White asked.

"Don't think about dying! Think about coaching Shane's Little League team someday!" Marlow answered, referring to White's older son. But he knew no words could divert the man's attention from the spikes.

Two firefighters joined Marlow and Brown, locking their arms under White's hips. "The ambulance is on its way," one said.

Charleston County paramedic Dick Edwards and his crew were dropping off a patient at a city hospital when the radio dispatcher directed them to a construction site

"Fastest way through those bars is with an acetylene torch."

where a worker had fallen onto rebars. Eight years before, Edwards had seen a victim after such a fall, and the image was still clear: a dark-haired young construction worker, two spikes through his chest. He had died instantly.

As Edwards pushed through the crowd, he stared in disbelief. It was the other case all over again, he thought—but this man was alive! He made immediate eye contact to keep the victim from staring down at the spikes piercing him.

"We're going to get you down in no time," Edwards told White while trying to figure out how. His partner checked White's vital signs, and Edwards began to assess the wounds. Although there was very little blood, he saw that the spikes in the man's thighs were near the main femoral arteries. If these were severed, White could bleed to death in minutes. Just as serious, the spike in White's chest appeared to run just past his heart. Somehow, Edwards thought, they had to get White down without jostling those rods.

Suddenly, he heard a voice over his shoulder. "Fastest way through those bars is with an acetylene torch." It was site foreman Danny Presson.

Edwards considered how the steel bars would conduct the heat. Would they literally cook White's insides? But he also thought the vibration of a high-speed power saw might be even more dangerous.

"Do you have a hose?" he asked.

Presson nodded. As construction workers ran for the tanks that fueled the torch, he began dousing the rebars with water. Knowing that sparks would fly in all directions, he also sprayed the pants of the men holding White.

"Cut at the base, where the rebar enters the cement," Edwards directed. Although it meant they would need to trim the bars a second time before White could be loaded into an ambulance, it was impossible to cut closer to him while he was in such a precarious position, caged in by the rebars.

Presson knelt with the torch in his hands. He counted at least seven

Even the slightest extra movement could prove fatal. spikes he'd need to cut between him and the ones on which White hung. A firefighter grasped each rebar in turn, with a bare hand, ready to call out if he felt the rod heating up. Despite years of experience, Presson had never been so nervous in his life.

"They're about to start cutting," Marlow told his friend. White's lips were turning a deep blue, and he was having trouble breathing.

As the torch sliced through each spike, Tim Marlow thought of all the times his family had shared with the Whites—afternoons waterskiing at a nearby lake, card games after dinner. Was it possible John would never be with them again?

He heard White start to speak, his tired voice sounding as if he was preparing once and for all to die. "Tell Mom I love her. And Betty. And the boys. Tell…"

"No! You're going to tell them yourself!" Marlow said, cutting him off. The idea that this accident had helped White see, at the price of his life, what mattered to him most just didn't seem fair.

Finally, Presson was ready for the final, most difficult cut—the spike in John's chest. Even the slightest extra movement could prove fatal. The rescuers braced a body board against White's back, ready to rotate him onto the board the moment the rebar was cut.

The superheated flame went through the last spike like a power saw. White screamed in pain as it came loose and pressed against the inside of his chest.

"Grab it!" Edwards yelled. A firefighter held the bar in place as

Marlow tightened his grip around White's body.

"You're fine, John, you're fine," Marlow told him, trying to control his own panic.

He helped the crew carry White to a pile of plywood ten feet away, where paramedics began dispensing intravenous fluids. Then Marlow pulled a paramedic aside. "I'm going to call the family," he said. His efforts to boost his friend's morale had drained him, but he ran for the phone in the construction trailer.

It had been close to 40 minutes since White had fallen. Edwards was holding one of the young man's wrists, and he could feel how clammy the skin had become. "We're going to have you in the ambulance any second now," he told the fading White.

They would have to rush to trim the rebars close to White's body. Charleston County Fire and Rescue Squad volunteer Chuck Reynolds, who had experience with acetylene torches, took over from Presson.

Paramedics covered White with fire-retardant bunker coats. Firefighter Raymond Lloyd wrapped a wet rag around his hand and grasped the rebar in White's left leg. He kept a steady trickle of water from the hose on the bar as Reynolds swiftly cut off a two-foot section.

"Did that feel okay?" Edwards asked White.

The man nodded, and Edwards motioned Reynolds to proceed. Quickly, the paramedic sliced the rebar in the other leg and moved on to the one that pierced White's neck and chest.

"You're going to feel the sparks this time," Edwards warned.

Again White nodded, and Reynolds began cutting. Sparks flew. Edwards could see welts forming under White's chin where the bunker coats couldn't protect him.

Finally, Reynolds shut off the flame. The last length of rebar had been trimmed. Between 12 and 18 inches of steel still protruded from White's neck and each of his legs, but now he could be placed inside the ambulance.

"All right, let's move!" Edwards ordered, and the construction crew and firefighters carried White on the body board up from the foundation pit. As they prepared to slide him into the ambulance, Marlow returned. "Your mom's on her way. And Betty knows you love her," he told his brother-in-law.

At the Medical University of South Carolina Hospital, White was rushed to surgery. Dr. E. Douglas Norcross, director of the trauma unit, worked on the rebars that sliced through White's legs, while thoracic surgeon Thomas Riggs attacked the bar in his chest.

Just as Edwards had feared, the spikes through White's legs were perilously close to severing femoral arteries; the one in the left actually touched the critical blood vessel. The rebar through his chest had nearly cut the superior vena cava, one of the principal veins surrounding the heart. The two surgeons worked together, and finally, after 3 hours and 35 minutes, the operation was completed.

White's pelvis and collarbone had been broken, but his injuries could have been much worse had the rescue team not been so careful to prevent the rebars from moving inside White's body at the accident site. "The work of the EMS people and the firefighters was amazing," Dr. Norcross said. "I've never seen anything like it."

John White remembers the surge of emotion he felt in the hospital when he heard his wife's voice on the phone. "I couldn't stop crying," he recalls. "I told her I loved her, and I'd be home soon."

After ten days in the hospital, he was strong enough to return to Georgia. When Betty saw him in the doorway—thin and pale, his arm in a sling—he looked so frail that she had to fight the urge to cry. For a long moment, they stood holding each other. Then their two boys—Shane, five, and Matt, three—raced to their father, and the family was together again.

Today, three years later, White has recovered from his injuries and gained a new life. Reconciled with Betty, he has found work that allows him to be home every night. Their third son, Danny, was born in January 1991. Today White coaches the Little League baseball and football teams of both Shane and Matt.

Best of all, Tim Marlow was proved right. John White can now tell his family every day that he loves them.

Originally published in the December 1993 issue of *Reader's Digest* magazine.

A Boy and His Dinosaur

by Dave Barry

*Even a baby diplodocus
has to grow up sometime.*

We have been deeply into dinosaurs for some time now, with many plastic dinosaurs around the house. Sometimes I think we have more plastic dinosaurs than plastic robots, if you can imagine.

This is my son's doing. Robert got into dinosaurs when he was about three, as many children do. It's a power thing: Children like the idea of creatures that were much bigger and stronger than mommies and daddies. If a little boy is doing something bad, such as pouring apple juice onto the television remote-control device, Mommy and Daddy can simply snatch the boy up and carry him to his room. But they would not dare try this with tyrannosaurus.

No, sir. Tyrannosaurus would glance down from a height of 20 feet, flick his tail, and Mommy or Daddy would sail through the wall leaving cartoon-style Mommy- or Daddy-shaped holes. And tyrannosaurus would calmly go back to pouring apple juice onto the remote-control device.

So Robert spends a lot of time being a dinosaur. I recall the day we were at the beach and he was being a gorgosaurus, which, like tyran-nosaurus, is a major dinosaur, a big meat-eater. (Robert is almost always carnivorous.) He was stomping around in the sand, and along came an elderly tourist couple, talking in German. They sat down near us. Robert watched them.

"Tell them I'm a gorgosaurus," he said.

"You tell them," I said.

"Gorgosauruses can't talk," Robert pointed out, rolling his eyes. Sometimes he can't believe what an idiot his father is.

Anybody who has ever had a small child knows what happened next. Using the powerful whining ability that Mother Nature gives to young children to compensate for the fact that they have no other skills, Rob-ert got me to go over to this elderly foreign couple, point to my son, who was looking as terrifying as a three-year-old can look lumbering around in a bathing suit with a little red anchor on it, and say, "He's a gorgosaurus."

The Germans looked at me the way you would look at a person you saw walking through a shopping mall with a vacant stare and a chain saw. They said nothing.

"Ha ha!" I added, so they would see I was in fact very normal.

They continued to say nothing. You could tell this had never hap-pened to them in Germany.

"Tell them I'm a meat-eater," the gorgosaurus whispered.

"He's a meat-eater," I told the couple. They got up and started to fold their towels.

"Tell them I can eat more in ONE BITE than a mommy and a daddy and a little boy could eat in TWO WHOLE MONTHS," urged the gorgosaurus, this being one of the many dinosaur facts he got from the books we read to him at bedtime. But by then the tourists were striding off, glancing back at me, and talking quietly to each other about which way they would run if I came after them.

I came after them.

"Ha ha!" I called out after them reassuringly.

Gorgosaurus continued to stomp around, knocking over whole cities. I had a heck of a time getting him to take a nap that day.

Sometimes when he's tired and wants to be cuddled, Robert is a gentle plant-eating dinosaur-baby diplodocus. (Diplodocus looked sort of like brontosaurus, only sleeker and cuter.) This one has lost its mommy and daddy, and wrapped in its protective blanket, it understands it's going to live with us forever and ever. The blanket wriggles with joy.

Lately at our house, we have become interested in what finally happened to the dinosaurs. According to our bedtime books, all the dinosaurs died quite suddenly about 65 million years ago, and nobody knows why. Some scientists think the cause was a Death Comet that visits the earth from time to time. Robert thinks this is great. A Death Comet! This is serious power. A Death Comet would never have to brush its teeth. A Death Comet could have pizza whenever it wanted.

Me, I get uneasy reading about the Death Comet. I don't like to think about the dinosaurs disappearing. It's yet another reminder that nothing lasts forever. Even a baby diplodocus has to grow up sometime.

Originally published in the November 1995 issue of *Reader's Digest* magazine.

Antonia's Mission

by Gail Cameron Wescott

*Once a privileged Los Angeles housewife,
Sister Antonia left that life behind
to reform prison inmates.*

A riot was raging through La Mesa prison in Tijuana, Mexico. Twenty-five hundred fed-up prisoners packed into a compound built for 600 angrily hurled broken bottles at police, who fired back with machine guns. "There was blood everywhere," remembers one inmate, "people lighting fires, people going crazy."

Then, at the peak of the pandemonium, came a startling sight: A tiny, five-foot-two, 63-year-old American woman in an immaculate nun's habit calmly strolled into the battle, hands outstretched in a simple gesture of peace. Ignoring the shower of bullets and flying bottles, she stood quietly and ordered everyone to stop. Incredibly, they did. "No one else in the world but Sister Antonia could have done that," says Robert Cass, a former inmate, now rehabilitated and living in San Diego. "She has changed thousands of people's lives."

In Tijuana, when Sister Antonia walks along a sidewalk, traffic in the street routinely stops; people there affectionately claim her as their own Mother Teresa. For the past quarter-century, she has lived, by choice, in a ten-foot concrete cell at La Mesa, without hot water, surrounded by murderers, thieves, and drug lords, all of whom she lovingly calls her "sons." She attends to their needs round the

In her converted cell in a Tijuana prison, Sister Antonia counsels inmate Jorge Villalobos.

clock, raising bail money, procuring antibiotics, distributing eyeglasses and false teeth, counseling the suicidal, washing bodies for burial. "I live on the premises," she explains with no hint of complaint, "in case some-one is stabbed in the middle of the night."

It is a world away from the plush precincts of Beverly Hills, where Sister Antonia—then Mary Clarke—grew up. Her father, from humble beginnings, owned a prosperous office-supply company. "He always said that it's easier to suffer when you are rich," she remembers. He also told her that once a Beverly Hills girl, always a Beverly Hills girl. She believed him.

"I was a romantic," she says, "and still am, really—always looking at the world through rose-colored glasses." Clarke grew up during the heyday of Hollywood—big stars tap-dancing down the stairs, bells ringing for me and my gal—and also during World War II. A vibrant beauty by her teens, she spent her weekend evenings dancing with young soldiers at the canteen and dreaming about the future. Her dream included a husband, many children, and a picture-book house.

It all came true. After graduating from high school, Clarke married and raised seven children in an airy Granada Hills home. Twenty-five years later, the marriage ended in divorce, a subject that remains painful for her and which she declines to discuss. "Because a dream ends doesn't mean that it didn't come true once," she says, blue eyes flashing. "What matters now is my second life."

With her marriage over and her children, with whom she stays in close touch, grown, she turned instinctively to helping the less fortunate. The suffering of others had always affected her profoundly. "I walked out of *Mutiny on the Bounty* because I couldn't stand seeing men tied to the mast and lashed," she says. "If others are humiliated, you're humiliated, too. I still can't bear to see prison movies, though I live in a prison." She had kept her father's business going for 17 years following his death at age 50, but had no desire to expand it. "It takes the same amount of energy to make business calls as it does to make calls to get beds donated to hospitals in Peru," she points out. "There comes a time when you can't just be a spectator. You have to step outside the lines."

In her case, she took a giant leap. In the mid-60s, she began traveling across the Mexican border with a Catholic priest to take medicines and supplies to the poor. She had fallen in love with the country before ever laying eyes on it. In a long-ago childhood game about ultimate places to live, she had inexplicably chosen Mexico. "At the time," she notes, "the only Mexicans I knew were gardeners." Now she found herself deeply drawn to the people.

Her second life began the day she and the priest got lost in Tijuana. Looking for the local jail, they wound up by mistake at La Mesa. "It's only 10 miles from the border, but like 100 if you don't know where you're going," she explains. She was instantly moved by what she saw. "In the infirmary, men were desperately sick, yet would stand when you entered." Soon she was spending nights there, sleeping on a bunk in the women's section, learning Spanish, assisting the inmates and their families in any way she could.

In 1977, convinced that she had found God's true purpose for her, Mary Clarke became Sister Antonia, making private vows with the bishops of Tijuana and San Diego. La Mesa prison became her permanent home, the place she even chooses to spend Christmas Eve. "Her children understand her priorities," says her friend Noreen Walsh-Begun. "They realize that she cared for them, and now it's her turn to care for others."

She had been a squeamish mom. "Oh, my, when any of my children needed stitches or were bleeding, I'd almost faint." But nothing that has happened inside La Mesa has been too shocking to handle. "I have seen a lot," says Sister Antonia. She was especially close to a warden who was dragged from his car nine years ago and brutally executed. "There is nothing now that I cannot face head-on."

"I don't know how anyone keeps up with her," says Cass, the former inmate, who recently named his newborn daughter after Sister Antonia. She's awake before dawn, praying and speaking in the chapel. For 25 years, she never missed the morning *grito*, when the guards lined up and new prisoners walked through a gauntlet-like column, saying their names and why they were incarcerated. "It was terrifying and humiliating for them," Cass says, "but Sister Antonia would be right there, advising them what to do ('Look them in the eye, don't show any attitude'), providing some bread and comfort. She's always rushing, yet always has time for you. I've seen her late at night when someone is stabbed—which is not uncommon—insist on running out to find lidocaine, no matter how exhausted she is, rather than let the victim be sewn up without anesthetic. She's not loved without reason."

Love, says Sister Antonia, is what she offers everyone. "I'm hard on crime but not the criminal," she says. "Just this morning, I talked to a young man, 19 years old, who had stolen a car. I asked him if he had any idea what a car means to a family, how long it takes to buy one. I said, 'I love you, but I don't sympathize with you. Do you have a girlfriend? Well, maybe someone will steal her while you're in here.' Then I hugged him." She hugs everyone, including the guards, whom she also instructs and counsels.

For years, Sister Antonia zipped around Tijuana in what was once a New York Checker cab, repainted royal blue. "One day I backed into a police car," she says, laughing boisterously, "and my immediate thought was, *Oh, thank God,* which I realize is not a typical response, but I love the police and they love me."

Eight years ago, she started Brazos Abiertos (Open Arms), a charitable organization for the widows and children of policemen killed in the line of duty. "We have nothing but love and respect for her," says Brazos president Roberto Sanchez-Osario. "She recognizes that both the delinquents and the police are human beings—and she creates the bridge."

Antonia's Mission

Mexican prison inmates and their families are not, Sister Antonia observes, a popular charitable cause. A charismatic speaker, she has nonetheless attracted a whole network of supporters who contribute everything from mattresses to medicines to money. A local dentist has provided thousands of sets of false teeth at cost for prisoners who had never seen a toothbrush. "You have to be able to smile in order to get a job," snaps Sister Antonia. "You must have teeth." An American eye doctor has sent thousands of pairs of glasses, and plastic surgeons have donated their services. "No one can say no to her," says Joanie Kenesie, a San Diego widow who is now Sister Antonia's chief assistant.

Wanting other women in midlife to share in the joyous satisfaction she has experienced, Sister Antonia recently founded Servants of the Eleventh Hour, an order for older women. Eight sisters have now taken vows along with 16 associates, including an oncology nurse who works at the AIDS hospice.

Her second life began the day she and the priest got lost in Tijuana. Looking for the local jail, they wound up by mistake at La Mesa.

Recent arrival Kathleen Marie Todora, a 69-year-old widow and mother of four from Baton Rouge, says, "I tried two other orders and was told I was too old before I heard of the Servants of the Eleventh Hour. I could not wait to get here. My car burned up in the desert 28 miles outside San Diego, and it didn't matter. Just left it there. Joanie came and got me. I think Sister Antonia's probably the most unique human being I've ever met in my life. A saint really, which we are sure she will become. She has opened a door with this order. We are getting inquiries from all over the country."

Originally published in the June 2004 issue of *Reader's Digest* magazine.

Mother Antonia passed away in 2013, at the age of 86, from a neuro-muscular disorder. She spent more than 30 years serving the inmates of La Mesa penitentiary in Tijuana, Mexico. The Eudist Servants of the 11th Hour, the order of nuns founded by Mother Antonia for older single, widowed, and divorced women, continues her work.

Submerged Subway

This submerged retired New York City subway car can look shocking and out of place at first glance according to Jeff Tinsman, artificial reef program manager at the Delaware Division of Fish and Wildlife. But he says, "We look for materials that will enhance fish habitats, and subway cars are unique. They almost always land upright, and with all the door and window openings, they become condominiums for black sea bass and tautog. After 40 years on the rails, these cars have a second life in the briny Atlantic."

Photograph by Stephen Mallon

Humor Hall of Fame

For the longest time, I thought my mother, father, and cat all had the same handwriting. Then I found out Mom was just signing cards for all of them.

—@MICHELLEISAWOLF

All her life, Victoria was told that the women in her family were able to walk on water on their 21st birthdays. It didn't seem possible, but her mother assured her it was true. So on her 21st birthday, Victoria takes a boat out onto the lake, steps off, and sinks. Back on land, Victoria confronts her mother. "You told me that every woman in our family could walk on water on her 21st birthday."

"It's true," says her mother.

"But when I just tried it, I nearly drowned!"

"That's because your sisters and I were all born in December. You were born in July."

—SHARON DELANEY-CHRONIS

On his 18th birthday, my son announced that he was no longer obligated to observe the curfew we'd imposed on him. "I'm 18," he announced. "And you can't stop me from leaving the house if and when I want to."

"You're right," I said. "I can't stop you from leaving. But I can stop you from coming back."

—PAUL ENNIS

I knew my kids watched too much TV when my seven-year-old told me to pick him up from school at 3 p.m./2 p.m. Central.

—JOANNE LEVI

"Oh my god, we forgot the kids."

Flight 93:
What I Never Knew

by Lyz Glick and Dan Zegart

*A 9/11 widow reflects on the man
she loved and lost and the legacy he left.*

Early one afternoon in July 2002, I received in the mail a white loose-leaf binder entitled "Unassociated Personal Effects of Flight 93." The return address was Douglass Personal Effects Administrators, a company in El Segundo, California. It was the mortuary handling the crash of United Flight 93, the hijacked plane that went down in a Pennsylvania field on the morning of September 11, 2001.

My heart began pounding. My husband, Jeremy, had died on that plane after trying to take it back—along with a group of other passengers—from the gang of assassins who had murdered people on the plane and intended to use it to kill more people on the ground. Piecing Jeremy's story together had become my life's work. I wanted our daughter, Emmy, just three months old when Jeremy died, to know about her father. I managed to wait until she went down for her nap that afternoon before opening the binder. In it were color photographs of everything found at the crash site that was not clearly linked to a particular person.

As wrenching as this was for me, I knew that I'd done the hardest

57

thing already: I had said goodbye to my soul mate, the only man I ever loved. Jeremy's wedding ring didn't survive, but 70 other pieces of jewelry did, along with a bewildering array of socks, hats, shoes, and other items of clothing that somehow made it through the crash and the fire that followed. There were also things like keys, books, and dozens of snapshots of children. I had packed Jeremy's bag for his business trip to California—a salesman for an Internet services company, he hated packing—so I knew exactly what he'd had with him. For a while I scrutinized a pair of khaki pants, but they were the wrong brand and size.

Then, on the second page of the men's underwear section, I came across a pair of black briefs. They were savagely torn and badly discolored, but there was no doubt they were Jeremy's.

I felt queasy and had to put the binder down. I got up and walked around the house until I felt better; then I sat down and finished the job.

Near the end, at the bottom of one page, was an American Express datebook, its cover burned and curled away. "Many travel dates," read the notes next to the picture. "Numbers for Jim Best, Rob Crozier, Greg Fitzgerald." Jimmy! One of our closest friends. Rob, a frat brother of Jeremy's at the University of Rochester. Greg, a neighbor of ours. There it was, bound in leather, or what was left of the leather now. Jeremy's datebook.

When the book was later sent to me, I studied its pages. It had travel pictures, a view of the Colosseum in Rome. "San Mateo" slanted diagonally across four days in July, a reference to a California business trip of Jeremy's. There were meetings with corporate clients in August, one with Bristol-Myers Squibb. "Craig dial-in, Claudette, Bob"—a conference call. A picture of a Buddhist temple in Thailand near which Jeremy had absentmindedly scrawled his own e-mail address.

It was all thoroughly mundane, a record of the things my husband did to make a living. Yet it was exciting, somehow, to see his familiar hand, the little architectural doodles he had made, the quickly executed scrollwork and crosshatched O's. It was better than a wedding ring because I felt Jeremy so particularly in these things. And I thought, I'll tell Emmy better than a wedding ring because I felt Jeremy so particularly in these things. And I thought, I'll tell Emmy he took the ring with him and left us this instead. I wanted her to know everything—including what her father did in the last moments of his life.

*　　*　　*

Sunday, September 9, 2001, was a good day for the three of us. Emmy was just 11 weeks old and we were enjoying her enormously. She was starting to sleep through the night, and I was feeling better physically after a difficult pregnancy. Jeremy, who was thinking of changing jobs, had gone on two interviews and felt they went well. The next day he had another interview in Newark. Since Sunday was rainy and cloudy, we just lay around our house in northern New Jersey, near Greenwood Lake, and at midday I bounced into the living room with my digital camera. I found Jer—all his friends called him Jer—stretched out on the couch. Emmy was on his chest, with Maxine, our first pug, on his leg, and Eloise, our newer pug, at his feet.

"Take pictures, take pictures," Jeremy said.

"Jer, do you know how many pictures I have of you lying in this position with the baby and the two dogs?" I asked. But after three miscarriages in two years, Emmy was doubly precious to us, so I took a few more anyway. We talked about how I'd get to go skiing this year, which I couldn't do last year because I was pregnant. We laughed a lot, and watched Emmy, and then went to bed early.

The next day, September 10, was busy. After Jeremy's interview in the morning, he would be catching a flight to California, a business trip he was taking reluctantly. He was convinced that his company, in a troubled economy, might be laying people off and could do that to him, so why bother with the trip? But I doubted they'd fire him; he was doing too well for them, bringing in new business. I told him he'd better go. I would take Emmy up to my parents' house in the Catskills, in Windham, New York, and he could meet us there when he returned.

For some reason, he particularly wanted to take care of Emmy that morning. So he fed the baby her milk and bathed and dressed her. He packed up both our cars, made sure Emmy was tucked into her car seat, and kissed her. Then he stood in the street in front of the house, waving, as we drove off.

The drive to Windham was uncomfortable. It was hot. Emmy cried a lot, and I had to go to the bathroom but felt I couldn't stop because how can you drag a baby and two pugs into a rest room? *This is insane,* I thought. *How do single mothers do it?* When I got to Windham, Jeremy called, excited because his interview had gone smoothly. Forty-five minutes later, he called again. His flight to San Francisco had been canceled due to

"Listen, there are some bad men on the plane."

a fire at Newark. He didn't want to take the next available flight and get in at 2 a.m. "Screw it," he said. "I'm going to go home, get a good night's sleep, and get up early tomorrow." He would grab the first flight out of Newark. United Flight 93.

The first thing I remember when I woke up Tuesday morning was trying to figure out whether to go out and buy coffee. There wasn't any in my parents' house, and I was annoyed. I'd been up with Emmy much of the night.

I was in the kitchen, fumbling with the lid of the doughnut box, when I heard my father say something about the World Trade Center. I looked in the living room at the TV and saw the image of the fire poking through the blackened holes in the tower's silver skin. I saw people waving shirts from the windows and felt the terrible sensation of height. I saw people on the ground watching: a blond guy in a blue suit, next to a paramedic, next to a guy in a white muscle shirt, all staring up. The phone rang, and my dad said into it, "Oh, thank God it's you." I ran into the living room. He held out the phone, his face pale. "Jeremy," he said.

I grabbed the phone. "Jer," I said.

"Hi," he said. "Listen, there are some bad men on the plane."

"What do you mean?"

"These three Iranian guys took over the plane. They put on these red headbands. They said they had a bomb. I mean, they looked Iranian."

I was crying now, not completely irrational, but on the cusp.

"I love you," he said.

"I love *you,*" I said.

*   *   *

After we'd said "I love you" for four or five minutes, I was in a different place. It was like we had meditated together. Physically, I was shaking and nauseated, but I also knew I could make myself do whatever was necessary to help Jeremy.

Jeremy stopped saying "I love you." "I don't think I'm going to make it out of here," he said. And then, "I don't want to die." And he cursed.

"You're not going to die," I told him. "Jer, put a picture of me and Emmy in your head and only have really good thoughts."

"Yeah," he answered.

"Don't think about anything bad," I said.

"You've got to promise me you're going to be happy," he said. "For Emmy to know how much I love her. And that whatever decisions you make in your life, no matter what, I'll support you."

This bounced right past me at the time. Everything had been going so well. Jer and I had gotten married on Labor Day weekend, 1996, in an old stone church near Windham in front of 250 guests. We'd known each other since ninth-grade biology, when he

> "You've got to promise me you're going to be happy," he said.

was a skinny kid with an enormous curly-brown Afro that was too big for his head. It was like a bowl sitting above his ears. I remember thinking, *What's up with this kid's hair?* But he was funny, with an agile mind, and we'd become fast friends, dating all throughout high school and at various times during college. He was protective—you never felt as safe as when Jer was around. For many years he'd been a judo champ, but that alone didn't explain this quality. What I loved about him was that when I talked to him, he paid attention with his heart. Now, on the plane, Jeremy was planning for two possible outcomes—not just the happier one.

At this point, apparently Deena Burnett told her husband, Tom, who was sitting near Jeremy, about the World Trade Center. Both towers had been struck, but neither had collapsed. "A passenger said they're crashing planes into the World Trade Center," Jeremy said to me. "Is that true?"

I was standing there in the living room, watching it on my parents' big-screen TV. I thought, *Do I tell him?*

"Are they going to blow the plane up or are they going to crash it into something?" he almost screamed at me.

"They're not going to the World Trade Center," I said.

"Why?"

"Because the whole thing's on fire."

By now my dad had retrieved a cell phone from his car and my mom had gotten a 911 guy on the line.

"Where are you?" the 911 guy wanted us to ask Jeremy.

"We've turned, we're not going to California anymore," Jeremy said. "I'm pretty sure a minute ago we went by Pittsburgh, and I think now we're going south."

"What do you see?"

"I can see a river. We're flying high, I think—yeah, we're high up, but you can see it's definitely rural down there." He said there were maybe 30 or 35 passengers. He was calling on the seat-back phone, not his cell. He'd left everything up front when the passengers were herded to the back. For some reason, however, no one was guarding them back there.

"What about the pilots?" I asked him. "Has there been any communication?"

"No. These guys just stood up and yelled and ran into the cockpit. After that, we didn't hear from the pilots."

He didn't tell me that the men had stabbed a passenger and probably a stewardess. Maybe he didn't know what had happened. Jer tended to tune out on planes. He always flew with a pair of oversize headphones, listening to music. I could imagine him sitting there half-asleep, kind of being startled awake.

"Who's flying the plane?" I asked him.

"I don't know," he said.

Just then, we saw something on TV about a plane crashing into the Pentagon, and I thought, *Thank God it isn't Jeremy's plane.*

When I told him about this new attack, Jeremy cursed again. The Pentagon was probably the jolt that made him see clearly that his fate and that of his fellow passengers in the rear of the plane were completely in their own hands. "Okay, I'm going to take a vote," he said. "There's three other guys as big as me and we're thinking of attacking the guy with the bomb. What do you think?"

"Do they have machine guns?" I asked. My mind summoned up a stereotype of an Iranian hijacker with an AK-47.

"No, I didn't see guns. I saw knives. I don't know how these people got on the plane with what they have." He joked, "I still have my butter knife from breakfast." There was a pause, and then he said, "I know I could take the guy with the bomb. Do you think it's really a bomb?"

Then he heard screams in the background, and he thought, They're doing it.

"I don't think so. I think they're bluffing you."

The whole time on the phone, I just heard Jer's voice, clear as a bell, as if he were in the next room. I had no sense of what was happening in the background. There must have been a moment when he polled "the three other guys as big as me," but if he told me about it, it didn't stick in my memory. I also don't recall mentioning that one of the twin towers had fallen during this interval or even knowing about it.

"Okay, I'm going to do it," Jer said.

*   *   *

There was no question in my mind that Jeremy could take down some guy with a knife. Along with his best friend, Kim Bangash, Jeremy had spent three summers at the Iowa Intensive Wrestling Camp, grueling month-long programs that featured Dan Gable, an Olympic gold medalist. In judo, Jeremy had trained in close hand-to-hand combat.

"I think you need to do it," I told him. "You're strong, you're brave, I love you."

"Okay, I'm going to put the phone down, I'm going to leave it here, and I'm going to come right back to it," Jer said. I handed the phone to my dad, ran into the bathroom, and gagged over the sink.

When my father put the phone to his ear, he heard nothing on the line for two or three minutes. Then he heard screams off in the background. And he thought, *They're doing it.* It was bound to be noisy. Perhaps a minute and a half later, there was another set of screams, muffled, like people on a roller coaster. Then silence.

Ten minutes later, an operator broke in to say that the FBI wanted my father to stay on the line because it was the only remaining connection to the plane. My dad took the phone outside, by the stone wall in our yard. He stood there for two hours. Then he brought the phone back and hung up.

When I opened the bathroom door I found myself surrounded by emergency medical technicians who checked my pulse and advised me to lie down. Evidently, our 911 call had summoned them. I told them to get the hell away from me. I snatched up my purse and car keys and told my mom to keep an eye on Emmy because I was going to meet Jeremy's plane.

"Where do you think I should drive, Mom? You think he'll come in at Newark? Or do you think they'd bring them into Philadelphia?"

"Lyzzy, you need to stay here," my mother said. I didn't push it. I thought, *Mom's right. I'm still breast-feeding Emmy every few hours. I can't leave.*

So I sat on the living room couch and ran through the various possible scenarios. *If the plane did crash, maybe he has no legs. That's fine. Or, if he's burned over 90 percent of his body, that's all right, I'll take care of him for the rest of my life.* I used one of the emergency workers' phones to call Jeremy's mom and tell her what I knew. I also managed to reach our high school friend Jimmy, and Shari, a dear friend from a trip to Australia, and Kim Bangash, and Diana Dobin, members of our old high school circle. People began to make their way up to Windham.

A minister then appeared from the local Presbyterian church, a woman. "I heard there were survivors," she said.

I thought, *Well, of all the people on the plane, of course Jeremy will be among the living.* That fit nicely with the rest of my thinking. The minister brewed some tea and prayed, a rather formal kind of prayer.

All my energy seemed to have deserted me. I just sat on the couch like a catatonic and drank tea. After a while, I got up and headed for the kitchen and almost collided with my dad, who was coming the other way. He must have just hung up the phone. He was crying. He gave me a hug. I watched him cry, a bit dumbfounded.

"Wait, you think he's dead?" I said.

He couldn't manage anything but to cry harder. I must have asked the same question five times. I was trying to figure out how we got to this place from where we were before. What exactly had happened? And then, when it finally sank in, I collapsed on the floor.

I remember very little after that. Our friends straggled in throughout the day, and they all stayed over. Shari slept in the bed with me. We lay there with the lights out, two friends holding each other. It was pitch-black, but there were these little sparkles above us, an iridescent dust, like a presence.

"Do you see what I see?" Shari asked.

"It's like golden dust," I said.

"Yeah," she said.

"It's him," I told her. I turned on my side, and it felt like Jeremy was spooning me, cradling me from behind.

I slept deeply, in a kind of blackout. When my eyes opened again, it was with the immediate realization that I would never see Jeremy again.

I needed to think about Jeremy, and I needed to be around other people who also needed to think of him. So when the airline people invited me to see the crash site in western Pennsylvania, my first impulse was to say no. But then I thought I might regret not going.

*   *   *

Since I wouldn't fly, United sent three black limousines to collect me, along with Emmy, my father, and Jeremy's parents. It was raining on September 19, the day we arrived in Shanksville, a rural hamlet 80 miles from Pittsburgh, in a caravan of tour buses. We passed miles of people who stood in the rain and watched us go by, waving little flags and crying. The buses stopped. We got out and walked down the dirt road until we came to a low bluff. Under a canopy was a makeshift memorial on hay bales, things people had left or sent to the site—letters, poems, flowers, baby shoes.

A field of tall yellowing grass framed by woods lay below, with a farm behind it. The trees at the back of the field were burnt black and stripped of leaves and branches. Bright orange plastic flags marked where a piece of steel, a melted driver's license, a tooth, a ring, a bit of bone had been found. Aside from a thousand-pound chunk of jet engine, which landed in a pond, the earth so far hadn't yielded anything bigger than a few inches in length. The plane had come down at a steep angle, I learned, hitting the ground at roughly the speed of sound, which snapped the cockpit off the fuselage and sprayed the woods with fire. Most of the aircraft and its contents were pulverized into small, coarse, hot pieces. There was no wreckage. Nothing to see.

We weren't allowed to walk down to the field because it was still considered a crime scene. The hole in the ground wasn't visible, but you could see trucks and bulldozers around it. Human remains were found in the field and the scorched woods. In this case, remains meant anything that contained human DNA.

After carrying Emmy around for an hour and a half, I was glad to get back on the bus. I realized Jeremy had merely passed through here, and took comfort in knowing he wasn't in such a remote gray place. I knew he was telling me not to waste my time standing in the rain looking for him.

Over the next months, during which I met President Bush in 9/11 ceremonies in Washington and appeared on *Dateline* and *Oprah*, I spent a lot of time searching for Jeremy. Often I heard his voice in my head, comforting me during those moments when my pain was almost unendurable.

I'm sure I will never really make sense of September 11. Did someone declare war on us for a principle? Because they were jealous? To show how tough they were? Did we in this country somehow overstep, push too hard, tread on ancient sensibilities? The world Jeremy and I knew was never more than the rooms we lived in, a few places we walked, a few friends and family we loved. Now it's gone, and no reason of state could ever really make sense of why.

It has helped that the older Emmy has gotten, the more I've seen how essentially unaffected she's been by all that happened. She's an even-keeled, cheerful child. There have been no tantrums. I tell my friends, "This is God's way of saying, 'You know what? I did this terrible thing to you. So here, have this on the house: an incredible personality for your daughter. Enjoy.' "

At age two, Emmy forgot what her father looked like. Before, she had always been able to point to his picture. It happened several times that she walked over and touched the TV when Jer's picture flashed on it.

One day I pointed to a photo of Jer kissing her. "Who's that?" Emmy said.

"That's your daddy," I said.

"His name's Jeremy," Emmy remembered.

"That's right. He's your daddy," I repeated.

And Emmy said, "Well, where is he?" I stood there like something stuffed.

Finally she said, "Oh, he's coming later." And then she picked up her blanket toy, Blue Dog, and walked off into her room.

I think Jeremy always suspected he had a higher purpose. I don't believe it was an accident that he was on Flight 93, though it was an accident—the fire at Newark—that put him there. It wasn't mere luck that an airline passenger with precisely the right physical skills to abort one of the terror missions happened to be on the only plane hijacked that day where there was an opportunity to do that.

Jeremy was 31 when he died, had been married to me for five years, and knew his daughter for barely three months. Yet I consider us blessed. He and I left nothing unsaid or undone, and he managed to give Emmy and me everything we need. And sometimes, when I'm watching and listening, I can still feel him near me, leading me forward into the rest of my life.

Originally published in the September 2004 issue of *Reader's Digest* magazine.

Emmy has delivered talks for the TedxYouth@SRDS (Saddle River Day School). She discussed how she has dealt with the grief of losing her father before ever having the chance to meet him. In 2019, she was on national tour of the Broadway production of Fiddler on the Roof, *in the role of Bielke.*

Lyz remarried in 2005 to Jim Best, Jeremy's best man at Lyz and Jeremy's wedding. Best officially adopted Emmy when she was four years old, and together Lyz and Jim have two children. Lyz started the nonprofit organization Jeremy's Heroes in his honor to ensure all children have the opportunity to improve themselves and their communities through sports, using compassion, courage, and character.

DO ANGELS EXIST?

Yes—in folklore, fairy tales, and religious text, and on a lonely stretch of highway in Oklahoma. Driving my old station wagon on a seemingly endless highway in rural Oklahoma, my front hood popped open into a vertical position while I was doing fifty-five in the right lane. In a split second, darkness enveloped me. Shaken, I eased onto the right shoulder. In the middle of nowhere, with no tools, I gazed at the horizon. I saw cornfields, but not a soul in sight. Suddenly, a man appeared out of seemingly thin air. Without uttering one word, he reached into the side pockets of his overalls and came up with an assortment of tools. With the dexterity of a mechanic, he fixed my broken hood latch. I raised my face to thank him profusely, but all I saw was empty space where he stood a few seconds ago.

—Steve Gaal *La Quinta, California*

FEATHERED FRIENDS

On a self-imposed COVID-19 virus isolation, I felt increasingly depressed from the "living alone" routine. After a long spiritless walk, I remembered to feed the birds before settling in for the evening. Loading the feeder, I noticed a chickadee (my favorite bird ... pure joy!) alighting on a nearby branch, waiting expectantly. As I stepped away, the bird flew to the feeder, pausing on a perch. Looking me straight in the eye, it sang a high-pitched "cheep cheep" then grabbed a seed and flew off. A thank-you I'll never forget! Tears welling up, I knew God had not forgotten me. His little messenger reminded me of that.

—David Gregorski *Coventry, Connecticut*

Best Teacher I Ever Had

by David Owen, from *LIFE*

A teacher shows his students
the importance of asking questions.

Mr. Whitson taught sixth-grade science. On the first day of class, he gave us a lecture about a creature called the cattywampus, an ill-adapted nocturnal animal that was wiped out during the Ice Age. He passed around a skull as he talked. We all took notes and later had a quiz.

When he returned my paper, I was shocked. There was a big red X through each of my answers. I had failed. There had to be some mistake! I had written down exactly what Mr. Whitson said. Then I realized that everyone in the class had failed. What had happened?

Very simple, Mr. Whitson explained. He had made up all that stuff about the cattywampus. There had never been any such animal. The information in our notes was, therefore, incorrect. Did we expect credit for incorrect answers?

Needless to say, we were outraged. What kind of test was this? And what kind of teacher?

We should have figured it out, Mr. Whitson said. After all, at the very moment he was passing around the cattywampus skull (in truth, a cat's), hadn't he been telling us that no trace of the animal remained? He had described its amazing night vision, the color of its fur, and any number of other facts he couldn't have known. He had given the animal a ridiculous name, and we still hadn't been suspicious. The zeroes on our papers would be recorded in his grade book, he said. And they were.

Mr. Whitson said he hoped we would learn something from this experience. Teachers and textbooks are not infallible. In fact, no one is. He told us not to let our minds go to sleep and to speak up if we ever thought he or the textbook was wrong.

Every class was an adventure with Mr. Whitson. I can still remember some science periods almost from beginning to end. One day he told us that his Volkswagen was a living organism. It took us two full days to put together a refutation he would accept. He didn't let us off the hook until we had proved not only that we knew what an organism was but also that we had the fortitude to stand up for the truth.

We carried our brand-new skepticism into all our classes. This caused problems for the other teachers, who weren't used to being challenged. Our history teacher would be lecturing about something, and then there would be clearings of the throat and someone would say "cattywampus."

If I'm ever asked to propose a solution to the crisis in our schools, it will be Mr. Whitson. I haven't made any great scientific discoveries, but Mr. Whitson's class gave me and my classmates something just as important: the courage to look people in the eye and tell them they are wrong. He also showed us that you can have fun doing it.

Not everyone sees the value in this. I once told an elementary school teacher about Mr. Whitson. The teacher was appalled. "He shouldn't have tricked you like that," he said. I looked that teacher right in the eye and told him he was wrong.

Originally published in the February 1991 issue of *Reader's Digest* magazine.

One Minute Left

by Sara Jameson

What began as a father-son scuba diving adventure soon turned into a deadly countdown.

David Meistrell, 17, hung a three-foot-long mesh bag from the weight belt of his black rubber wet suit. Around the gently rocking dive boat, California's Santa Monica Bay sparkled under a nearly full moon. "Let's go catch more lobsters, Dad," David said with a grin.

Joe Meistrell, 49, smiled at his only child. In his 25 years as a marine biologist, Joe regularly dived in these waters. But he, too, was excited about another trip 80 feet below to the *Avalon*, an iron steamship wrecked in a storm 30 years before. On their first dive, they had pulled three spiny lobsters from the 265-foot hulk.

As they prepared for their second dive on that night of October 6, 1995, Joe's thoughts went back to an old snapshot showing little David in a wading pool, wearing a snorkel and mask and holding a plastic lobster. Even then the boy had been eager to hunt lobsters. By the time he was 14, he was a certified diver.

Joe checked David's air tank. "Okay, you can go now," Joe said, "but don't get out of sight." David waved, then splashed overboard. Joe followed quickly.

Only a luminescent line of bubbles and the glow from the light stick tied to David's air tank marked his descent to the silty bottom. At 70 feet down, he leveled off and kicked ahead with powerful thrusts from his fins, disappearing into the darkness. Joe swam harder to catch up. Faintly visible below, the twisted remains of the *Avalon* came into view.

Earlier, on the dive boat, Joe had cautioned David that they should stay only 18 minutes on the bottom. Their tanks would run longer, but Joe wanted to be conservative about their exposure to the nitrogen gas mixed with oxygen in their tanks. They had already stayed down 33 minutes on their first dive.

A hand-size dive computer, dangling on a hose from Joe's tank, calculated their bodies' nitrogen saturation. Its two-inch screen would warn Joe if they should make a decompression stop at 20 feet before their return to the surface to avoid the "bends," a painful, potentially fatal condition when nitrogen bubbles into the bloodstream and tissues. Ascending too fast could also kill by rupturing the lungs.

For 10 minutes they swam above the mangled, rusty wreck. Then they went to inspect the nearly intact bow, aiming their flashlights through several irregular six-inch holes corroded through the thick metal of the port side. Inside, they saw lobsters scurrying away, startled by the sudden beam. Hunting would be excellent here.

But when Joe looked down by his left foot, where his son had been a moment before, David had vanished. *Where has he gone?* Joe wondered.

* * *

David assumed his father had seen him follow a lobster into an 18-inch-wide opening in the hull, where the ship's bow had buried itself in the sea floor. The boy edged up an angled passage into a cramped space some 20 feet across, cluttered with the wreck's fallen ribs and cross braces, chunks of rusted iron, and collapsed bulkheads.

He grabbed a lobster, careful not to let its long spines pierce his gloves. Turning in the tight space, he snaked back to the opening. He'd pass the lobster to his father, then scoot back for more.

* * *

One Minute Left

A thin line of silt eddied across Joe's flashlight beam as he inspected the 18-inch hole. *Did David go in there after a lobster?* he wondered. *The hole looks awfully small. Maybe he swam around to the other side.*

Joe moved a few feet left and looked around the bow at the vast deck stretching away into the muddy gloom. David was not in sight. Joe shivered. *Don't worry,* he told himself. *He can't be far.*

David Meistrell and his dad, Joe

Suddenly David's hand popped out of the hole holding a squirming lobster. *Thank God,* Joe thought, sighing with relief. He grabbed the lobster and put it in his game bag, expecting David to follow. Instead, his son disappeared again. Joe shined his light into the hole but saw only muddy water.

They had now been at the bottom for 13 minutes. "Come on out," Joe muttered to himself. "We've got to go." Yet David didn't reappear. Two more minutes passed.

Should I go look for him? Joe wondered. He was glad he had made David wear the new 80-cubic-foot tank. The kid used air faster, especially when he got excited. His own 72-cubic-foot tank was older, but unlike David's, it had a feature that warned him when he was running out of air.

Another minute passed. *Could David be stuck inside?* Joe wondered. *I'd better check.* But as he started to pull himself through the hole, his air tank caught on the top of the opening and stuck.

Joe pushed and tugged but couldn't get free. Soon he was panting, sucking hard at his mouthpiece, straining for each breath as he struggled. His airflow dwindled.

Still wedged in the opening, he reached back over his left shoulder and pulled a valve to free his last 450 pounds of air. Breaths came more easily again, but Joe knew he'd be lucky if his air lasted another seven minutes.

With a great surge, he broke free and backed out. He trembled from the exertion, sweating despite the cold water. He'd never felt so alone. The question he had been avoiding refused to go away. *What if I run out of air and David still isn't here?*

Joe knew in his heart that he would wait, however long it took. Even if his own air ran out, he would never leave without his son.

Excited by his catch, David had turned back to continue hunting. Two more lobsters backed away to his right, blinding him in a blizzard of rust. He spun around, disoriented, stirring up more rust and sediment.

I'd better get out of here, he thought, and turned to where be thought the entry had been. But it wasn't there. He groped against a solid surface. The hull? The deck? Panicked, he dropped his game bag and swam faster. He bumped into a corner, hitting his head on a pipe, still unable to find the entry.

Maybe I can find another opening, he thought. He swam in a direction he hoped was up. Suddenly his head popped out into a two-foot-wide triangular pocket of air where his exhaled bubbles had collected under the tip of the bow.

He checked his air-pressure gauge. Only 500 pounds. That wouldn't last more than three minutes if he kept breathing this fast.

He snatched off his mouthpiece and sucked in a breath of trapped air. Though it was high in carbon dioxide, it would still have some oxygen for a while. Breathing it would save what was left in his tank. *Anyway, I'd rather pass out from carbon dioxide than die inhaling water,* he thought.

Then be began to scream. "Help me, Dad! I can't get out. Don't let me die!"

* * *

Worried from his wait, Joe left the entry hole and swam up the nearly vertical side of the ship. Suddenly he heard David's screams. Relief drowned Joe's surprise as to why the words sounded so clear. Usually the water muffled sounds. He didn't care why. His son was alive!

Joe peered through a six-inch hole in the metal, his flashlight probing the murky water. He caught a glint of something shiny and recognized David's wet suit not two feet away. Only an inch of steel deck separated them, but it might as well have been a mile.

"Go down," Joe yelled around his mouthpiece, the words garbled in the water. He saw his son turn toward him. Sticking his hand through the hole, Joe pointed down toward the entry. When he looked in again, David had disappeared.

Joe raced back down to the opening, searching for signs of movement. Nothing. *Don't panic, David,* he thought. *Take your time.* Joe's air-pressure gauge dropped past 200 pounds–enough for maybe two minutes.

David groped around the ship's beams, his pulse racing. Seconds passed, then more. *Am I going the right way?* he wondered. Fear cramped his muscles.

In despair, he fought his way back to the air pocket, snatched off his regulator, and gasped the stale, metallic air. "Help! Dad! I'm trapped. Don't leave me. I don't want to die!"

After waiting what seemed an eternity at the entry, Joe wedged his flashlight into a crevice as a beacon for his son. *It hardly shines through the muddy water,* he thought, *but I've got to try.*

Then he swam back up the hull, feeling his way along the rough metal to the smaller hole. David's cries rang out as he arrived. Reaching in, Joe touched David's waist. He stared into his son's blue eyes for a long moment, willing him to understand.

Then Joe stuck his whole arm through the hole and once again pointed down toward the entrance. He felt his son grab his arm tightly, working down to the fingertips. Finally David let go. *This is it,* Joe thought as the air came hard again from his regulator and the pressure gauge dropped toward zero. *If David doesn't find the entry this time, we will surely die.*

Joe swam down to the hole. Kneeling by his flashlight beacon, he waited, his heart beating out the seconds. He sucked but got no more air. The last bubbles rose from his regulator.

David bumped along blindly, feeling his way along an overhanging ledge. Ahead he saw a faint glow; it was the opening. *Dad's out there!*

Shaking with relief, he started to twist his body through the passage. Then his tank screeched and he jerked to a stop, his tank wedged tight.

David tugged frantically. "Dad, pull me through!" he yelled.

Lying by the hole, holding his breath, Joe stared. *Did something move? It's David!*

He reached out, but the boy had stopped. "Don't stop now!" Joe screamed around his clenched teeth. He reached in, grabbed David's shoulder strap, and yanked. Metal scraped, held, then came free. David popped out in his arms.

Pulling his son to his chest, Joe flicked open the buckles on their heavy lead weight belts and let them drop. Kicking hard off the bottom and finning frantically, he shot for the surface, hugging his son.

Joe's lungs screamed for air, and his dive computer flashed "ASCEND SLOWER." But Joe ignored it. He raced for their lives.

As they rocketed upward, the sea pressure fell. Now Joe's tank was more pressurized than the water around it, and it shot forth a last bit of air. With that final breath, he revived. Kicking, he exhaled hard so his lungs wouldn't rupture with the rapid decrease in pressure.

Father and son exploded into the night air, ripped out their mouth-pieces, and gasped hungrily for air. After three deep breaths, Joe tore off David's mask and searched his face for the frothy blood that signals ruptured lungs. He saw only David's happy tears, mirroring his own.

Joe Meistrell knew it was a miracle they had survived. His son learned something more. Two weeks later, in an essay for his college-entrance exam, David wrote: "I am alive today because of my dad's willingness to sacrifice himself. He has made me realize the most important things in life are the people you love."

Originally published in the April 1997 issue of *Reader's Digest* magazine.

Joe and David both still live in California. While David took a year hiatus from diving after the events of this story, Joe had a project that required diving later that week. After 35 years, he finally retired in 2006. David now works as a firefighter and paramedic for Long Beach Harbor.

Uncle Jim's Wink at Life

by John L. Phillips

Be honest, be brave, be kind, look around—
the words were never uttered, but the
message always got through.

I was ten years old, and I'd been caught in a lie. I stubbornly denied breaking a window in Harold Colby's barn, but my parents knew perfectly well that I had done it.

In those days, in the little town of Pultneyville, New York, a broken window was a big deal, and I was close to miserable.

I suspected, too, that my parents had told Uncle Jim, whom I worshiped. But coming back from a trip to the store, riding beside him on the front seat of his dark-green DeSoto Firedome, I glanced over a time or two, fast. I could see a bemused smile at the corner of his mouth.

"Telling the truth is always easier," he said, straight out of the blue. He took his eyes off the road for a second and grinned at me. "So it's perfect for a lazybones like you and me."

I swallowed, watching the mailboxes go by, waiting. But that was it—no scolding, no moralizing. My uncle began to hum, and I was awash in relief. Like you and me. My pal was still my pal.

It wasn't long before I got the chance to test Uncle Jim's thesis. One day I spotted a pair of brown leather gloves on the windowsill in the post office. Old Mrs. Jameson had come in wearing them and had left barehanded, struggling with a bulky package. I tried the gloves on. They were perfect.

That night I had a losing bout with my conscience. The truth is easier for a lazybones like you and me. The following day, I returned the gloves and told Mrs. Jameson the truth.

A month later, a small package arrived for me. Inside were the gloves and a note: "I needed another pair and thought you might like these, Mrs. J."

When my uncle asked where I got the snazzy gloves, I told him the story. "See?" he said, delighted. Yes, I did see. I still do.

* * *

James Bellows Little would have winced at the idea that he ever taught anybody anything. He had a lifetime allergy to cookie-cutter wisdom. But he always applied a light touch to common sense as it angled through his prism.

He did it almost every time I saw him. His eyebrows would arch invitingly as he waited for me to get it, whatever it was—how to use a thesaurus or operate a Coleman stove, how to gauge an opponent across a tennis net or a shift of wind across a mainsail. I listened and watched, and once in a while, I even learned.

Uncle Jim even taught me to see through tears. My father died when I was 12, and as my mother's brother, Uncle Jim must have felt an urge to step in, but he didn't. He stayed in, providing a steady hand and a calm presence.

Only late in the game did I realize how deftly he'd tailored what he did and said to the needs of a kid who hadn't really known he had any. My uncle seemed to think, for instance, that I could stand a little help on gullibility, so he literally used his head.

One day when I was seven, I asked him why his head was bald but his chest was hairy. "Oh," he said breezily, "during World War II, I had the hair on my head transplanted. The Army Air Corps did it for free, and that way I'd never have to bother with barbershops. Not a bad deal, huh?" he asked with a wink.

It was a good three years before I began to have serious doubts.

Uncle Jim ran an industrial rubber-goods company in downtown Rochester, and in those days before major highways, the rush-hour commute to his house on Lake Ontario could be brutal. I was with him one afternoon when, never exceeding the speed limits, he made it without catching a single red light.

Over and over he reminded me that friendship is a currency that never depreciates.

"How'd you do that?" I wanted to know.

"Rhythm drive," he said cheerfully. "I don't know why I have it, but I do. So does your mother. Your Uncle Bill doesn't."

He glanced at me with an almost straight face. "Maybe you've got it, but we won't know for a few years."

Rhythm drive! I bought it on the spot and clung to it until I was old enough to get my driver's license. Eventually I'd see for myself that daily commuters need a notion like rhythm drive.

Rush-hour traffic? Baldness? If you can't beat 'em, celebrate 'em! That was Uncle Jim's way.

Over and over he reminded me that friendship is a currency that never depreciates. And he had his own way of showing it. Just back from a trip, for example, he'd stop the first friend he saw and insist on buying him lunch. If the guy didn't have time, he'd offer to buy him a hat. This was how he told his pals he missed them and how good it was to see them again.

To bolster my self-assurance, every now and then Uncle Jim would offer to bet all the change in his pocket against all the change in mine. No fair checking to see how much I had in my corduroys, either. It was a dare, and it made a kid feel like a gunslinger. He always decided what the bet was about, but I didn't find out until I'd said yes.

"Want to bet?" he'd say all of a sudden.

"Okay." And the game was on. "What's the capital of ... Ohio?" "Ummmmmmm. Columbus!" "Hmm," he'd say, feigning surprise, then reach into his pocket. "Hey, what do you know—27 cents!"

It wasn't the money; it was the reminder that sometimes you just have to jump in—even when you don't know how cold the water is. I can't remember ever losing one of those bets. Somehow Uncle Jim made it work out that way. It was a confidence game in the best sense. Most kids need things like that somewhere along the line. I sure did.

In time, my uncle would teach me many manly things—how to knot a bow tie, how to handle a tractor, how to fold a gabardine suit so it doesn't wrinkle, how to look life in the eye—and tell if it's winking back.

He loved beauty, too, and wasn't afraid to show it. Thrusting a pair of gardening gloves and my aunt's rubber boots at me, he'd lead me on a search for wildflowers. Back at the house, he'd put a huge Mason jar on the table, then seek my counsel on how best to arrange our trove. Be honest, be brave, be kind, look around—the words were never uttered, but the message always got through.

By example, too, Uncle Jim reminded me that men read books and value them for their beauty and inspiration. I was proud to be among those who knew behind which living-room volumes—some well-thumbed works of Dickens—he kept his stash of macadamia nuts.

His prodding reminded me that my father had been a voracious reader and a good gardener. Would I otherwise have spurned such "sissy" pursuits? Possibly. Uncle Jim wasn't taking chances. He helped me arrive at my dad's conclusion: These were things worth making time for.

Uncle Jim and I hadn't talked much about my father in the years since his death. But that changed one afternoon when we were cutting brush at his place at the lake.

"When Monty died, you lost a father, and your mom lost a husband," he said. "I lost a friend. But your dad lost the chance to see how his hopes would turn out. All of a sudden, it was the end of a life, and it was too soon—he never got to know. That's the tough part."

He looked at me. There was a touch of anger in his face. He, too, resented my father's having drawn so short a straw. I was startled to realize that, independently, I had the same feelings. Maybe I was growing up.

We walked across the broad lawn toward the lake. At the end of the bluff were a pail of old golf balls and a couple of drivers whose shafts were more rust than metal. From a height of 100 feet above the narrow, rocky beach, we teed up and swung from the heels, trying to give each ball one long, last ride.

My uncle hit what for him was a monster—not a high, arching shot but a Ben Hogan bullet. The ball clotheslined out, out, out over the dancing blue water, then fell, leaving a tiny, defiant signature of spray.

It might have gone 270 yards or so over ground—not bad for a short-hitting 20-handicapper using an old club and a mangled ball. I was still trying to keep my eye on the spot where it had plopped when Uncle Jim said, "How do you like that? The drive of my life, and it still winds up in a water hazard. Talk about life being unfair!" Then he whooped with laughter.

* * *

On one August day, on a fishing trip near Henderson Harbor not far from the St. Lawrence River, the two of us were in a battered 12-footer powered by a small outboard. I was a bit hangdog at our slow puttputting along. Uncle Jim said speed was fine if you wanted to go fast, but slowing down made any journey less of a blur. "It helps you focus," he said.

I thought of that decades later when he was dying, becalmed by a failing heart in his 82nd year. Was he seeing more, even as he slowed?

Jim Little was an observer who touched those he loved by sharing what he saw. I understood some of what he showed me pretty fast, but other things took decades to become clear.

From time to time in his later years, he would send me something I'd sent him 30 or 35 years earlier. A drawing of his house on the bluff. A crayon rendering of a sailboat with a stick figure at the tiller and "JBL" on the transom.

At first, these mementos triggered feelings of affectionate amusement. But as they accumulated, I came to recognize them as the clearest signposts Uncle Jim had set out for me. Time has passed, they gently reminded. You're not a short pants nephew anymore. Matter of fact, you've got nephews of your own, so hop to it.

Those aging scraps lie flat in a wooden box near my desk. But my mind's eye sees them as my heart knows them to be—tightly rolled into a baton that has finally passed to my hand.

Originally published in the September 1993 issue of *Reader's Digest* magazine.

The Smell of Space

Mike Hopkins, an astronaut from Houston, Texas, shares, "Space has a smell to it. I don't know how to describe it—an ionized metallic-type smell that's unique. When we first opened the hatch of the International Space Station, I commented on the scent, and the folks I was with said, 'Oh yeah, that's the smell of space.' No one told me about that."

Photograph by Glenn Glasser

Space-Camp Kid

"I'm one of the engineers at NASA's *Jet Propulsion Laboratory* and was part of the team for the *Curiosity* rover, which landed on Mars in 2012," says Bobak Ferdowsi of Pasadena, California. "My parents have always encouraged me to do what I love. They even sent me to space camp, where I had my first kiss! I remember that distinctly—I don't know if everybody can say that. It's a pretty nerdy, awesome experience."
Photograph by Glenn Glasser

Humor Hall of Fame

"The WIFI password is: 'buysomethingorgetout'."

My wife and I had been texting back and forth when unbeknownst to her, I had to stop for a few minutes. When I returned to my cell phone, I found this text message awaiting me: "CGYT?" "Huh?" I responded. She shot back: "Cat got your thumb?"

—REP. PAUL BRAUN ATHENS, GEORGIA

"Adam and Eve: the first people not to read the Apple Terms and Conditions."

—**CHURCH SIGN,** via *Planet Proctor* newsletter

After closing his framing store for the day, the owner took a call from a customer who wanted to pick up an order that wasn't ready yet. The owner didn't want to admit that the job wasn't finished, so he told the customer that she had called his home number—that the store was closed and nobody was around to help her.

"Hold on," she interrupted. "I'm on my cellular, and I can see someone inside. I'll try to get him to let me in."

—JOHN FORSYTHE

Green Eggs and Sam

by Penny Porter

A runt chick shows a family nature's awe and beauty.

The egg on our chicken-coop floor was far from ordinary. An ugly mud-green, it looked as if it had been left by some alien creature. Nudging it with my sneaker, I wondered, *Where did it come from? Had Mother Nature made a mistake?*

"Mama! You found Sam," five-year-old Becky piped up behind me. Holding up her much-read Dr. Seuss book, *Green Eggs and Ham,* she pointed at the scraggly creature on the cover named Sam, then at the egg. "Sam's in there," she insisted. "I know he is. It's green."

My husband, Bill, and I and our six children raise cattle and horses on our Arizona ranch. But I'd recently decided I wanted chickens, too— and not just everyday Plymouth Rocks, White Leghorns, and Rhode Island Reds, which lay white or brown eggs. I wanted Araucanas, the new, amber-gold breed from Chile, which lay rainbow-colored eggs.

I pictured these beautiful eggs hovering in the refrigerator like small, bright balloons, adding magic to our lives. Every day would be Easter.

"Please, honey," I'd said to Bill, "let's order a hundred chicks. I could sell eggs and make a little money."

He looked skeptical but finally relented. I ran for the checkbook before he changed his mind.

Six months later, my chicks had grown into fat hens. Brown and white eggs appeared every day. But where were the magical colors? The mud-green egg on the floor wasn't even close to turquoise or sea-foam green, much less yellow or pink.

"Looks like a hand grenade," Bill said as he poked his head into the chicken coop. His words made me feel strangely protective. I cupped the egg in my hand. A curious warmth surged through its smooth, elliptical walls, and it took on magic of its own. *What is inside?* I wondered. There was only one way to find out—wait for it to hatch.

* * *

Becky thought "Sam" might be lonesome on his arrival, so we nestled him among three other eggs—two brown, one white—in the incubator in our kitchen. We turned the eggs several times a day, adding teaspoonfuls of water to keep the humidity just right.

On the 21st morning, we heard the tapping of tiny beaks against shells. The eggs quivered and rocked. At last the brown and white eggs burst open, releasing three soggy chicks. Becky named them A, B, and C. But the green egg stopped moving. "Mama!" Becky cried. "Sam gave up!"

"No, honey. He's just resting."

Tears welled in her eyes. "He can't get out. He's gonna die!"

Pressing the egg to my ear, I could hear mournful cheeps inside. *Was the shell too thick?* I wondered. *Should I help?* Poultry books say "never interfere" because "no hatch" is often nature's way of ridding a species of the weak and the imperfect. But I had a child with dark eyes pleading, "Mama, do something."

Praying I was doing the right thing, I cracked the egg open. A tiny gold beak popped through. Seconds later, Sam rolled out, a scraggly female chick with pure-white eyes embedded like seed pearls in ash-gray down.

"She's blind," Bill said. "You'd better get rid of her now before the other chicks peck her to death!"

I knew Bill was right. Chickens peck at anything in their search for food. Even if Sam survived "peephood," a blind chicken could never bluff her way past the knifelike beaks of full-grown hens.

I sensed something special about Sam, however. When she nestled in my hand, she dozed peacefully, enjoying the warmth of my palm like a baby bird beneath its mother's wing.

Since chicks eat and drink at frequent intervals, I decided to find out if Sam could locate food without the noisy cheeping of A, B, and C to guide her. When she was four days old, I placed her on the kitchen table about a foot from a soda-bottle cap full of mash. Seconds later, she scuttled toward the mash and pecked up every speck.

Maybe, just maybe, Sam could live a life of her own. And since I was responsible for that life, I had to keep her safe. I put her in a wire cage on the porch.

As time passed, the children took Sam out frequently. They laid her in a doll buggy on her back, claws skyward. Sam remained content while the girls danced around singing, "I am Sam. Sam I am."

One afternoon Becky said, "Sam likes to ride on the swing, Mama." Indeed, wings outstretched, ghost eyes wild, our Araucana chick clutched the rim of the rubber tire Bill had tied to a tree. "She thinks she's flying," three-year-old Jaymee squealed, giving a too-hard push that tossed poor Sam to the ground. But she was on her feet instantly, flapping her wings and staggering back toward the children's voices.

When the girls tired of the fun, Sam crouched on the porch alone, as though trapped within invisible barriers she dared not go beyond.

Early one April morning, a stray Siamese cat arrived at our kitchen door. His body was so starved, it hung over my arm like an empty sock. But what fascinated me was the nonstop purr, even as he slept. The girls named him Ping-Sing, and were delighted to have two pets to play with. Although Sam was safe in her cage, Ping was still a cat that ate birds, and I warned, "Be careful when you take Sam out of her cage. Make sure Ping is outside."

The day came when I overheard Becky say, "Jaymee, maybe Ping and

Sam could be friends."

Too late to protest, I peered out on the porch to see Becky shoving two-month-old Sam toward the cat. The Siamese purred like a chain saw, hot glitter blazing in his eyes. The young chicken approached, bewitched by Ping's strange vibration. Nose met beak, and Sam stabbed. Ping recoiled, instantly subdued. By afternoon, Ping and Sam were wedged side by side in the doll buggy, enjoying a friendship ride.

To our amazement, Sam began to shadow Ping as radar tracks a distant object. When Ping lay down on the stoop, Sam nestled nearby. When Ping got up to drink water, so did Sam. The two became inseparable, and our blind chicken happily discovered life beyond the cage.

Meanwhile, as my hens continued laying eggs, all the colors I'd dreamed about filled my basket to the brim. I watched for more mud-green eggs, but never found one.

Then January cast a shadow on little Sam's life. Seeing the sign at the end of our road—ARAUCANA EGGS FOR SALE—a passer-by stopped and bought three dozen in assorted colors. He was ready to leave when he glanced at Ping and gasped, "Where'd you find that cat?"

"He found us," I said, "and Sam can't live without him." But Ping was already cradled in the old man's arms. "His name's Elvis," he said. "Can't stop singin'—in case you didn't notice."

I choked back useless arguments and waved good-bye to Ping.

Now Sam's lonely battle with life began in earnest. Cheeping the loss of her Siamese friend, Sam paced in her cage. She stopped eating. When I saw too many castoff feathers blanketing the cage floor, I worried. I let her out, hoping for a miracle.

At first Sam hunkered down near the porch. One day her curiosity drew her toward the sounds of my free-roaming flock, but angry ducks and stabbing beaks forced her to flee.

Several weeks later, we watched her wait for the hens to go to their nests. Then, squeezing cautiously through the trapdoor into the coop, she found the grain in the feeder.

Green Eggs and Sam

When night came, however, I still gathered up Sam and put her back in her cage. She'd snuggle with pleasure in my arms. But as the weeks passed, I noticed a resistance each time I carried her off. Then came the unexpected peck on my wrist. Was she telling me to leave her alone?

One summer evening, I was later than usual locking the coop for the night. To my surprise, Sam was roosting on the feed trough, sound asleep. She looked so content, I left her there. At last, she was one of the flock, ready for life on her own.

By her second September, Sam still hadn't laid an egg. At the same time, she became obsessed with a hole between the railroad ties that supported the bucket of Bill's tractor, parked next to the chicken coop. As the days grew cooler, and bobcats, coyotes, and raccoons left telltale tracks along Sam's favorite paths, she seemed to find this to be a warm, safe hiding place.

One October night, I awoke to screeches of terror from my flock. I grabbed my flashlight and Bill's rifle and dashed outside. In the beam of my light glowed the eyes of a raccoon inside the coop. As the raccoon prepared to rip off my rooster's head, I fired a shot into the air. He fled.

The next morning at breakfast, Becky asked, "Did he get Sam?"

Cold fear gripped me. I didn't know. I'd long ago stopped worrying about leaving Sam with the flock.

We hurried to the barnyard. Near the tractor, golden feathers lay scattered like fallen leaves. "Oh, Mama," Becky said sadly. "Sam's gone."

"Maybe she's underneath," I said to Bill. He climbed up into the cab. Hydraulics whined, and the giant shovel rose from its resting place.

That's when I saw them: four little mud-green eggs, cradled in a straw-banked nest. A farewell gift from Sam? *Maybe I should hatch them,* I thought. But this was not to be.

Who, after all, could replace her? As she scuttled bravely to the edges of her unseen world, Sam, a mere chicken, had demonstrated how extraordinary life is.

Originally published in the May 1999 issue of *Reader's Digest* magazine.

TWO SETS OF PARENTS

I was born to a young soldier and his young wife. Two years later, I became the only daughter of a retired sergeant and his wife with three sons. At the age of twenty-two, after getting married and giving birth to my own daughter, I reunited with my birth parents, who were still married. They apologized for giving me away and asked for forgiveness. I advised them that everything happens for a reason and I had forgiven them long ago. Reader, my two sets of parents have taught me very different life lessons. My birth parents taught me to be resilient and flexible when life changes unexpectedly. My adoptive parents taught me to forgive when those changes are caused by others or even me. I feel blessed to have two sets of parents who have given me tools for survival. Thank you for letting me share my story with you.

—Kimberly Harris *Palmetto, Georgia*

A DOLL NAMED REBECCA

My third-grade teacher and I had a magical bond. She moved after that year, though, and we lost touch. Thirty-one years later, we reconnected through Facebook. I sent her a picture of a doll she'd bought me back then to prove I'd kept it all this time. She immediately sent me a picture of the same doll! Turns out, she'd bought two dolls because they looked like her "little Jill," and she'd kept one to remember me by. Unknowingly, we'd both also named the doll Rebecca. You never know whose life you're going to impact in profound ways!

—Jill Beeckman *Freeland, Michigan*

Mercy for a Thief

by Jen McCaffery

A bar owner's determination to find a lost wallet helps a young man change his life.

Afrantic call came into Jimmy Gilleece's bar this past March. A newly married woman who had spent the afternoon at the dive beach bar in Wrightsville Beach, North Carolina, couldn't find her wallet. She didn't care about her ID, credit cards, or $150 in cash—but her wedding ring was tucked inside.

Gilleece, 42, didn't like the idea that a theft could have occurred at his place, Jimmy's at Red Dogs. So he set out to find the wallet. He spent hours scouring footage from 16 different surveillance cameras, watching the woman's every step in the bar until she went to sit on a bench outside and left when her ride arrived. Within minutes, a young man in a hoodie approached the bench, shoved something in his pocket, and walked off. Gilleece posted a clip on the bar's Facebook page. "I didn't want to crucify him," he said. "I just asked if anybody knew who the guy was."

Within hours, Gilleece got a text from 17-year-old Rivers Prather, who'd heard about the post from his sister. Prather owned up to having taken the wallet and told Gilleece he'd done it because he hadn't eaten in two days. He said he saw the ring but thought it was fake, so he took the money and threw the wallet off the public docks into the ocean. Then he bought a sandwich.

Rivers Prather, left, with Jimmy Gilleece, says, "I'd be sitting in a cell right now if it weren't for Jimmy."

Gilleece, unsure whether he believed Prather, told the teen to meet him at the docks. There, they got to talking, and Prather revealed that he wasn't getting along with his family and had been living in the woods for a week. Gilleece, a father of two with another on the way, took stock of Prather—his small stature, his ruddy cheeks—and saw him for what he was: more of a kid than a criminal.

But the stakes were high. The police were already on the case, and because of the missing ring, Prather could be facing felony charges. "He would be going to big boy jail, all 130 pounds of him," Gilleece says. "I had to help him somehow."

Gilleece recruited two local divers to search the waters where Prather had thrown the wallet. Meanwhile, the police had heard that Gilleece and Prather had spoken and wanted Gilleece to bring the teen down to the station. Instead, Gilleece called the police and told them, "He's going to be at the docks with me tomorrow."

Gilleece saw Prather for what he was: more of a kid than a criminal.

A detective was waiting for them there the next day at noon. A crowd had gathered to watch the two divers search in the strong current. More than an hour passed, with no sign of the ring. Gilleece grew worried, especially when the detective began peppering Prather with questions, trying to get him to admit to keeping the ring. Each passing minute increased the chances that she would arrest the young man.

And then a diver popped up. In his hand was the wallet, and inside was the ring. Cheers erupted from the spectators. Even the detective was happy.

When Gilleece called the wallet's owner, she burst into tears. She promptly dropped the felony charges against Prather for stealing the ring, and he was permitted to go through a misdemeanor diversion program for the theft of the $150.

But it wasn't over for Gilleece. He'd been troubled about Prather sleeping in the cold woods. Gilleece knew his home was big enough to give Prather a place to live for a while. He told the teen he could stay with his family until the boy got on his feet again. He also gave the kid a job at his bar.

"Most people would have given the footage to police, and he chose to help me," Prather told CBS News. "I say thank you to him every day."

Originally published in the October 2018 issue of *Reader's Digest* magazine.

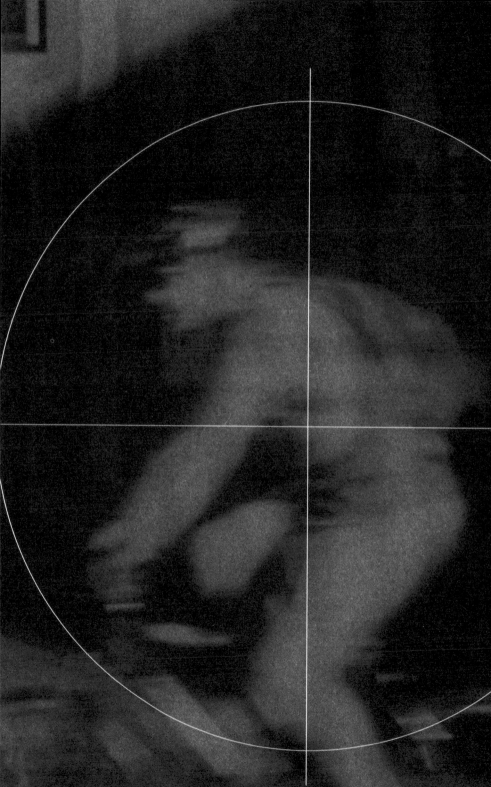

Sniper on the Loose

by Kathryn Wallace

*As a murderer terrorizes a city, one man
has a haunting thought:*
Could my friend be the killer?

It was a stifling hot July evening, but Ron Horton was comfortable inside one of his haunts: Stingers pool hall in suburban Phoenix. A 47-year-old construction superintendent, Horton was raising three young sons on his own and liked to spend the little free time he had with fellow bikers at a few bars in the area.

He was a favorite among the crowd—a stand-up guy you could count on. Horton's modest home, close to downtown Phoenix, was a place where friends could find a beer or a bed anytime. "We are all closer than blood," Horton says of his biker buddies. "Any one of them would give me their life's savings if they thought I needed it, and I'd do the same thing for them."

On this night, two summers ago, Horton was chatting by the bar with a few of those friends when one of them said to the others, "You heard about that guy shooting people? Isn't it nuts?"

Horton perked up. "What's going on?" he asked.

"There's some wacko who's killed a bunch of animals, and now he's shooting people—about a dozen shot and six dead. And the police don't have any idea who this guy is."

Another buddy chimed in. "Two people got shot Saturday night, and another guy on Monday night," he said. They discussed the murderer's MO: random gunshots at anyone unlucky enough to find themselves in his crosshairs—men on bicycles, women walking alone, anyone.

"Where are these shootings happening?" Horton asked, dreading that he might already know the answer.

Phoenix Valley, one of the guys said, "mostly on the west side." Horton's stomach knotted as he thought back to a bizarre conversation he'd had four months earlier over beers with an old friend—a conversation he'd dismissed as twisted barroom humor but now realized may have been the confession of a killer.

* * *

Up to that moment, Horton's life was gratifyingly calm and steady, especially compared with his hard-partying days as manager of the Mason Jar rock bar. Back then, he often returned home with the sunrise, and, he says, "I was medicating myself to stay awake."

But then Horton met Debbie at a bar across the street, and the two wound up building a life together—until Debbie stunned Horton by moving out, leaving him to care for their three children. Horton quit the Mason Jar and took work as a construction contractor, a job that allowed him regular hours so he could be with his sons. He spent as much time as possible with them, coaching their Little League teams, helping with homework, and even trying his hand at chicken soup if one of the boys got sick. His mother warned him that his devotion was too consuming. "Have a life of your own or you're going to resent your kids," she said, and Horton listened to her.

"I ventured out slowly," he says, and he began to forge new friendships. On one of those first outings, six years ago, Horton struck up a conversation at a local bar with Samuel Dieteman, a husky guy with an easy smile who was serving drinks. Sammy to his friends, Dieteman liked to laugh, tell stories, and pull pranks, and his playfulness appealed to Horton. So did Dieteman's commitment to his friends. "If you gave him a ride or bought him a drink, he was your buddy for life," Horton says.

"He'd fall all over himself to pay you back." Horton brought Dieteman into his expanding circle of friends, and though Dieteman didn't have a motorcycle, he was embraced by the biker group as one of the family.

As difficult a stretch as Horton had experienced, he discovered that Dieteman had faced even more: He married young, divorced early, and tangled with the law—everything from bar fights to doing jail time.

Dieteman told Horton it was his chance for a fresh start when he moved to Phoenix in 1999 to live with his mother and stepfather. Trained as an electrician, the 24-year-old landed a high-paying job at Honeywell and also took part-time work at a neighborhood pub in downtown Phoenix—the hangout where he met Horton.

But it didn't take long for life to turn sour again. He lost his job at Honeywell in 2005, and the pub closed. He told Horton that, later that year, tensions with his parents boiled over, and his stepfather kicked him out of the house. Now 30, Dieteman was both jobless and homeless. "He didn't want a handout, but he needed help," Horton says. "I told him he could stay with me and put in my ceiling fans as a trade. He liked that idea, and I trusted Sammy. He got along with my kids, and that means a lot to me."

Before long, though, Dieteman "was spending all his time at bars, the first one there and the last one to leave," says a mutual friend, Gary Gang. "He'd hit rock bottom." He was also pushing his friends away and had decided to move out of Horton's home, telling him, "I don't deserve to live in a house. I don't deserve to live."

"He didn't think a lot of himself," Gang says. "I never knew why he felt that way. But you wanted to help him. You wanted him to succeed."

By December 2005, Dieteman had disappeared. For months, no one saw him or heard from him. And then in May, Horton received a phone call out of the blue. Dieteman asked if he could meet Horton at a restaurant called the Rib Shop.

If Horton was surprised by the call, he was completely unprepared for Dieteman's new swagger and confidence. "He told me he'd met a guy who offered him a job and also had a room for him. I thought, That's great— Sammy had landed on his feet," Horton says. Life, Dieteman said, was good.

Over drinks, the two caught up and shared some laughs. At one point, Dieteman leaned in close and said to Horton, "Do you know what it's like to kill a man?"

"How would I know?" Horton responded.

"I didn't know either until a couple of months ago," Dieteman said and then launched into a story about a brutal murder he claimed he'd committed. Horton listened, assuming it must be a bizarre attempt at humor. He played along and waited for the punch line.

> *His friend leaned in close. "Do you know what it's like to kill a man?"*

"Why'd you do it?" Horton asked.

It was this new thing with him and another guy, Dieteman told him. "We call it random recreational violence—RVing." The two drove around town targeting people for no particular reason. "We use a .410 shotgun because the pellets are hard to trace," he said.

Horton felt sure it was all drunken nonsense and tried to dismiss the odd conversation. But some of the details lodged in his brain, particularly Dieteman's story about a woman whom he'd mistaken for a man and had shot in the back. "Sammy said that bothered him," Horton says. "He told me he lost sleep over that one."

Soon after, Horton recounted the conversation to Gary Gang, who agreed that it had to be Dieteman's idea of a sick joke. Sammy, a cold-blooded murderer? Not possible.

Horton didn't see Dieteman again for several weeks, until he got a text message from him on June 19, suggesting they meet up at the Rib Shop once again.

There, Horton found Dieteman drunk and irate. He'd had a fight with his roommate and gotten kicked out. Dale Hausner, his roommate's younger brother, was on his way to get him and would put him up in his apartment in Mesa, on the east side of Phoenix. Dieteman's tirade ended abruptly when Dale came into the bar, and the two left with barely a word. It was half past midnight. Horton recalls that "everyone at the bar said [of Hausner], 'That was one scary-looking dude.'" He remembers the night clearly because of the ominous text message he received from

Dieteman minutes after he left the bar. It read simply, "I'm angry, and someone is going to get hurt."

* * *

It was a few weeks later that Horton heard from his friends in Stingers pool hall about a murderer on the loose in Phoenix. At home later that night, Horton made a point of turning on the news. He was transfixed by a map plotting the attacks of the man cops were calling the Serial Shooter. The locations formed a large circle, and the area of town where Dieteman now lived was dead center.

Horton telephoned Gang, who had also been monitoring the news. "He knew why I was calling," Horton says. Both of them were heading toward the same mind-boggling conclusion: Sammy was responsible for the violence terrorizing Phoenix.

The next day, Horton missed work after a sleepless night struggling with his conscience. He sat in his living room for hours with his cell phone in one hand and, in the other, a slip of paper on which he'd scribbled the number of a witness tip line he'd gotten from a newscast. The police promised anonymity for the caller. What should he do?

He thought about how it was still possible Dieteman was just telling tales and that by calling the cops, he would be stirring up needless trouble for a friend. Plus, there was an unspoken code among bikers: You never snitch on someone you know.

But then Horton thought about all those innocent people dying and told himself that if Dieteman was the killer, he might be able to stop him.

"I sat there and went over all of it a long time," Horton says. "I knew I could lose my friends for doing this to Sammy. But I have to be able to put my head in my pillow at night."

He finally dialed. After an operator assured him that his number was not being recorded and no one would call him back, he provided Dieteman's name, along with the disclaimer that he wasn't certain he was the Serial Shooter. Horton also said there could be at least two shooters out there.

After the call, he felt a combination of dread and relief. "I wash my hands of this," he told Gang. "It's on the cops now to track down my lead."

Except they didn't. Horton spent a good part of the next several days in his car, driving to different work sites, and he listened to the news non-stop. "I watched the news all night, too, looking to see if the cops moved on my tip." But the police were reporting they still had no suspects. Horton thought maybe he'd been so worried about getting involved that he'd been too vague with his information. In fact, he'd given the cops too little to go on—not much beyond Dieteman's name—and his tip was buried in a stack of thousands of others.

Meanwhile, the Serial Shooter struck again, targeting three new victims in downtown Phoenix. All were hit from behind—one in the head, the other two in the back. Amazingly, they managed to survive. When he heard about these shootings, Horton felt responsible. "I knew something that might have stopped them," he says. "I had blood on my hands."

He called the tip line again, but he couldn't provide the kinds of details the police needed. Dieteman's cell phone no longer worked—Horton had tried that number already—and he had no idea where in east Phoenix Dale lived. He didn't even know Dale's last name.

Horton's anxiety only grew when, on July 12, he heard on the radio about yet another victim, who was targeted on a deserted street the night before. Racking his brains to think what he could do next, he suddenly remembered a detail he hadn't revealed in the earlier calls to police. He phoned the tip line once again and said that Dieteman had told him his murder weapon was a .410 shotgun. The operator was silent for a moment and then asked Horton if he was willing to speak to an officer. Now his answer was yes.

"This is Officer Darrell Smith," said a voice on the phone. He proceeded to tell Horton that police had intentionally kept the media in the dark about the suspected weapon, so Horton's knowledge really got their attention. The two agreed to meet at a Mexican joint where no one who knew Horton would see them and get word back to Dieteman.

Obscured by the restaurant's dark lights, Horton sat down with Smith and the lead investigator on the case, Detective Clark Schwartzkopf, and shared everything he knew. The detectives took in the details of Horton's two bizarre encounters with his friend, then asked him to step out to their car. There they showed Horton a heavily pixelated photo. "Is this Sammy?" they asked. The Federal Bureau of Alcohol, Tobacco, Firearms and Explosives was investigating fires deliberately set in two local Wal-Marts in June—near an area where the Serial Shooter had struck that same day. Horton stared at the photo. It was Sammy. Peering closer, Horton

The text message read simply, "I'm angry, and someone is going to get hurt."

thought he could recognize the second man in the photo, too: Dale, Sammy's friend who'd picked him up from the bar in late June.

"At that point, I was certain," Horton says, and he told the cops that he'd do everything he could to help them catch Dieteman, even though he still didn't know Dale's address or last name.

Horton's biggest concern was how to investigate Dieteman's whereabouts without raising suspicions. He knew he was now wading into dangerous waters and decided to send his sons to live with their mother in case Dieteman heard about Horton's calls to the police and responded in a ruthless way.

The obvious place to start the search for Dieteman was at the various bars where his crowd hung out. Horton buttonholed every friend he could find and casually asked about Dieteman. No one knew anything— he had done another disappearing act. Phone calls to other buddies came up empty as well.

Horton talked to Smith constantly, too, reviewing again and again all that he knew about Dieteman. On Sunday, July 23, he got an upsetting call from Smith: The previous morning before dawn, the Serial Shooter had injured a man who was riding his bike. "This thing was urgent," Horton says. "People weren't going out after dark in Phoenix. It changed damn near everyone's life."

It took a week more, but on Friday, July 28, Horton finally hit pay dirt. A fellow biker had gotten a text message from Dieteman and, knowing Horton had been looking for him, passed the number on. Right away Horton sent

Dieteman a greeting. "Hi, Sammy—it's Ron. Are you alive?" No response. After several more unanswered text messages, Horton was about to give up. Finally, on Sunday night Dieteman responded. He'd been in Vegas, he wrote to Horton. Anxious to continue the conversation, Horton quickly typed, "Did you win or lose?" About 45 minutes later, Dieteman sent a two-word response. "I lost." After a few more attempts to engage Dieteman, Horton wrote, "You're obviously busy. Call me when you're free."

Horton phoned Smith and said, "He's up to something. Sammy always responds right away to text messages, writes a whole book." Stay on it, Smith told him, because Sundays and Tuesdays were big days for the Serial Shooter. Seven of the past 17 victims had been shot on one of those days.

The next morning, Smith called with news. The shooter had murdered a 22-year-old woman in the bedroom community of Mesa. She'd been shot in the back while walking to her boyfriend's house. "The scene was a real heartbreaker," Smith said quietly.

Even now, Horton can't talk about this death without breaking down. "He was hunting her when he was texting me," Horton says. "I could've stopped him from shooting her if I'd been more aggressive."

Horton fired off a text message to Dieteman that was like a friendly taunt. "What? Are you too good for your old friends?" A couple of more digs along those lines were followed by a suggestion that they meet for a beer. Sammy finally sent back a one-word response: "Can't." Horton asked him what was going on. Dieteman told him he was eating. They texted back and forth, Horton offering to pick him up and let him crash at his place that night if a ride was the obstacle. After a half hour, Horton got the response he'd wanted. Yes, Dieteman would meet him, but no, he didn't need a ride. They'd meet at the Stardust Bar in one hour.

Horton immediately got Darrell Smith on the phone. "It's on."

＊　＊　＊

"I had no idea the machine that would swing into motion," Horton says. There were officers in the bushes outside the bar, police tracing Dieteman's phone through his text messages, and undercover officers at every cross street leading to the Stardust. Part of that intense police cover was protection for Horton. "I've never lost anyone in 28 years, and I don't want to start with you," a detective said to Horton.

Uncomfortable facing Dieteman alone, Horton brought Gary Gang with him to the Stardust. Standing nervously at the bar, the two finally caught sight of Dieteman walking toward them. He was his old self, full of jokes and happy to see his friends. Dieteman wanted to know about the others from the old crowd, how they were doing, and he talked of his recent visit with his kids. Horton tried to seem relaxed as they

> *"I knew something that might stop the shooter. I had blood on my hands."*

talked, but he noticed that the bar was filling up with undercover agents who looked too much the part. "One guy had this big cop mustache and was drinking water instead of beer and just staring at Sammy," Horton says. "Gary and I kept exchanging looks. We were sure Sammy had to see these guys. What would he think?"

When Dieteman excused himself to go to the bathroom, Horton placed a hurried call to Smith and demanded that he get the most obvious cops out of the bar right away. A minute later, Horton saw a nearby cop touch his hand to the wire in his ear, pay his bill, and leave.

In another quick conversation, Smith asked Horton if he could find a way to get Dieteman and Hausner together at the end of the night. They couldn't risk grabbing them before they had certain proof of their guilt or a judge might just let them walk, Smith explained. The killers needed a bit more rope to hang themselves.

Horton had already offered to let Dieteman crash at his house, so he had to quickly come up with a

On a carefree walk to her boyfriend's house, Robin Blasnek, 22, was shot from a passing car. She turned out to be the serial killer's last victim.

new plan. After more drinks, Horton casually suggested that the three of them hit a casino across the valley—a spot that would put Dieteman far closer to his own home. That sounded good to Dieteman, but Gang decided not to join them. Having arrived on his motorcycle, Horton

The final showdown took place at this apartment complex, where Samuel Dieteman (at right, in a police mug shot) lived with Dale Hausner.

rode it back to his home and returned soon after with his truck to take Dieteman to the casino. It was a very odd feeling, Horton recalls, when he stepped into his truck with his old friend, knowing that hundreds of police officers would be aware of every turn his vehicle took but that none of them would have a clue about what was happening inside.

Horton was glad he'd thought to put a .32 under the driver's seat that night, just in case. When they were inside his truck, he instinctively reached down and touched the hidden weapon. "I was tempted to end Sammy's shooting spree right there," Horton says, "and save everyone in Phoenix the trouble of settling the matter in court." Reason prevailed, and he drove them on to the casino, where they spent several more hours gambling. At one point, Dieteman was playing slots and, after several losses, complained that they were all cold. Horton put his dollar in the same machine and pulled the lever, instantly winning $300. "Lady Luck isn't smiling on you tonight," Horton said.

After a few hours, at about 2 a.m., Horton told Dieteman he needed to head home to get a few hours of sleep before going to work. Could someone pick Sammy up and give him a lift home? Just as Horton hoped, Dieteman arranged for Hausner to come get him. They said their good-byes and Horton walked out, relieved that the tense charade was over. Within minutes he had dialed Smith again. "I put them in one place," he said to the officer. "Now don't lose the sons of bitches."

Two more days passed, with Horton nervously awaiting word. Had the police screwed it up somehow? Then his phone rang at 3 a.m. "We got 'em!" Smith said. The cops had put Hausner's apartment under 24-hour surveillance from a next-door apartment. When they moved in, they found an arsenal of weapons, spent gun casings, a map with every shooting pinpointed, Serial Shooter news clippings, and gunpowder residue. The evidence couldn't be better.

"You saved a lot of lives, Ron," Smith said. "You let people walk the streets again." He then added that there'd be a press conference in the morning.

His mind spinning, Horton knew he'd never get back to sleep, so he turned on his TV. In an hour, a ticker ran along the bottom of the screen: "The police made two arrests in the Serial Shooter case—Dale Hausner, 33, and Samuel Dieteman, 30."

It was August 3—almost 15 months after the Serial Shooter had claimed his first victim in Phoenix and four weeks since Horton had first called the tip line. At long last, the rampage was over.

Originally published in the October 2007 issue of *Reader's Digest* magazine.

Dale Hausner died of an overdose of amitriptyline in his prison cell on June 19, 2013.

Samuel Dieteman is serving a life sentence at the Arizona State Prison in Safford.

Humor Hall of Fame

"...and then we'll clear the blockage by inserting a tiny balloon."

Like many freelance writers, I charge an hourly rate for my work. A doctor had hired me to develop a brochure, and I made an appointment with him to go over the text. When I arrived at his office, the waiting room was full, so I took a seat. An hour went by before I got in to see him. "I'm so sorry for the delay," he said.

"That's all right," I replied. "I was the only one in the waiting room charging you."

—TRISH LESTER

A doctor dies and goes to heaven, where he finds a long line at St. Peter's gate. As is his custom, the doctor rushes to the front, but St. Peter tells him to wait in line like everyone else. Muttering and looking at his watch, the doctor stands at the end of the line.

Moments later, a white-haired man wearing a white coat and carrying a stethoscope and black bag rushes up to the front of the line, waves to St. Peter, and is immediately admitted through the Pearly Gates.

"Hey!" the doctor shouts. "How come you let him through?"

"Oh," says St. Peter, "that's God. Sometimes he likes to play doctor."

—PATRICIA THOMAS IN *WORLD MEDICAL NEWS*

And a Child Shall Lead Them

by Henry Hurt

*On the edge of civilization, faith and
family love work a modern-day miracle.*

Black as the tropical night, the cat patted gently at shadows dancing
from the oil lamp's flickering orange flame. Made from a small jar with
a wick of tightly twisted paper, the lamp sat on a table beside the bed
where eight-year-old Rona Mahilum was sleeping. Nearby, five of her
brothers and sisters nestled on woven mats, making the two-room, wood
and thatch hut a peaceful cocoon of sleeping children.

They were alone in a vast night on the edge of civilization, high up a
mountain on the Philippine island of Negros Occidental, 300 miles south
of Manila. The children's parents, Rolando and Nenita, along with two
older children, had set off along the jagged paths earlier that day last
May to sell bread and coffee at a fiesta in Alimatok, a village over an
hour away on foot.

In the isolation of the Mahilum hut, the soft glow of lamplight had
brought comfort to Rona and the other children as they drifted off to
sleep. But now, deep into the night, blazing oil suddenly spilled onto
Rona's bed and splattered the floor.

Rona jumped up. She knew instantly that the meddlesome cat had knocked over the lamp. Hearing sizzling, she realized that her shoulder-length hair was on fire. The blaze leapt to her nightclothes.

Rona hit at the flames searing her head and shoulders. Safety was but a step to the door. Then, in the terrifying light, she saw her brothers and sisters stirring.

With flames in her hair, her nostrils filled with smoke, Rona grabbed the first child she could, five-year-old Cheryl. She rushed down the ladder steps into the yard, where she laid the child under the big banana tree. Then she ran back through the smoke,

Nenita and her daughter Rona

squinting and holding her breath, and lifted both Ruben, four, and Rhocelle, one, to safety.

The initial flash of flame had died down, and the fire had begun its slow, serious business of spreading through the house. Rona entered again, then carried Roberto, seven, outside. Dazed and coughing, he watched as his sister, her hair and clothes still smoldering with smoke and small flames, ran back into the house for nine-year-old Roda. Unable to lift her, Rona frantically pushed her older sister to the window and rolled her out.

With all the children rescued, Rona grabbed the family's plastic pail. ran to the nearby stream, and returned to the house to douse the flames again and again. Finally her small body was overcome, and she collapsed facedown in the charred, smoking rubble.

* * *

Dark-haired, with bright, smiling brown eyes, Rona Mahilum had worked alongside her mother in the sugar-cane fields since the age of four. Rona worked from dawn to dusk, but no matter how tired she became, she remained cheery—laughing, singing, and playing mischievous tricks. She was an excellent worker, always willing to help others. Quick and smart, she scurried through the fields, her little hands snatching weeds from among the cane stalks. Her diligence did not go unnoticed. Soon her daily wage of 5 pesos was increased to 8 pesos (30 cents). For a child to get a raise was unusual, and her parents were proud.

When Rona turned six, her mother cut back her work in the cane fields so she could attend school three days a week. The teachers spoke well of Rona, often mentioning her good nature. To Nenita, nothing was more important for her children than the chance to learn to read and write.

A better life: that was the theme of Nenita's every hope for her children, as she and Rolando struggled to keep them in school and get them to Mass at the church three miles away in the tiny settlement of Divina Colonia. Such aspirations stood as a beacon over their living conditions, as did the manner in which Nenita lived her own life—sacrificing to give her children advantages, however small, that her own parents never dreamed of.

Now, as she negotiated the long, dark path home, lighting her way with a small oil lamp, Nenita's thoughts were hopeful. She had left Alimatok around midnight, securing a few pesos at the fiesta. Her husband and older children would be along later.

Then she smelled something burning. "Not regular wood smoke," she says. "Smoke that meant something else." She moved more quickly, nearly running as she came into the clearing and saw her house.

The hut was gutted, its roof nearly gone. Beneath the banana tree lay her children—all but one.

"Where's Rona?" Nenita screamed. "I don't know," Roda answered groggily.

Frantic, Nenita clambered over the collapsed doorway of the hut, her nostrils filled with the odor of burnt flesh and hair. Holding up her lamp, she looked at the devastation. There was no sign of Rona.

Desperately, Nenita began digging through the rubble. A black, round hump, like a pile of charcoal, caught her eye. Praying it was not her daughter, Nenita crouched down.

It *was* Rona, pulled up into a ball, facedown. Most of her hair was burned off. A thick, black crust, split by ugly cracks, covered her back and scalp.

Rona had not shown a flicker or a twitch. Nenita felt for a pulse but found none. Weeping, she cried out in her native Ilonggo, "God, I entrust my child to you!" She then carried her daughter from the house and laid her on a large green banana leaf.

"Rona is dead," Nenita told the other children. Overcome by weeping, she lay down, holding Rona's limp hand and begging God to give life to her child. Could he possibly hear such a small voice from such a tiny speck of the universe?

*　*　*

Rona's father, Rolando, returning home toward morning, accepted the news of his daughter's death as God's will. He offered to dig a grave near the house. But Nenita could not yet accept that God would put such a wonderful child on earth only to allow her to die.

For reasons not entirely rational, she decided to take Rona down the mountain to the village of Bato, some six hours away on foot, where there was a small hospital. Perhaps a doctor would at least confirm there was no life in her little girl. *Yes*, she thought, *I will go as soon as the sun is up*.

In the morning sunshine, Rona's wounds were wretched to behold. Her left ear was a tiny nub of charcoal. Heavy, black crust covered her back and head, oozing fluid.

Nenita gingerly washed the soot from the girl's face, which somehow had been spared the flames. Even though she believed Rona was beyond pain, she didn't want to carry the child in a fashion that would rub her burns. Nenita positioned her daughter upside down—her belly against her mother's back, her face against her mother's upper legs. The child's feet hooked over her mother's shoulders, allowing Nenita to grasp them as she walked.

Alone, she trudged along the steep, jagged paths, along soaring hills and precipitous valleys. Midmorning, she reached Alimatok, the scene of the previous night's fiesta. There she located her daughter Christina, 14, who had spent the night with a friend.

Now she and Christina walked on toward the next village of Santiago, their sure steps avoiding sharp rocks and knee-deep wash ruts.

A heavy rain broke loose in midafternoon. Cold drops slammed down, battering Rona's encrusted back. Christina held up huge banana-tree leaves for cover. Finally the sad little entourage stopped to wait out the storm.

As she slid Rona off her back, Nenita saw that the child's eyes were open and looking at her. "Momma," came a small voice, "where are we?"

A glorious shiver ran through Nenita's body. "We're going to see a doctor," she said gently. Her spirit soared as she thanked God for such an overwhelming blessing. Then she called out joyfully to Christina, "Rona is alive!"

"Yes," came the small voice again. "I'm alive now, but I'll probably be dead again."

Now that Rona had regained consciousness, her pain was terrible. There was no more resting for Nenita, who again positioned Rona on her back and set out through the rain and mud with ever greater purpose.

*   *   *

Dr. Agnes Bustillo was in her quarters at the small one-story hospital when word came that she was needed. It was just before 7 p.m. Examining Rona, Bustillo found she had third-degree burns over her scalp and back. Her left ear was virtually gone. The burns were over 15 hours old, and infection was mounting.

"It is remarkable that Rona has lived this long," Bustillo told Nenita, but the girl needed to be in the hospital. "If she is not admitted, she will die."

Dr. Agnes Bustillo

Explaining that her family did not have money, Nenita asked that Rona simply be given first aid. Even for that, she'd have to borrow the pesos to pay. "I cannot throw away the future of all my children to help just one," she said forcefully.

This discussion took place in front of Rona, whose eyes showed she understood—and agreed. Treatment for her could mean no more school-books for her brothers and sisters.

Indeed, life in Negros Occidental was rife with harsh choices. But under no circumstances was Dr. Bustillo going to let Rona go without treatment. She assured Nenita that the bill would not be burdensome.

Bustillo was impressed by how cheerful Rona was in spite of her terrible pain. After four days, though, the doctor insisted Rona be transferred to the more modern hospital in Bacolod, 50 miles away.

The burn treatments were agonizing. Worse, as her back and head healed, horrible scars shortened her shoulder and neck muscles, pulling her head into a hunched position.

A local newspaper and radio station had carried stories about the courageous little girl who was burned saving her brothers and sisters, and funds were raised to help pay the hospital bills. So in June, Rona and Nenita left the hospital with some simple medicines for her wounds and set off on the long journey home. There Nenita went back to work, struggling to pull together pesos for the children to go to school.

As she helped tend the family garden and fetched water from the spring, Rona's smiling bright eyes never faded. She delighted in her brothers and sisters, and they in her. But no amount of good cheer could obliterate the crippling effect of her injuries.

July turned into August, and the medication began to run low. Because of the constrictions in her shoulders, Rona's gait grew ever more halting and clumsy. But a return to the hospital for reconstructive surgery was completely beyond the Mahilums' finances. Nenita prayed that God would do what she could not: help her child.

On a Sunday afternoon in mid-August, the mayor of Manila, Alfredo Lim, sat at home reading an editorial in the newspaper *Today*. A tall, graying man of Chinese ancestry, Lim felt his eyes fill with tears.

His city had recently voted to give an award to a Filipino boxer who had just taken a silver medal at the Olympics in Atlanta. The man seemed to snub the city by not accepting the money. Now the newspaper had a solution.

It urged Mayor Lim to give the money to someone who really deserved the gold: a little girl who three months before had won her scars and her honor not in a boxing ring but in a ring of fire.

A tough former cop and police official, Lim had gained the sobriquet

"Dirty Harry of the Philippines" for his war against prostitution, drug dealing, and other crime. He proclaimed an undying commitment to protect the innocent. And, says one longtime observer, "he almost never uses normal channels."

Now Lim began calling the editorial office of *Today*, but no one he spoke to that Sunday knew the exact whereabouts of the burnt child. So he did, for him, the next logical thing: He chartered a plane.

On August 20, Nenita was scrubbing clothes in the river when people came running to say the police were looking for her at home. Strange men in uniform were rarely seen so far up in the mountains. What the police said also seemed incomprehensible: The mayor of Manila was on his way to see her. He also wanted to see Rona.

After frenzied discussion, Nenita walked home to find Rona. Along with the policemen, the two started the long journey down the mountain—this time not on foot but on board a truck.

When they reached the tall grandfatherly mayor, he leaned down to Rona's level, and her smiling eyes immediately captivated him. He could see the heavy red scars covered her neck and back, that the healing was pulling her shoulders upward, that she couldn't raise her left arm.

"I want to take you both to Manila," he told Rona and her mother.

* * *

The water bed in Rona's hospital room takes a pounding as she and her sister Roda do jumping jacks. In the month since she arrived in Manila, doctors have begun a series of surgeries to reconstruct Rona's shoulder and neck muscles. The city of Manila is paying all medical expenses. Gifts amounting to 2.7 million pesos ($100,000) have been given to the family.

Rona has faced the medical procedures with the same courage she had when facing the fire. Asked about her extraordinary bravery, she speaks with a simplicity as profound as her mother's faith. "I did it because they are my brothers and sisters, and I love them."

Originally published in the January 1997 issue of *Reader's Digest* magazine.

Rare Whale

"This is a Southern right whale, which is recovering from near extinction, thanks to the ban on commercial whaling," says Leigh Henry, senior policy advisor at the World Wildlife Fund. "I love this photo because it conveys trust between whale and human, a trust we have a responsibility not to betray. I work every day to ensure that my daughters grow up in a world where encounters like this remain a real possibility, not photographic history."

Photograph by Brian Skerry

Lucy, Me and the Chimps

by Janis Carter

A young woman introduces a chimpanzee to the wild by eating ants and sleeping in trees with her.

Ifirst met Lucy at the University of Oklahoma. She was ten at the time and was being given lessons in sign language by one of my professors. I was a graduate student in psychology studying this teacher's methods.

Born in captivity, Lucy had been taken from her chimp mother when she was two days old and reared as a human by psychologist Maurice and sociologist Jane Temerlin, who were researching the effect of heredity and environment on behavior. As Lucy matured, her human parents faced a critical problem. Captive chimps approaching puberty often become unmanageable. The Temerlins eventually were unable to fulfill all of Lucy's emotional and physical needs. What to do? There were few options: a life of confinement in a research facility or zoo—or be put to sleep. Her human family wanted something better for Lucy.

About this time they heard of a British woman who trained and released orphaned chimps in Niokolo Koba National Park in Senegal. Although she had never attempted to return a chimp with Lucy's background to the wild, her success gave us an incentive to try.

Arrangements were made to take Lucy to Africa in 1977. To prepare her, the Temerlins got another chimp to live with them for a year and accompany Lucy to Africa. This was Marianne, a young female born and raised at the Yerkes Regional Primate Research Center in Atlanta. Marianne gave Lucy her first opportunity to interact with one of her own kind.

The author introducing a new food to one of her charges.

At first Lucy, Marianne, and I lived in the Abuko Nature Reserve in The Gambia, one of the smallest African countries. Because chimpanzees disappeared from The Gambia in the early 1900s, Gambian officials were eager for our project to succeed. Our family of chimps soon began to grow. We were joined by Dash, Lily, Lakey, Karen, Marti, Geza, and Kit. Some had been home-reared, some caught at young ages in the wild by illegal traders and then confiscated by concerned governments.

We remained at Abuko for 18 months, slowly becoming acclimated to African life. Then, early one morning in March 1979, I climbed into my Land Rover for a 170-mile journey to our permanent home: a remote island in the Gambia River.

As we set out, three warm, nervous bodies were attached to mine. Lakey rode on my lap, clutched to my stomach; Lily perched on my shoulders, legs draped around my neck; Dash sat next to me, an arm tightly looped through mine. Lucy, Marianne, and the others would join us later.

After eight hours of hot, dusty driving, we arrived at a group of islands known as The River Gambia National Park. A Wildlife Conservation Department boat transported us to the tip of a 1,200-acre island where my camp—actually a wire-enclosed cage—had been set up. From the beginning, the chimps would have to accept that I alone lived in the cage.

As the boat disappeared, I felt a stab of fear and loneliness. We were now totally alone in unfamiliar jungle without even a radio. Clinging bodies reminded me, however, that there were others possibly more afraid than I. When it grew dark, I slipped into the cage and into bed, exhausted. As I lay there, I heard the grunts of a hippo and the cries of a hyena. The chimps, curled up on the cage directly above me, shrieked in alarm. When I awoke in the morning, I saw three chimps, entwined, fast asleep with my mosquito net as a cushion.

A chimp's bond with its mother is strong and persists even after the offspring reaches maturity at 13 to 15 years of age. This long dependence is necessary for a chimp to learn to function as an adult. Chimps reared in captivity or captured when very young are deprived of this opportunity to learn. When they are released, someone must teach them.

One of the most basic skills is recognizing food sources. To motivate my charges, I served as their model. As we walked through the forest, I would spot a tree sprouting fresh new leaves and begin to give food barks. Trying my best to give a convincing performance, I would climb a low branch, tear off young leaves, and chew them voraciously, while emitting satisfied grunts. For the wilder chimps, this was usually sufficient, and they would climb up above me, devouring leaves as they went. The home-reared chimps were curious yet hesitant. They would sit cramped close to me, inquisitive faces almost touching mine, watching.

When Marianne and Lucy arrived, Lucy also lagged behind. She seemed unwilling to gather food herself. To encourage her, I improvised. Late at night, I crept out and tied clusters of ripe fruit to low tree branches. The next morning, I led the group to the area and gave loud food barks, pointing to the fruit for Lucy's benefit.

Although Lucy had some climbing experience, she had difficulty with the thick, trunked baobab tree, whose fruit, flowers, bark, and leaves were chimp favorites. She would sit under the tree and wait for the cast-off food of the others. She wanted me to help her. MORE FOOD, JAN GO, she signed, pointing to the others devouring the tree's tasty fare.

Lucy had to learn to gather her own food. I communicated NO. She persisted, leading me to the tree and placing my hands on the trunk. MORE FOOD, JAN GO, she signed. In order to assist her without actually gathering her food, I got a large piece of timber and started dragging it to the baobab. Lucy seemed to anticipate my action and helped me take the timber to the tree, where she immediately propped it up against the trunk, giving her access to the food. With experience, Lucy began to have more success.

Insects, particularly ants and termites, are also part of a chimp's diet. One day Dash, Lily, and I encountered a nest of safari ants. I watched as Dash broke a branch off a bush, cleaned it of leaves, and inserted the stem into the nest. When he withdrew the stem, it was covered with ants—which he quickly gobbled up. Lily sat nearby, satisfied merely to watch.

In a few days, Lily's curiosity took over. She edged closer while Dash and I were fishing for ants. In her first attempt, Lily stuck her fingers directly into the ant hole. I winced as she shot into the air with a wild shriek. Later, after another painful failure, she learned the appropriate skills.

One of the most difficult challenges was teaching the chimps to nest in trees. At first they nested on the cage roof. After several days, I put thorny branches over the roof, forcing them to find nesting sites in the trees. It worked.

Lucy and Marianne proved more difficult. Lucy desperately wanted to come into the cage with me. She sat next to the wire crying the first night. After some time, she very delicately removed some of the thorn branches from the roof, clearing an area directly over me on which to sleep.

The next day, I wired the thorns securely to the cage. That night, as dusk neared, I dragged branches up to a wooden platform constructed in a tree ten feet above the ground and began making a nest. Lucy finally climbed up to share my bed. After an hour with her, I tried to slip away. Lucy followed.

It was clear I would have to spend the entire evening on the platform. But when I did, I felt hairy bodies, one by one, slowly and quietly squeezing onto the four-by-four-foot perch. Within an hour after dark, six of us were packed on the tiny platform—all pushing, pulling, and fighting for enough comfortable space.

I let the others join us for several nights until I was convinced that Marianne and Lucy were comfortable with the platform. I then attached thorns to it, allowing only enough space for two bodies—Lucy's and Marianne's. Since there was no longer any extra room on the platform, the other chimps relocated high in the trees.

Lucy and Marianne used the platform every night. After eight months, I decided to take it down and test their ability to select an appropriate nesting site. The next morning, I found Lucy, Marianne, and Marti perched on the tree ladder that led to the platform, all fast asleep.

But one evening shortly thereafter, I set my alarm for midnight and found Marianne curled up in a tree hole, an ideal spot for a snake. Lucy was stretched out flat on the ground nearby. I scooted them both up a tree. I repeated this procedure every two hours that night and for six consecutive nights, until I was so tired I could not keep up with the group when they foraged during the day.

Again I set the clock for midnight. Again I located Marianne and Lucy in their respective areas. I quietly crept up to each and pinched a piece of skin with a pair of pliers, hoping to simulate the bite of an animal and thus frighten them. Success at last: In a week, both were sleeping in trees.

Only by denying Lucy my attention could I get her to seek the company of chimps and realize that her needs could be met by them rather than by humans. My task had been made easier when the two infant males, Marti and Geza, arrived in 1979. This exceptional event fulfilled needs on both sides. The orphans received much needed attention and physical comfort; Marianne and Lucy were provided with an excellent opportunity to develop maternal skills.

Today, as I travel with the group, I hear them giving food grunts as they approach a favored wild plant, eating until they are full of fare they once adamantly refused. Marianne recognizes a cobra in the vegetation close ahead of us and gives an alarm call—a skill that took her nine months to acquire.

These once captive animals have learned much of what is needed to survive in the wild. Initially strangers, they have formed strong ties with one another—ties that will help protect them in the future.

Chimpanzees are extinct in four African nations. Exploited for medical research and for the pet trade, and with their natural habitat being cleared for timber and cultivation, their numbers are also declining rapidly in other areas. It is imperative that wild chimps be relocated to protected reserves. I hope my work will demonstrate the feasibility of future projects on an even larger scale, and that my successes and setbacks will serve as guidelines.

Lucy often peers down at me now as she forages for food high in a tree. On occasion, she climbs down and, with one arm wrapped around my neck, gently puts food in my mouth. As she leads the group to a new area, I feel a sense of pride and relief. I follow now, they lead. I no longer provide the emotional contact that was so necessary in the early days. This is deliberate on my part to prepare them for my eventual departure. Yet I cannot deny that, as we grow apart, I feel an aching loneliness.

More than the others, Lucy had difficult periods in her adjustment. I often wondered if she would ever make it. Now as I watch her with her adopted son walking close beside her, I am convinced it has been worth everything.

Originally published in the August 1982 issue of *Reader's Digest* magazine.

Janis never left Gambia and established a sanctuary for chimpanzees, the Chimpanzee Rehabilitation Project in the River Gambia National Park. It is home to 100 chimps, as well as other animals, including monkeys, baboons, hippos, and birds.

The Prisoner of Mensa

by Rick Rosner

Rick Rosner has the second-highest IQ in the world (192), according to the World Genius Directory.

History remembers moments of genius. Isaac Newton saw an apple fall to the ground and formulated his theory of gravity. Archimedes was taking a bath when he had his eureka moment: Water displacement can measure the purity of gold. Who knew? But in contrast, over the past 10,000 years, humans have experienced about 100 quadrillion run-of-the-mill, nothing-much-happened moments, which is a lousy ratio of genius to not-genius moments. The fact is, the world is set up for non-Einsteins, not geniuses. The words *tortured, evil,* and *eccentric* are more frequently associated with genius than bubbly or well-adjusted.

My mom was aware of this. She freaked out when I taught myself to read at age three. But while I crushed IQ tests, I was a playground loner and target of projectiles. A moment of genius at age six: "Here comes a rock, thrown by a bully on the other side of the chain-link fence. The fence is divided into two-inch squares, and the rock is one and a half inches in diameter. The odds that the rock won't be deflected by the fence are negligible (25 percent squared, or 1 in 16), so I don't have to duck." Then the rock passed clean through the fence and clonked me on the head.

Having the world's second-highest IQ, I can tell you genius has its drawbacks. My less bright friends put it like this: "There's the right way, and there's the Rosner way." The Rosner way includes trying to get a girl to make out with me at a junior high basement party by pitifully asking, "How do you kiss—suction or pressure?" Instead of a kiss, for the rest of the year, I got "Suction or pressure?" yelled at me by kids I didn't even know.

> *Instead of a kiss, I got "Suction or pressure?" yelled at me by kids in my junior high I didn't know.*

As with many brainiacs, my people skills needed work. I addressed this problem after college by becoming a nightclub doorman. At the doors, I caught thousands of underage people using fake IDs. The challenge of detecting liars within ten seconds of meeting them fascinated me. High-IQ people can easily become gripped by obsessions. I became obsessed with IDs, spending ten years developing a statistical algorithm to help me spot fake or borrowed IDs with 99 percent accuracy. But after a decade of research, I was still getting paid $8 an hour, the same as all the other bouncers who didn't have statistical algorithms.

When I was writing for the quiz show *Weakest Link,* we had a quota of 24 questions a day. This didn't seem like enough for someone with my big brain, so I set my own quota of 60 to 100 questions a day. I didn't know that my bosses were evaluating writers based on how many of our questions were rejected. Writing three times as many questions as everyone else, I made the top of that rejection list and was fired.

For more than a year, I trained to get on *Jeopardy!,* studying hundreds of books and spending dozens of hours clicking a handheld counter to make my thumb faster on the buzzer. After five auditions, I got on the show ... and lost (by chickening out on a Daily Double and then surrendering the lead by failing to identify the flag of Saudi Arabia). I also lost my extra pair of pants, which were mistakenly taken by another contestant.

I studied for almost as long to get on *Who Wants to Be a Millionaire.*

For my $16,000 question, Regis Philbin asked me, "What capital city is located at the highest altitude above sea level?" I answered, "Kathmandu." *Millionaire* claimed the correct answer was Quito. However, the world's highest national capital is generally considered to be La Paz, Bolivia, which wasn't included among the possible answers. I sued the show, backing up my claim that the question was flawed with thousands of hours of research, comparing my question with more than 100,000 other *Millionaire* questions. I eventually learned that judges don't have much patience for quiz show lawsuits. I lost in court, appealed the judgment, and lost again. The legal proceedings cost me tens of thousands of dollars, making me the biggest loser in the history of *Millionaire*.

Not everything has backfired because of my genius. I've had a 25-year career as a TV comedy writer. When pumping out thousands of jokes, it helps to be obsessive and have a skewed point of view. I have a lovely wife and daughter who rein in my most unreasonable schemes. Having earned 12 years of college credits in less than a year and graduating with five majors, I'm always able to help with homework. I've even used my research ability to concoct a mixture of 20 medicines and supplements that helped our dog survive for 117.5 dog years.

In 20 years, my mental power will be commonplace. Thanks to our increasingly brilliant devices, we'll all be potential geniuses with access to all the information and wisdom in the world. And just like me, you'll use your vast computational resources to do mostly dumb stuff.

See you at the 2036 Four-Dimensional Candy Crush Championship, everybody!

Originally published in the October 2016 issue of *Reader's Digest* magazine.

POW Poet

by Dawn Raffel

John Borling, who spent nearly seven years as a prisoner of war, found an extraordinary way to stay sane—even as he was plotting an escape.

The cells were horrific: cramped, dark, and blisteringly hot. The prisoners—hundreds of American servicemen captured by the Vietcong—endured torture, hunger, and crushing isolation. During the endless days and nights, in the bleak procession of weeks, months, and years of not knowing whether they'd ever go home or see their loved ones again, one thing pierced the utter desolation: the small sound of taps on the wall. From man to man, from cell to cell, a code was passed, a way to say "hello," to say "I am still alive."

The tap alphabet was first brought into the North Vietnamese prison by a pilot who'd been shot down in 1965. These bare-knuckled ABCs were surreptitiously taught to new arrivals. With little explanation, one man would tap out the rhythms until the next man understood. Desperate, they learned fast. They also learned that to tap was to risk being beaten. The guards in the infamous Hoa Lo prison, sarcastically called the Hanoi Hilton by the POWs and the same prison in which Senator John McCain was held, dispensed brutal punishment if they heard any sounds

First Lieutenant Borling in 1966

127

from the prisoners. And yet the taps persisted—a lifeline out of hell.

Air Force pilot John Borling, imprisoned for nearly seven years after his plane was shot down northeast of Hanoi in 1966, briefly occupied a cell next to Jeremiah Denton, Jr., who later became a senator. "We were dying from the heat," Borling says as he describes a typical tap exchange. When the guards opened the cell doors, the prisoners, who spent their days in total darkness, were blinded by the sunlight. "I tapped 'hot' on the wall to Jerry," says Borling, "and one of us tapped 'dying,' and one of us tapped, 'Pray for rain.' " Incredibly, within an hour, there were thunderclouds and a drenching, cooling rain. "The temperature must have dropped 15 degrees," Borling says. "Kept us alive. And it stayed cool for weeks."

Borling calls the cup above his "only constant companion" in prison.

But Borling took tapping far beyond simple declarations. He imagined beauty under monstrous circumstances to show that his spirit couldn't be destroyed. A self-described and wryly self-deprecating "old fighter pilot," he had always loved literature. Imprisoned with no pen or pencil, nothing to write with but his mind and heart, he composed verse in his head and tapped it out on the walls. "In order to stay human, in order to stay sane, in order to stay competitive, I needed to create," he says. The poems were gifts for the other men, and they were also for his wife, Myrna—a legacy in case he didn't make it out alive but someone else did. (Myrna later told him that she knew all along that he was alive; "she could feel me," he says. Still married after all these years, they have two grown daughters.)

Some of Borling's prison poems are about flying planes and the freedom that represents. Others are what he calls "the dark and bitter stuff." He also wrote holiday poems. "We couldn't celebrate them, but the poignancy of Christmas and New Year's and Hanukkah and Easter was there with us," he says. "I would create those poems and pass them through the walls as a present, and the guys would tap back, 'Thanks very much. When are we going to have the suicide pact?' Because you want to laugh, you want to cry."

Borling says writing was "a way to make time an ally" and to open an armored heart. But he also risked life and limb in an effort to escape. At one point, his captors had tied him to a board; Borling painstakingly worked a nail out of the wood and hid it in his mouth. Later, he used the nail to free himself from the hell cuffs—so named because they caused extraordinary pain and sometimes broke bones—and from the manacles on his ankles, giving his body and spirit a rest before slipping them back on as the guards returned.

Knowing the prisoner in the next cell, a man named Darrell Pyle, was also suffering terribly, he used the nail to bore a tiny hole in the wall between them. "It was Sunday," Borling recalls, "and we said the Lord's Prayer through this little speck of a hole, and then I passed the pick through to him and told him how to work his cuffs." The two men hatched a plan. On a rainy Saturday night, they propped their bed boards so they could climb into the ceiling, and then made it to the roof. They had planned to get to Hanoi's Metropole Hotel, where foreigners stayed, and claim asylum or at least tell the story of how they were being tortured. But Pyle couldn't get out of his leg irons—the guards had changed the locks—and the men were caught. They were badly beaten and thrown back into their cells.

After 1970, with Ho Chi Minh dead, the prisoners received slightly better treatment, Borling says. Around the same time, Americans at home began wearing metal POW bracelets, copper bands engraved with the names of missing soldiers. Finally, on February 12, 1973, the first 142 of 591 POWs—including Borling—were released, to the joy of their families and the nation. One man had been held since 1964. By March 29 of the same year, Operation Homecoming was complete. The returning POWs were hailed as heroes. "There was a great outpouring of respect and affection on the part of the country, which needed a boost after that long, hard war," Borling says.

*   *   *

You might think the first thing a freed prisoner would do—after calling his wife!—would be to request a good meal, but Borling asked for a tape recorder. Initially, he didn't recognize the machine. Seven years earlier, when he was shot down, a tape recorder was still a bulky device with reels. After someone at the military base showed him how to use a cassette, he recorded the poems he'd recited for years in his mind.

Then it was time to go home and celebrate. "President Nixon had a big party for us," Borling recalls. "He opened up the entire White House, and we went wandering into the Lincoln Bedroom, looking in the drawers. One of our guys did a handstand on the Steinway eagle-leg grand piano in the East Room." The party ended at about 11 p.m., when

Borling (circled) with his squadron in 1966, the year he was shot down; the tap code was based on an alphabet grid (below left); after Borling's release, people sent him POW bracelets bearing his name.

Nixon declared he had to go to bed. "By the way," adds Borling, "about 50 children were born nine months later."

* * *

You might think another thing a freed prisoner would do would be to find a desk job. Not Borling. He went back to active duty for another 23 years before retiring with the rank of major general. Now 73, he's still writing poetry and still keeps in shape; he ran the Chicago Marathon at 70 and plans to do it again when he's 80.

Through the decades, the former POWs stayed in touch. "I remember long, intense talks about how can we better serve the nation, how can we use this experience to be, in a humble sense, motivators to the higher calling that is America," says Borling.

Remarkably, these men who had given so much believed they owed something to their country, rather than the reverse: "We all felt that we had a lifetime of paying back that we had to give."

Borling's belief in the importance of service inspired him to start SOS America (Service Over Self), a foundation that advocates a year of mandatory military service for young men to make them, he says, "better citizens, husbands, and fathers."

It was perhaps inevitable that Borling would return to Vietnam. In 2002, he traveled there with a group of White House Fellows. Ironically, the group stayed at the Metropole Hotel in Hanoi, the same hotel that had long ago beckoned in his imagination as a place of refuge. In the morning, before everyone else got up, Borling went for a run, back to what had once been the Hanoi Hilton. A hotel now stood at the back of the grounds. Borling went in. Up on the fourth floor, he found tennis and volleyball courts and a swimming pool. "As best as I could determine, I was standing in what was once a terrible place, where they took you in initially and hurt you. Looking down into the prison courtyard that's now a children's playground, I thought, God must have a great sense of circularity or a hell of a sense of humor—and isn't that fine?"

Originally published in the May 2013 issue of *Reader's Digest* magazine.

NIGHT BLOOMING

Out my bedroom window to the thick, cool grass; the hot night air is spiked with jasmine. He sneaks out the back from his house next door (his parents drink and my mom sleeps the exhausted sleep of single mothers), pimply, shower-damp, brown-eyed, and sixteen, smelling of soap and nerves. We're clumsy, thrilled, ragged with yearning, first love eventually followed by first heartbreak. Flash-forward, astonishingly, forty-some years, a brave new world of cell phones, the Internet, and Facebook, and there's his daughter posting about her father, that he's a good man, a widower now for two years. She makes him chicken enchiladas and French toast. She misses her mom. Her friends LOL and "Like" her. I conjure him with grayed, thinned hair and laugh lines carved deep in sun-wrecked skin. I'm fourteen again, inhaling jasmine, the night-blooming kind.

—Alicia Gifford *Burbank, California*

AWARD-WINNING DAUGHTER AND FATHER

When I was a little girl, my father always let me help him with car and home repairs. Afterwards, he used to say, "I couldn't have done it without you!" If he deemed a job too dangerous, he would seat me out of harm's way and have me read poetry aloud to him. He insisted this eased his work and would thank me just the same. I didn't write my own poetry until my father's last years. Now I have two published poetry collections and several awards. I couldn't have done it without YOU, Dad!

—Laura Grace Weldon *Litchfield, Ohio*

The Man in the Cab

by Irving Stern, from *New York Newsday*

*A cabbie asked one simple question
and transformed his son's future.*

For 28 years, 3 months, and 12 days, I drove a New York City taxi. Now, if you were to ask me what I had for breakfast yesterday, I probably couldn't tell you. But the memory of one fare is so vivid, I'll remember it all my days in this world.

It was a sunny Monday morning in the spring of 1966. I was cruising down York Avenue looking for a customer, but with the beautiful weather, it was kind of slow. I had stopped at a light just opposite New York Hospital when I spied a well-dressed man dashing down the hospital steps. He was hailing me.

Just then, the light turned green, the driver behind me honked impatiently, and I heard a cop's whistle. But I wasn't about to lose this ride. Finally, the man reached the cab and jumped in. "LaGuardia Airport, please," he said. "And thanks for waiting."

Good news, I thought. On Monday morning, LaGuardia is hopping, and with a little luck, I could get back-to-back fares. That would make my day.

As always, I wondered about my passenger. Was this guy a talker, a mummy, a newspaper reader? After a few moments, he started a conversation. It began ordinarily enough: "How do you like driving a cab?"

From left to right: Irving Stern with Robert at his graduation, 1969, at home in Brooklyn, 1966; and Dr. Robert Stern in 1975.

It was a stock question, and I gave him my stock answer. "It's OK," I said. "I make a living and meet interesting people sometimes. But if I could get a job making $100 a week more, I'd take it—just like you would."

His reply intrigued me. "I would not change jobs if it meant I had to take a cut of a hundred a week."

I'd never heard anyone say such a thing. "What do you do?"

"I'm in the neurology department at New York Hospital."

I've always been curious about people, and I've tried to learn what I could from them. Many times during long rides, I'd developed a rapport with my passengers—and quite often I'd received very good advice from accountants, lawyers, and plumbers. Maybe it was that this fellow clearly loved his work; maybe it was just the pleasant mood of a spring morning. But I decided to ask for his help. We were not far from the airport now, so I plunged ahead.

"Could I ask a big favor of you?" He didn't answer. "I have a son, 15, a good kid. He's doing well in school. We'd like him to go to camp this summer, but he wants a job. But a 15-year-old can't get hired unless his old man knows someone who owns a business, and I don't." I paused. "Is there any possibility that you might get him some kind of a summer job—even if he doesn't get paid?"

He still wasn't talking, and I was starting to feel foolish for bringing up the subject. Finally, at the ramp to the terminal, he said, "Well, the medical students have a summer research project. Maybe he could fit in. Have him send me his school record."

He fished around in his pocket for a card but couldn't find one. "Do you have any paper?" he asked.

I tore off a piece of my brown lunch bag, and he scribbled something and paid me. It was the last time I ever saw him.

That evening, sitting around the dining room table with my family, I pulled the scrap from my shirt pocket. "Robbie," I announced proudly, "this could be a summer job for you." He read it out loud: "Fred Plum, N.Y. Hosp."

My wife: "Is he a doctor?"

My daughter: "Is he an apple?"

My son: "Is this a joke?"

After I nagged, cajoled, yelled, and finally threatened to cut off his allowance, Robbie sent off his grades the next morning. The fruit jokes continued for a few days, but gradually the incident was forgotten.

*　*　*

Two weeks later, when I arrived home from work, my son was beaming. He handed me a letter addressed to him on richly embossed paper. The letterhead read "Fred Plum, MD, Neurologist-in-Chief, New York Hospital." He was to call Dr. Plum's secretary for an interview.

Robbie got the job. After working for two weeks as a volunteer, he was paid $40 a week for the rest of the summer. The white lab coat he wore made him feel a lot more important than he really was as he followed Dr. Plum around

Irving Stern, (left), and his son, Dr. Robert Stern

the hospital, doing minor tasks for him.

The following summer, Robbie worked at the hospital again, but this time, he was given more responsibility. As high school graduation neared, Dr. Plum was kind enough to write letters of recommendation for college. Much to our delight, Robbie was accepted at Brown University.

He worked at the hospital for a third summer and gradually developed a love of the medical profession. As college graduation approached, Robbie applied to medical school, and Dr. Plum again wrote letters attesting to his ability and character.

Robbie was admitted to New York Medical College and, after getting his medical degree, did a four-year residency specializing in obstetrics and gynecology.

Dr. Robert Stern, the son of a taxicab driver, became OB-GYN chief resident at Columbia-Presbyterian Medical Center.

Some might call it fate, and I guess it was. But it shows you that big opportunities can come out of ordinary encounters—even something as ordinary as a taxi ride.

Originally published in the July 2013 issue of *Reader's Digest* magazine.

Robbie—now Dr. Robert Stern—and Dr. Plum exchanged Christmas cards every year until Plum's death in 2010. Dr. Stern is currently an OB-GYN specialist in Fishkill, New York. His son is a cardiologist; his daughters are an endodontist and an attorney. "This may all be due to Dr. Fred Plum, whom I will never forget," he says.

From Darkness to Light

by Christopher Carrier

*After so many years, and so much pain,
could he find the strength to forgive?*

The day David McAllister died brought both great sorrow and relief to me. It rained in Miami that September morning in 1996. There was no funeral procession for the old man, no flowers, no tearful eulogies. But it wasn't because of the weather that no one else showed up to pay last respects. In death, McAllister was reaping the bitterness he had sowed all his life. He was a thief, a con man, and worse, driven by a malignant energy fueled by anger and hate. Yet today I realize that few things have affected me as powerfully as did the death of that old man.

The story really began 22 years earlier, on a sunny afternoon in December 1974. A ten-year-old boy had just climbed off the school bus on Aledo Avenue near his house in the tree-laden Miami suburb of Coral Gables. Hugh was the lanky kid's middle name, and that's what his father, a corporate attorney, often called him. He had brown hair, trusting eyes, and a ready smile.

That afternoon, Hugh's mind was on Christmas, only five days away. He wasn't aware of the man walking toward him until he spoke.

"Hi, I'm a friend of your father's," the stranger said, smiling. In those days, no one in Coral Gables worried much about strangers, especially one as well dressed and polite as the graying, middle-aged man standing before him. Hugh smiled back.

"We're throwing a party for your dad," the man continued. "But I have some questions about what gifts to get him. Could you help me pick them out? We'll come right back."

Hugh agreed, eager to do something for his father. They walked to a motor home, which was parked two blocks away, and got in. The man drove north and said little as city streets gave way to open fields. On a remote stretch, he pulled over. "I think I got off on the wrong street," he said, handing Hugh a map. "See if you can find the main highway." While Hugh studied the map, the man got up and walked back through the motor home.

A moment later, Hugh felt a sharp pain, like a bee sting, in his back. He felt another sting, then twisted in his seat and recoiled in horror. The man, his eyes cold and intense, stood over him, holding an ice pick in his raised hand.

Hugh tried to protect himself, but the man pulled him to the floor. The ice pick plunged again and again. Yet even in his fear, Hugh sensed it was not penetrating deeply. The man held the pick over Hugh's chest for a moment, his hand shaking, then put the weapon down. Without saying a word, he let the terrified boy go back to his seat, then continued driving, farther away from the city.

"Your father cost me a lot of money and made things hard on me," the man said in a flat voice. Hugh shrank back into his seat, too frightened to speak. His wounds were not serious, but he ached with fear. The man turned onto Interstate 75—known as Alligator Alley where it crosses the Everglades, home to many thousands of alligators and hundreds of crocodiles.

After a moment he said, "I'm going to drop you off a few miles from here. I'll call your dad to come and get you." They drove for some time, then they turned onto a dirt road and pulled into a secluded clearing. "Let's get out of here," the man told Hugh.

Relieved to be out of the motor home, Hugh walked a short distance and sat facing a thicket. He did not see his assailant coming toward him with a small-caliber pistol. Nor did he feel the bullet as it tore through his left temple.

For six days, Hugh's mother and father did not know if the boy was alive or dead. Hope faded with every passing day. No one had witnessed the abduction, and police had no leads. It was as if their youngest son had vanished off the face of the earth.

Police had no leads. It was as if their youngest son had vanished off the face of the earth.

The day after Christmas, they got a call from the Coral Gables Police Department (CGPD). Hugh had been found sitting on a rock next to a road in the Everglades.

The story of Hugh's abduction and survival made headlines in Miami. After lying unconscious in the Everglades for almost a week, the boy had awakened and staggered to the road, where a passing motorist picked him up. The bullet, which exited Hugh's right temple, had severed the left optic nerve, leaving him permanently blind in his left eye. But everyone agreed it was a miracle he had survived.

In the ensuing days and weeks, detectives worked closely with Hugh in trying to identify his attacker. He described the anger the assailant expressed toward his father and gave a detailed description of the man to the police artist, including the faded tattoo on his arm. Detectives developed a list of potential suspects. Among them was a male nurse hired by Hugh's father to care for an elderly uncle. Recently, Hugh's father had fired the nurse for drinking on the job. To detectives, the firing provided the perfect motive—revenge.

The suspect owned a motor home just like the one Hugh described, and he had a police record that included armed robbery, auto theft, forgery, and a jail escape. His name was David McAllister.

For weeks, Hugh studied hundreds of photos, but perhaps because he was still traumatized by the kidnapping, he was unable to identify McAllister as his attacker. Without a positive ID, detectives felt they did not have enough evidence for an arrest.

As the months, then years, went by, McAllister continued to walk the streets a free man.

* * *

Few people were more deeply affected by the case than Major Chuck Scherer of the CGPD. Scherer, who as a sergeant had helped in the investigation, had two children about Hugh's age. He was horrified by the crime and, like the other investigators, felt strongly that McAllister was responsible.

When police had gone to question him, McAllister opened his door with a smirk. "Well," he said, "what kept you? I've been waiting two weeks." Then he denied any involvement with the assault.

McAllister's cocky attitude quickly got under Scherer's skin. For the next several years, Scherer kept tabs on him, hoping he'd slip up. From talking to the man's acquaintances, Scherer was able to piece together a picture of a mean, spiteful, functioning alcoholic. McAllister had no friends, and his family wouldn't have anything to do with him.

Scherer took some comfort in the fact that life had sentenced Hugh's kidnapper to a lonely and unhappy existence. Still, he was determined one day to make McAllister face up to his crime.

For Hugh, life continued on a downward spiral. He no longer felt safe and rarely ventured outside alone. Nearly every night for the next three years, he slept on the floor at the foot of his parents' bed, fearful of every sound.

As he grew older, he became more self-conscious about his injured eye, which drooped half-shut, and he found few reasons to smile. He sensed that people stared at him and was convinced he could never lead a normal life. Eventually, his fear turned to resentment that his innocence had been stolen. Despite the support and encouragement of his parents and friends, he continued to live in the grip of insecurity.

When he was 13, Hugh realized there was one place outside his home that offered a measure of security: his neighborhood church. He was struck deeply by the Christian message of hope and forgiveness, which seemed to speak to him directly. Ever since the attack, he had been looking for a way to cope with his fear and anger. Here, at last, he found it.

One evening, at the urging of several friends he met at church, he told them his story. He spoke haltingly, not knowing how they would react.

When he finished, to his surprise, they were very supportive and full of encouragement. With tears in his eyes, he realized for the first time that his miraculous survival could be a source not of fear and hatred but of inspiration.

He grew to realize that sharing his faith was what he wanted to do with his life.

Hugh graduated from high school and attended Mercer University in Macon, Georgia, where he studied Christianity and psychology. He went on to the Southwestern Baptist Theological Seminary in Fort Worth, Texas, where he was awarded a master's degree in divinity.

As his faith deepened, his fears diminished, and he began to smile again.

In 1991, Hugh met Leslie Ritchie, an attractive redhead who shared his faith and desire to work with young people. A year later, they were married, and in 1994, Leslie gave birth to Amanda, the first of their three children.

"I knew God must have had a reason for keeping me alive in the Everglades," he told Leslie, holding little Amanda in his arms. "Now I know what it is."

After moving back to Miami in 1995, Hugh took a job as a director of youth ministries at his local church in Coral Gables. His students often asked about his eye, and telling the story was a great icebreaker. Once they learned all he'd been through, the youngsters readily opened up to him with their problems.

* * *

In 1996, Hugh was 32 years old and deeply satisfied with his life. He had, for the most part, come to grips with the horror in his past, yet one question haunted him still: What would he do if he ever came face to face with the man who tried to kill him? The question inevitably came up whenever he told his story, and he would always reply, "I hope I would have the strength to forgive him. Otherwise, I'd end up living in a world of anger and revenge, just like him."

In his heart, though, he knew he couldn't be certain of the answer.

In early 1996, Hugh was surprised to get a phone call from Chuck Scherer, now an internal-affairs commander with the CGPD. Scherer explained that a colleague, knowing Scherer's interest in Hugh's case, had recently visited a nursing home in north Miami. David McAllister was one of the patients there. Scherer had driven to the home and spoken to McAllister. "He was cagey at first," Scherer told Hugh. He hesitated then said, "But McAllister admitted to kidnapping you that day."

Hugh was silent. Scherer added, "Would you like to confront the man who tried to kill you?"

A confusion of thoughts and emotions raced through Hugh's mind. But he heard himself answer, "Yes ... I want to meet him."

The next day, Hugh arrived at the nursing home. He felt his stomach tighten as he walked down the long hallway toward McAllister's room.

He had never been so nervous. Could he even shake the hand of the man who shot him and left him for dead? If not, was everything he had taught his students about forgiveness a lie?

As he approached the room, Hugh feared that seeing McAllister might open a floodgate of emotions. He stood outside the door and took a deep breath. It took all his strength and courage to enter.

He was not prepared for what he saw. Lying on the bed was not the monster of his nightmares but a withered 77-year-old man weighing less than 70 pounds. His face was a skin-tight mask. His eyes, rendered sightless by glaucoma, stared blankly at the ceiling.

Hugh introduced himself, and as he spoke, the old man showed flickers of his old cockiness. "I don't know what you're talking about!" he said when reminded of his confession to Scherer.

After several minutes, something seemed to give way inside the old man. He was quiet for a long moment, and his face softened. He began to tremble and then to cry. He reached out a frail hand, and Hugh took it in his own. "I'm sorry," McAllister finally said. "I'm so sorry."

Hugh gazed at him, feeling tenderness and pity. "I just want you to know that I have been blessed," he said. "What you did was not the end of meaning in my life. It was a beginning."

McAllister squeezed Hugh's hand. "I'm very glad," he whispered.

For the next three weeks, Hugh visited McAllister nearly every day. The old man visibly brightened when he heard Hugh's voice.

Although he was almost too weak to speak, McAllister told Hugh bits about his life. Growing up without a father, he spent much of his childhood in juvenile halls and was drinking heavily by the time he was a teenager. He was rejected by his family and had no friends. It was clear to Hugh that he regretted having lived a life full of anger and shame.

McAllister explained he'd always considered God to be something only "suckers believed in." But with Hugh's help, he began to pray.

One autumn afternoon at the nursing home, Hugh spoke of his own faith and his hopes that McAllister's budding belief would grow. "I'm planning on going to heaven," Hugh said to him, "and I want you there, too. I want our friendship to continue." That night, McAllister died in his sleep.

Even today it's difficult for me to walk down Aledo Avenue without thinking of that afternoon so long ago when David McAllister stepped out of the shadows. There's a part of me that is relieved he's finally gone, a part that finds, in his death, the assurance that the monster will never return.

But it was a different man who emerged, as if from the shadows, in the final days of McAllister's life. That man experienced far more pain than most of us could ever imagine. Perhaps, in a sense, he paid for the suffering he caused.

Strange as it seems, that old man did more for me than he ever could have known. In his darkness I found a light that guides me still. Forgiving David McAllister gave me a strength I will have forever.

You see, Hugh is my middle name. I was that boy.

Originally published in the May 2000 issue of *Reader's Digest* magazine.

Into the Wild

by Peter Michelmore

A two-hour hike turned into a six-day test of survival and sanity.

Hiking along a path through the rainforest, Dave Boyer and Crystal Ramsey were enraptured. Hardwood trees towered into a canopy tinted myriad shades of green. Bats hung upside down from vine-draped branches, and parrots and toucans screeched atop leafy crowns. On the moist forest floor, fluorescent green frogs darted after six-inch grasshoppers and spiders that looked like tiny monsters. It was the adventurous nature lovers' dream come true.

The two American college seniors were a week into a two-month stay at the Amazon Youth Hostel, a remote cluster of wooden cabins on stilts at the headwaters of Brazil's Rio Camerao Grande. Aiming to return well before sundown on this Tuesday in late May, Boyer carried just enough in his backpack—six snack bars, a two-liter water pouch, two water bottles, a bottle of insect repellent, a Swiss Army knife, and a camera. Strapped to his wrist was a compass. Both wore boots, light pants, and T-shirts. Ramsey, five-foot-ten, slender, had her long blond hair twisted around a ballpoint pen on her head.

They were told at the hostel that the trail, marked by white arrows, ended at a river, a two-hour walk away. But there was a crucial miscommunication about the word *river*. They never came to anything they considered a river. The rainforest was full of standing water. Perhaps they had waded right through it and walked on deeper into the jungle.

Finally, at midafternoon, they decided to turn back. Behind them was a wall of green—the brush seemed to have closed in over a path that could have been made by wild boars. They looked for their own footprints in the wet soil, for broken branches. They saw nothing, no familiar landmarks, not a single white arrow.

Boyer figured they'd taken a northwesterly course, so they headed southeast. But walking a straight line in the maze of trees was impossible. They had to detour right, left, double-back. Ramsey shouted for help, only to be answered by caws from unseen birds. "We have to be realistic," she said. "We may have to spend the night out here." They made a resting place out of six-foot palm fronds.

They looked for their own footprints in the wet soil, for broken branches. They saw nothing.

Everything changed with darkness. A cloud of red mosquitoes descended, stinging bare flesh, piercing their shirts. They smeared on repellent until the bottle was used up. Boyer snapped off fronds to swat at the swarm. In the tangled underbrush, they heard the rustle of leaves and sounds of animals moving about. To pass the hours, the couple sang Phish rock songs and repeated Jack Handey quotes from *Saturday Night Live*.

The two met as college freshmen in Florida in 1998 and fell in love. Sharing a passion for the natural world, they imagined hiking the Amazon as their ultimate adventure. "One day I'll take you there," Boyer promised.

During the two years they were together, they went to Spokane, Washington, so Ramsey could attend an animal handling school for big cats. Then the independent Ramsey went off to study cheetahs in South Africa, and Boyer enrolled at the University of North Carolina at Asheville as an economics major. On Ramsey's return, Boyer made good on his promise. Working nights at a video store, he saved what they needed for the Amazon trip.

* * *

Shortly after midnight, they heard an outboard motor to the east. It told them they were near a river. Neither realized that sound in the jungle echoes off tree trunks, distorting direction.

At first light on Wednesday, they each had a fruit roll-up, a drink from the water pouch, and then weaved their way east. Both were confident they'd be at the hostel for breakfast. At noon, there still was no river in sight and their water was gone. In the baking equatorial heat, they were becoming dehydrated. Water in a nearby stream floated with vegetable matter. Boyer cut the bottom from a water bottle, Ramsey stuffed in her sports bra and filtered the liquid through the cups. It tasted like chalk.

"We have to drink it anyway," Ramsey said, filling the pouch and the other bottle. The specter of diarrhea, vomiting, disease gnawed at her mind. She also took medicine for depression—now she had none. Her worst fear was that heat, stress, or hunger would bring despair.

Circling a swampy section, they found dry slope on which to spend night two. Boyer used his knife to fashion a tepee of fronds. To protect against mosquitoes, they slathered mud on their faces, hands, and feet. The tepee kept out a sudden shower of rain but not the mosquitoes. Once the mud had dried on their skin, the insects bored right through.

Day three, Thursday, they split a granola bar and collected more stream water. By heading southeast, Boyer felt sure they'd hit a river that would lead them to civilization. They trekked single-file through a section of forest so dense they had to squeeze sideways between trees. Thorns jabbed at their thighs and ripped their hands. Predator black ants dropped off bushes and scurried inside their shirts.

That night they used a sharp stone from a streambed to dig a trench in clay soil and then covered themselves with dirt. It was no barrier for the mosquitoes. A downpour of cold rain drove the swarm off briefly. They were soon back, even though the rain was unceasing. Ramsey began to shiver. Boyer hugged her close, tried to warm and comfort her. But she felt like her mind was unraveling.

Naile Queiroz Maldonado, a young Brazilian mother of three sons who owned the youth hostel, sent workers in search of the two Americans when they failed to return on that first afternoon. By day three, the search party had grown to 50 men from nearby villages, the river town of Maués, 17 miles to the north of the hostel, and a group from the fire department in Manaus, the nearest city, 180 miles to the west. An official there passed word to American authorities. A consul at the U.S. embassy in Brasília called the hikers' parents in the States on Friday, day four. From his home in Kernersville, North Carolina, Boyer's father paid for a plane out of Manaus to search for them.

When the rain let up following a night-long siege, Boyer and Ramsey found a patch of sunlight to dry out in. With Boyer's shirt off, Ramsey saw the price he had paid to shelter her. His back was a swollen mass of red flesh. Her own body was covered with welts. Hopelessness flooded over her. "It's another day," Boyer coaxed. "Let's give it a shot."

A noisy chatter started in the trees as they hiked on. Some 70 feet up, a colony of black and brown monkeys swung in the branches and peeked down at them with white-rimmed eyes. From her training, Ramsey knew that monkeys lived in the most remote areas of the jungle. She and Boyer were more lost than ever.

Saturday morning, day five, they were sharing their last cereal bar when the humming sound of a boat engine sent them running.

We're saved, Boyer thought.

They crashed through the brush, chased the hum across a mesa of white sand, and then plunged back into the jungle. But when they stopped to listen, all the two heard was the cry of birds. No other sound.

Their frantic dash ruptured blisters on Ramsey's feet. In her sweat-soaked socks, infection became more likely. Now every step was torture. She tied vines around her calves to cut circulation and to ease the blinding pain. Hobbling, she took a fall.

Boyer could see that Ramsey was wrecked—her face drawn, body limp with exhaustion. He was at the breaking point himself. "Just make it to the end of the day," he said. "Do it for me."

With the promise of finding open air again on that sandy mesa, Boyer tried to keep Ramsey moving. His own steps faltered, too. Peering at his compass, he saw they were headed west. "We shouldn't be going west," he said.

Ramsey took the lead then, climbing over fallen logs by pulling her legs up with her hands. By late afternoon, the canopy began to recede and they came to another sandy area, this one dotted with soft, spongy bushes. To be out of the trees made Ramsey deliriously happy. She flung off her boots and rolled in the sand. Under a starlit sky, the two fell asleep. On Sunday morning, while

Boyer and Ramsey—real survivors—know what it's like to be tested in the wild.

Ramsey was still sleeping, Boyer took a stick and wrote in the sand by her side "Six days lost."

They were on a slope above floodwater that almost covered bushes and lapped at tree trunks in a basin below. Descending, pushing through saw grass, they found that the water became deeper and deeper. Was this the flood plain of the river?

They began swimming in the dark water, resting by holding on to tree trunks. The coolness eased the pain in Ramsey's feet. But the thorns from half-submerged bushes shredded her clothes, tore at her hair.

They were working their way toward a gap in the canopy when they heard the drone of a plane. It grew louder, coming right at them. Then they saw it, just above the tree crowns, a white plane with red markings. Boyer scrambled up a dead tree, shouted, and waved as the plane made a second low pass—and flew on.

But Boyer was excited. "They're looking for us," he said, "and they're looking in the right place." Moreover, in the Amazon, pilots usually followed rivers—that might mean the open sky ahead indicated a river below. The two moved on, Ramsey so exhausted that sometimes Boyer had to drag her floating on her back.

Just after five that afternoon, they broke through. The forest opened to a blue sky and broad brown river. Boyer began cutting vines to lace logs for a raft. Then Ramsey shouted: "There's people!"

Two dark-skinned men slowly paddled toward them in dugout canoes. They grinned when Boyer shouted out in fractured Portuguese, and took the two bedraggled Americans aboard.

At a village an hour and a half away, women brought them bread rolls, fruit juices, and dry clothes. A couple cut thorns from their flesh with razor blades and treated their wounds with purple salve. And there Boyer and Ramsey slept soundly in hammocks off the wet decay of the jungle floor.

Taken to a hospital in Maués, the two were thoroughly examined. Doctors treated Ramsey's feet—still she couldn't walk for two days. Having lived on less than 50 calories a day, their ribs showed. Ramsey called herself "disgustingly thin."

The jungle had tested them and their relationship—but still had more to teach them, they decided. They returned to the hostel to complete their stay. And went hiking again—with guides and always marking their trail.

Originally published in the May 2003 issue of *Reader's Digest* magazine.

Dave Boyer became a middle school science teacher in Kernersville, North Carolina. He is married and has two young daughters. He and Crystal are still friends. He considers the experience one of the greatest things that ever happened to him.

Crystal Ramsey is now a veterinarian for Tri-County Animal Rescue in Boca Raton, Florida.

Humor Hall of Fame

"I'll have the fish."

A customer pulled up to my drive-through window at the fast-food restaurant where I work and requested something from the lunch menu.

"I'm sorry, but it's 10:15," I told her. "We're only serving breakfast now."

After thinking it over, she asked, "Do you have anything on your breakfast menu that tastes like lunch?"

—BETH TILSON MOULTRIE, GEORGIA

I ordered pizza, and the man answering the phone asked if it was for delivery or carryout. "Carryout," I replied. I was puzzled when he asked for my address, but I gave it to him anyway. Then he inquired if there would be a car in the driveway.

"This is for pickup," I tried to clarify.

"Okay," the man responded. "What color?"

—CAITLIN HASLER MUSKOGEE, OKLAHOMA

During dinner, I asked my three-year-old granddaughter if her meal was good. She picked over the plate before answering, "Not yet."

—WILLIAM YANNEY

151

LINDA'S SHOES

The first few years that I attended Gresham Elementary School, it was predominantly white. In fourth grade, the teacher came before our class to tell us that a colored family had enrolled in our school. She said that we should treat them as we would want to be treated. I was delighted when Linda was seated in front of me, and we soon became friends. One morning during recess, we traded shoes for the rest of the day. Linda's shoes were much cuter than my old saddle shoes, and they fit me perfectly. Linda remained the only African American in our fourth-grade class, but by the time I reached eighth grade, our school had become predominantly African American. Now, I was the only white student in my class. And only then did I have some sense of what it was like to be in Linda's shoes.

—Leslie Jones *Oshkosh, Wisconsin*

PHOTO FINISH

My son, Mark, volunteered to help Cherie, a young runner at a local Special Olympics. Cherie was happy and enthusiastic. Mark encouraged her, kept her calm, and helped her know when it was time to line up for her race. When the starting pistol sounded, she took off like a lightning bolt, leaving her fellow racers behind. As she neared the finish line, she stopped, turned around, and motioned for the other runners to hurry. She waited for them so they could all cross the finish line together.

—Debra Holley *American Fork, Utah*

A Simple Shortcut That Will Set You Free

by Elise Miller Davis

Honesty in all things, little or big, is as rewarding as a good-luck coin—for truth lies on one side, well-being on the other.

Some years ago, Dr. Henry Cohen, the well-known rabbi, asked my opinion of a short manuscript. "A boy sent it from Europe, hoping I could sell it for him," he said. "I haven't had time to read it."

After I had read only a few paragraphs, it was apparent that the article had been copied from a travel folder. But I didn't say so. I hedged. "I don't know about this," I said. "I'll send it to my agent for you."

Rabbi Cohen scanned the pages as I handed them back. After a minute, he looked at me in surprise. "Do you mean to tell me you'd take the time and trouble to send this to New York and impose on a man there to read it and write you a letter, only to have to return in a week or so to tell me what you can tell me now?" he asked incredulously. My embarrassment must have been apparent, because he smiled gently. "Always remember this," he said. "Honesty is the world's greatest labor-saving device."

I thought about his advice for some time afterward. For how long, I kept asking myself, had I been engaging in deceptions that were squandering precious time and irreplaceable energies—both mine and those of others? And all under the virtuous cloak of diplomacy. Gradually, I came to realize that honesty is more than a labor-saving device: It is the ultimate of economy in all human relations. For example:

Honesty Saves Time. I'm often interrupted by telephone calls from strangers offering everything from "free" dancing lessons to "free" cemetery lots. There was a time when I remained mute during such calls, listening to a memorized speech that took valued minutes and left me frustrated and resentful. Now, however, I interrupt my caller immediately. "It wouldn't be fair to take your time," I say, "when I already know I'm not interested." And I hang up.

A couple I know made a New Year's resolution to be completely honest in their social life. "It all began with a friend calling every Monday morning to make plans with us for the following weekend," the wife explained. "I'd say okay—whether we wanted to see them or not—because I could never come up with a quick excuse. Then my husband and I would spend all week trying to figure out a way to cancel. We finally realized that it is all right to refuse any invitation."

Honesty Is Good Manners. Some months ago, at a club meeting, I heard an exchange student speak glowingly about his year in our country. "But there's one thing I still don't understand," he added. "Americans often promise more than they deliver. 'Come to see me,' they're always saying, or 'We must get together.' Yet, few follow up. Everybody seems to want to be a good guy, but I find their dishonesty unkind. Maybe it's meant to be good manners, but it turns out to be bad manners."

An honest question deserves an honest answer—that's only common courtesy. A neighbor of ours recently acquired a new puppy. She called a veterinarian's office three times, but her calls were not returned. Finally, on the fourth call, she asked the receptionist outright, "Do you think the doctor already has too many patients?" A silence hung in the air. Then the receptionist said, "You've been frank, so I'll be frank. Yes, I think the doctor has more patients now than he can properly handle. If I were you,

I'd call one of the younger doctors at a less-established animal clinic."

Honesty Saves Needless Contriving. A friend of mine recently underwent the chores of moving. As the movers were gathering their barrels and boxes, she realized that she hadn't seen a valuable vase. Carefully, the four men went through every barrel of excelsior, every box of papers, while my friend and her young daughter searched closets and cupboard shelves. After an hour, on the verge of giving up, the woman's eyes caught the gleam of a bit of crystal on the kitchen floor. The girl looked at her mother and burst into tears. "I dropped it early this morning," she confessed. My friend was distressed over the loss of a treasure, naturally. But she was more distressed over the unnecessary trouble her child had caused. "You have wasted an hour for six people," she pointed out. "That's six hours—almost a day's work." The girl wiped her eyes. "But I think I learned a lesson, Mother," she said. "If the truth hurts, putting it off only hurts worse."

Honesty Generates Trust. A little boy who greatly feared the sight of blood was taken to a dentist to have a tooth pulled. Both his father and the dentist assured him there would be no blood. There was, of course, and the child was outraged. Now an 80-year-old man, he said to me, "I remember it to this day. Parents shouldn't lie to children even if they think it's for their own good. Lies deteriorate relationships, can ruin them permanently."

Honesty Brings Inner Peace. When she first went to Hollywood, an actress I know posed as a foreigner in an effort to appear more glamorous. "I knew nothing but hectic days and sleepless nights," she told me. "It was a horrible existence—trying to be what you're not." One day a columnist told her he knew the truth and was going to release the story. "The fact that people really believe you're British proves that you're a good actress," he said. "But you can't continue running scared. Because if you do, you won't have energy left for your real profession." The actress said that she would be grateful to the columnist for the rest of her life. "He forced me to admit the truth, and the truth set me free."

A final word of warning about honesty: Solicited or unsolicited, it should never be confused with rude, intrusive comment. "Aggressively outspoken people get satisfaction from saying that they don't like your new dress or your new chair," a minister told me. "Worse, there are those who say they wouldn't be your friend if they didn't tell you something ugly that was said about you. In my work, I sometimes have to tell a hard truth. But I don't do it unless I'm absolutely certain it's meant in a loving way. The rule I use—and think anyone could use—is to refuse to employ painful honesty unless the unpleasant task breaks my own heart. Hence, I'll never wound to gain feelings of self-righteousness or superiority. Or to punish someone I really don't like."

From time to time, each of us should step back and take a look at our daily lives. Are we wasting time and energy carrying out deceptions, both polite and impolite? Having stepped back myself, I have learned that being honest is not a talent, not an art, not even a skill. It is a habit. And like the forming of most habits, this one requires concentration and practice. But once formed, it is as rewarding as a good-luck coin—for truth lies on one side, well-being on the other.

Originally published in the April 1970 issue of *Reader's Digest* magazine.

A Life Apart

by Cathy Free

Conjoined twins Kendra and Maliyah Herrin made medical history when they were separated.

At a clinic in Salt Lake City, the ultrasound technician moved the transducer in slow circles over Erin Herrin's abdomen. Erin, 20 and already the mother of a 2-year-old girl, was 18 weeks into her second pregnancy.

"Wow! Do you see that?" said the sonographer, zeroing in on a pair of small, fluttering images. "Two hearts! Congratulations—you're having twins." Erin wasn't entirely surprised; she'd felt extra kicks this time, though her obstetrician had heard only one heartbeat during earlier tests. She grinned at her husband, Jake, 21, who stood holding her hand.

Then the sonographer stopped the exam. "Just a minute," she said. "I want the radiologist to take a look at this."

The Herrins waited anxiously as the specialist arrived and studied the ultrasound scans. "It looks like you're having conjoined twin girls," he said at last, his tone apologetic. "I really can't tell you much more than that." He scheduled an appointment for them to meet with a perinatologist the following Monday—four long days away.

On the drive home, Erin, a homemaker, ran down a preliminary list of questions: Where are the babies connected? Can they be separated? Will they ever have a normal life? Are they even going to live? Jake, a computer network manager, tried to reassure her. "Let's not panic," he said. "Maybe they're just attached by a bit of skin and there's a way to fix it."

As it turned out, the twins shared a great deal more than that. If they made it to term, their only hope of independence—from each other as well as from their caregivers—would be a surgical procedure of almost unimaginable complexity. In fact, it would be the first operation of its kind.

At the perinatologist's office, the Herrins learned that their twins were joined frontally at the abdomen and pelvis. They had two legs (each twin controlled one) and shared a liver and a large intestine. To deliver the girls, Erin would need a large vertical cesarean section, which could result in huge blood loss. The doctor told the couple that, because of the enormous complications, Erin would be risking her life to go ahead with the birth.

The Herrins' Mormon religion permits abortion in certain cases—when the fetus has defects that would prevent it from surviving beyond birth, for instance, or when the mother's health is in danger. But Erin said that was not what she wanted. So the perinatologist referred the couple to Rebecka Meyers, MD, chief of pediatric surgery at Primary Children's Medical Center in Salt Lake City. At their first meeting, Dr. Meyers told the Herrins their twins had strong vital signs and good odds of making it to term.

"Jake and I looked at each other and knew we had to go forward," Erin recalls. "There wasn't any doubt."

* * *

On February 26, 2002, Kendra and Maliyah were born by C-section, eight weeks premature. Together, they weighed six pounds four ounces. "They were beautiful," says Jake. "They just happened to be stuck together."

Too small to survive on their own, the twins were whisked off to the hospital's intensive care unit. Prematurity was far from their only problem. When they were three days old, tests showed that only one of the girls' three kidneys—the one on Kendra's side—was functional.

No one could be sure how long the organ would support both twins, but as the weeks passed, their condition stabilized. After two months in the ICU, the girls were strong enough to go home, and their parents were ready to think about the future.

Separation was central to the Herrins' plans. The ideal age for dividing conjoined twins is generally 6 to 12 months—old enough to withstand the traumatic surgery but young enough that it leaves fewer psychological scars—and the couple imagined that the girls would learn to walk with one leg apiece, aided by prostheses.

But when Erin and Jake shared their hopes with Dr. Meyers, she gently discouraged them. No one had ever tried separating twins who depended on a single kidney, she explained. Such a procedure would pose unprecedented challenges for Maliyah, who lacked her own organ. If the girls were separated, she would need dialysis until she recovered from the operation—and then a kidney transplant.

"I'd give both my kidneys if it would help her," Erin said.

Dr. Meyers assured her that one would be enough. "You might be the perfect donor," she said. "Unfortunately, that's not an option right now." Infants did not do well on dialysis, and Maliyah's body was too small to accommodate an adult organ.

"When will she be big enough?" Jake asked.

The doctor's answer made the couple's hearts sink: "Let's see how she's doing in four or five years."

If caring for newborn twins is challenging, handling two babies who share a lower body is even harder. "Holding them, trying to balance their little heads, I was overwhelmed," says Erin.

But the family adjusted. Before long, the twins discovered they could get around by scooting on their rear end. They learned to climb stairs, dress themselves, and jump on a trampoline. One day, at age three, Kendra called to Erin, "Look at us, Mom!" The girls had pulled themselves to a standing position—an achievement doctors had said would be impossible without surgery.

As the girls' fourth birthday approached, their parents looked forward to the day when each could function on her own. But then came an event even more unlikely than having conjoined twins: Like one mother in seven million, Erin became pregnant with twins a second time. She couldn't give a kidney to Maliyah until she'd recovered from delivering Austin and Justin. (Others had offered to donate, but Erin was the best match.)

She and Jake began to have doubts about the surgery. Kendra and Maliyah were learning to use a walker. They got along so well that their condition sometimes seemed less a curse than a blessing. "I knew I'd miss bathing them together, tucking them in together," Erin says. "And they were happy. I thought they were perfect the way they were."

There was also the trauma of the separation to consider. Dr. Meyers assured the couple that their daughters were strong enough to survive the initial surgery. Afterward, however, Maliyah would have to be on dialysis for months before she recovered enough to receive her mother's kidney. More operations would be needed to reconstruct the twins' bodies. Was it really fair—or necessary—to put them through all of this?

Although the Herrins had never intended to burden the girls with the decision, the twins wound up tipping the scales. "You mean I can be playing on the computer while Maliyah plays with Barbies in the other room?" Kendra asked one day when Erin raised the subject.

"And we can sleep in our own beds?" added Maliyah.

Erin nodded, and the twins giggled happily.

Cut-apart day, as the girls called it, was scheduled for August 7, 2006. Two months before the surgery, Kendra and Maliyah were admitted to Primary Children's, where doctors inserted balloon expanders into their torso, filling them with a little more saline solution every week. The devices gradually stretched the girls' skin so there would be enough to cover the tissue left exposed by the separation.

Preparing them psychologically was equally important. Erin made the girls a long paper chain so they could count down to the big day. The hospital's counselors gave them each a pair of dolls, sewn together, which they could separate when they felt ready. Kendra cut hers apart right away; Maliyah waited until shortly before the surgery.

At 7 a.m. on August 7, the twins lay on a gurney as a nurse wheeled them toward the operating room. They seemed calm, even cheerful. Hospital staffers had decorated the corridor with lift-the-flap posters celebrating the girls' individuality—Who likes caterpillars? Maliyah. Who likes butterflies? Kendra—and they stopped the cart under each one, making the trip into a kind of scavenger hunt. At the last moment, though, both twins broke down: "I don't want to go! Let us stay with you!"

Their parents stroked and soothed them while hiding their own anxiety. "Letting them go," says Erin, "was the hardest thing I've ever done.

*　*　*

"Separating conjoined twins is never standard," says Michael Matlak, MD, one of the surgeons who operated on the Herrin girls. No two sets of twins are joined in quite the same way, and there's always a chance that something will go fatally wrong.

Kendra and Maliyah's team included 6 surgeons, 5 other specialists, and more than 25 nurses and technicians. With Dr. Meyers acting as director, they spent 16 hours dividing the girls' torsos, rerouting their circulatory systems, and allotting each twin a share of liver and intestines. Then, just after midnight, they split into two teams—Maliyah's led by W. Bradford Rockwell, MD, and Kendra's by Dr. Matlak—to put each girl back together.

"My God, what have we done?" Dr. Matlak exclaimed when he saw the gaping fissures where the twins had been connected. The pediatric surgeon had performed half a dozen separations in the past, but he'd never encountered wounds as massive as these. He wasn't sure Kendra would have enough extra skin to cover the chasm running half the length of her body.

His colleagues fell silent, and Dr. Matlak walked out to compose himself. In a nearby room, he found the twins' parents and other family members gathered. The surgeon told them of his concerns for Kendra, and the group began to pray. Dr. Matlak returned to the OR, his doubts allayed. "All right," he said as he prepared to move Kendra into an adjoining room. "Let's close her up."

For the next ten hours, the two teams worked simultaneously to rebuild each girl's pelvis and abdominal wall. There was enough extra

"Sometimes I miss being stuck to Kendra," says Maliyah (front). "But it's fun to sleep in my own bed."

skin to cover both girls' incisions—in Kendra's case, just barely. At 9:30 the following morning, the twins slept in the ICU, in separate beds for the first time. The nurses pushed their cots together so that when they woke up, they could look at each other and hold hands.

When the Herrins saw their daughters, they held each other and wept. "Everything we'd gone through for the past five years came rushing back," says Jake. "It was such a powerful thing—like they were born again."

The twins' ordeal wasn't over. They stayed in the hospital another 12 weeks. Maliyah underwent dialysis three days a week, which often made her so ill that she had hallucinations. Kendra needed surgery for an intestinal blockage. The skin around both twins' incisions began to retract, requiring treatment with "wound vacs" to suction away dead tissue and stimulate new growth.

By April 2007, when Maliyah was ready to receive her mother's kidney, the couple was emotionally drained. "The girls had been to the brink of death and back, and the whole family had gone with them. We had to make one last push, but it was pretty hard for all of us," Erin says.

The transplant was successful, but only time could answer the question

"Because of what we've gone through with the girls, we're more optimistic about life," says Erin Herrin, above with husband Jake and their five children (from left): Justin, Kendra, Courtney, Austin, and Maliyah.

that haunted the Herrins: Had all the twins' suffering been worthwhile?

"Kendra, hurry!" Maliyah calls out, tapping at a keyboard in her parents' study. "I'm sending you an e-mail!"

Climbing into a chair nearby, her twin logs on to another computer. "Dear Kendra," says the message in her inbox, "you're my best friend. Love, Maliyah."

As she types a reply, Kendra glances toward her sister. "You can't look yet," she warns Maliyah. "It's a secret."

Originally published in the September 2008 issue of *Reader's Digest* magazine.

The six-year-old twins needed many surgeries in the years that followed, but they adapted well to life apart and enjoyed playdates, swimming lessons, and school, as well as playing with their siblings, Courtney, Austin, and Justin. But their special bond has lasted through the years. Maliyah experienced kidney failure and successfully received another transplant in 2018. The girls are now 18 and recently graduated from high school. They are deciding on their future plans, which may include college or vocational training.

Humor Hall of Fame

"That's my medal for having the most medals."

My sister had her kindergarten class write to my nephew Nate and his Marine buddies serving in Afghanistan. Nate's favorite letter was this one: "Dear Marine, thank you for being in the Army."

—MARI-ANNE KOPP
SAN RAMON, CALIFORNIA

Soon after our Marine Corps Reserve unit was deployed to Saudi Arabia, one of our officers introduced himself to the active-duty regimental executive officer. "I'm with the 4th civil-affairs group," he said. "As a civilian, I work for the world's second-largest security firm." "Congratulations," replied the exec officer. "Now you're working for the largest."

—CAPT. KEITH R. ANDERSON

As female Army recruits, we watched our femininity being taken away one piece at a time. Our civilian clothing, jewelry, and makeup were locked away. Our hair was hidden under caps, and battle-dress uniforms camouflaged our figures. We were issued the same boots and eyeglasses as the men. We were all soldiers now.

The final blow, however, came in a letter written by a fellow recruit's mother. After seeing a photo of our platoon, she wrote, "I had no idea there were so many men in your group."

Of the 42 pictured, only the drill sergeant was a man.

—AMY PITTMAN

While on maneuvers in the Mojave Desert, our convoy got lost, forcing our lieutenant to radio for help.

"Are you near any landmarks that might help us locate you?" the base operator asked him.

"Yes," said the lieutenant. "We are directly under the moon."

—JESSE JOE WINGO GAYLOR, MICHIGAN

"It's the officer's foxhole."

The Dog in the Flood

by Barbara Sande Dimmitt

He reached the roof, but could anyone save him?

Go get 'em, Rody," Jim Thompson said with a swing of his arm. The four-year-old border collie streaked across the sodden field, circled the cows, and soon had them on the move, heading for the corral.

"I'm bringing the cattle in from the pasture," Jim had told his wife, Janice, when a TV news report said the Feather River had begun to rise. "If we get the evacuation order, we'll let Rodeo drive the horses and cattle to high ground before we pack up the dogs and leave."

Storms had been pelting Northern California for days. The rain, coupled with record runoff from the mountains, had forced reservoir operators to open spill gates. Now it was up to levees to hold back the surging waters.

On this Thursday afternoon, January 2, 1997, the thundering roar of the Feather River filled Jim with foreboding. Their 80-acre farm in Arboga, with 80 cattle and four horses, bordered a sweeping curve of the river called Star Bend. In 1986, water from a levee break several miles away had submerged the land under 5½ feet of water.

Despite his anxiety, Jim paused to admire Rodeo's keen efficiency.

Friendly to a fault—Rodeo happily escorted strangers to the door—he was all business when it came to the cattle. Even as a puppy, Rodeo had known where his duty lay. Every morning when Jim, 57, looked out the window, he would see a black-and-white figure patrolling the herd.

At four o'clock that afternoon, Jim reluctantly left to tend the small grocery store he and Janice owned. Now Janice, 55, paced around the empty house, monitoring the flood coverage on radio and TV. Around 6 p.m., she fed the dogs in the carport. Four of their five dogs came to eat, but Rodeo was still in the corral. Janice went back inside.

About an hour later, she saw the headlights of several trucks moving toward the levee. *What's going on?* she wondered. At 8:30 p.m. she called a neighbor who lived closer to the levee. The woman shrieked into the receiver, "Get out now! It's breaking up behind us!"

Stunned by the panic in her neighbor's voice, Janice grabbed her purse and a plastic bag she'd filled with a few items and had left by the front door. She yelled for the dogs. Not one entered the circle of light around the house. *There's no time to find them,* she realized to her horror. *And it will take too long to reach the corral. What will become of the horses and cows?*

Breathing in gasps, Janice reached the car and turned the key. She and Jim had agreed she'd head for the store. As the engine roared to life, she heard a thunderous crack from the direction of the levee. She stepped on the accelerator. Then she heard a mighty rumble and knew the water was coming.

* * *

At five o'clock the next morning, the green-and-white helicopter of KCRA-TV, Channel 3, lifted into the sky over Sacramento. Pilot Michael Kidd and cameraman Ron Middlekauff felt a special sense of urgency. They knew they would be documenting events much graver than the fender benders and traffic tieups they normally covered.

Their audience would be anxious for the first images of the flooding around Arboga, about 35 miles north of Sacramento. Although the sun wouldn't rise until nearly 7:30, Kidd carved a smooth turn with the Bell JetRanger and headed north. He planned to have Livecopter 3 close to the levee break at first light.

Kidd, 35, was a crack pilot. He had trained on Cobra attack helicopters in the Army and now flew Hueys for the National Guard.

Middlekauff, also 35, had filmed the 1986 floods and was amazed at how far the water extended this time. "That must've been a heck of a break," he said grimly.

Ghostly treetops and roofs took shape in the predawn light. Middlekauff lifted the 35-pound camera onto his right shoulder. He aimed its lens through the half-open window to his left, grimacing at a twinge of pain. A few months ago, he'd injured his back, right shoulder, and left knee protecting his camera when he fell on a stairway. He was under doctor's orders to work light duty, but he didn't want to miss taping the flood. He peered through the viewfinder at the devastation below. "I think it's light enough for me to start shooting," he said.

"That must be the golf course," Janice murmured into the telephone as she watched Livecopter 3's camera pan down a line of nearly submerged rooftops and trees. She was in her son's house, still wearing her clothes from the night before. Jim, unable to sleep, had gone to the store early. He was watching Channel 3's report and called to be sure she was, too.

"I've flown around a lot over the past day or so," the Thompsons heard Kidd say, "but this is the worst so far. We're coming up now on the levee break."

"Jim, there's our house!" Janice said, staring at all that was visible of a white house with a steeply pitched roof. It stood alone, stubbornly resisting the torrent of brown water swirling around the top story.

"That can't be it," Jim said in disbelief. "Where's the barn? The barn's nearly as high as the house!"

The camera panned the surrounding area, and Janice realized how lucky she was to be alive. But she grieved for their animals. She prayed the end had come quickly for them.

As Jim and Janice watched the helicopter circle their house once more, the anchorwoman's voice broke in.

"What's that white spot? Could it be a dog?"

The camera zoomed in on a small black-and-white shape huddled on the porch roof mere feet from the rushing water. "Rodeo!" Janice shrieked into the telephone. "Jim, that's Rodeo! How in the world did he get up there?"

"Call Channel 3," Jim urged. Janice hung up, then dialed the station and asked to have a message delivered to the newsroom. A newsroom assistant asked if she would be willing to tell her story on the air. Surprised, Janice agreed.

"That's our house with the dog on the roof," Janice told the anchorwoman. "His name is Rodeo. We don't know how he got up there, but he must've really wanted to live. We know people come first, but maybe somebody might be able to help him."

Kidd held the helicopter steady to give Middlekauff a good camera angle. The bedraggled dog looked safe for now, but Kidd worried that the rising water might force the animal to the top section of the roof, where the pitch was so steep that he could slip and be gone in an instant.

The current was too powerful for a boat rescue to be practical. *Could I get close enough?* Kidd wondered. Resignedly, he answered his own question over the air. "It would be nice to set down and get that dog, but he's down too low. Our rotor blades would hit the roof."

Kidd and Middlekauff left to make a sweep of the surrounding area. About an hour later, they returned to find that the water had risen several feet on the Thompsons' roof.

Kidd broadcast Rodeo's location over the pilots' radio frequency in case one of the rescue helicopters could pick up a dog. He got no answer. *They're all probably looking for stranded peaple,* he thought.

Both men loved dogs, and now that they knew the border collie's name, they felt bonded with him. But it was time to tend to their responsibilities. They broke off their vigil and flew south. Middlekauff shot poignant pictures of horses wading toward high ground, unaware that fences blocked the path to safety. They showed a Coast Guard helicopter plucking a man and woman from the top of a submerged vehicle. They covered another helicopter as it raised several people off a rooftop with a hoist.

But neither man could shake the memory of the black-and-white dog on the roof. "If we leave now," Kidd said to Middlekauff late that afternoon, "we can get in one more report on Arboga." Except for refueling stops, they'd been up all day.

*   *   *

It was nearly 5:30 when the Thompson house came into view. Kidd was shocked. The water had risen six or seven feet more. There was no trace of the porch roof on which they'd last seen Rodeo. Water still raged through the breach in the levee.

That house is under tremendous pressure, Kidd thought, recalling the debris from other buildings they'd seen floating and snagged in trees. *It might not stand through the night.*

"I don't see the dog," he said.

"Neither do I," Middlekauff replied.

As the north side of the house came into view, pilot and cameraman exhaled in relief. Somehow Rodeo must have scrambled over the peak and down the other side. He now lay curled tightly around an attic vent protruding several feet below the peak.

It was getting dark. The features of Kidd's boyish face locked in concentration. He eased into a spiraling turn around the house, memorizing details, estimating distances.

"I think I can get in there," he told Middlekauff. "Do you want to try to grab him?"

Middlekauff had flown with Kidd for years and trusted his skills completely. His only concern was whether his own injured back, knee, and shoulder were equal to the task. "If you're not sure you can do it, don't try," Kidd said, as if reading his mind. The cameraman concluded that any pain he might experience now would be nothing compared with what he'd feel if Rodeo were swept off the roof during the night. "I want to try," Middlekauff said.

Kidd approached the north side of the roof in a gentle, diagonal descent to the left, all his senses alert. He wore the 31-foot-long helicopter like a shell, sensitive to its dimensions and the 33-foot swath of its main rotor blades. Rodeo was perched high enough that there was no longer any risk the main rotor, spinning 9½ feet above the skids, would hit the roof.

Still, there were plenty of hazards. A chimney with a TV antenna jutted from the near end of the roof. Kidd would have to keep the helicopter parallel to the roof line so the tail rotor would clear the antenna. Because Middlekauff had no harness, the pilot had to position the door directly opposite the dog. That would afford enough clearance for the main rotor to miss the chimney—as long as Kidd didn't let the helicopter drift backward. Unfortunately, the closer he got, the less visibility he would have from his seat on the right side of the cockpit, farthest from the roof.

"I'll pull away if he starts to spook," Kidd said. Both men watched Rodeo intently. The dog looked frightened but not panicked as he crouched in the downdraft. There was a steady intelligence in his upturned eyes.

"Looks like he's going to stay put," Middlekauff said, unbuckling his seat belt.

"I'll get you as close as I can," Kidd said. "Watch yourself." He felt the helicopter's center of gravity shift as Middlekauff opened the door. Kidd eased the last few feet down and to the left, listening for the slightest hint of spinning blades hitting brick or metal.

He settled the craft delicately until the front tip of the left skid barely touched the roof. Middlekauff eased his legs out. With his right hand, he clutched the handle of the door, which opened to a 90-degree angle. He planted his right foot on the skid and reached for the roof with his left foot. With his left arm outstretched, he hung spread-eagled out of the helicopter.

"Come here, boy!" Middlekauff called, barely able to hear himself over the deafening *whap-whap* of the helicopter blades. Rodeo lay as if glued to the attic vent, just out of reach. He looked up with pleading eyes, his body trembling.

Middlekauff called again and again to the dog, glancing up periodically in case Kidd signaled the need to cast off. A minute passed, and Middlekauff kept reaching toward the flattened form of the dog.

Inside the helicopter, Kidd was using all his skill to compensate for Middlekauff's shifting weight. He kept his bearings by watching an attic vent visible through the low window on the opposite side of the cockpit.

The Dog in the Flood

He estimated he'd been hovering almost two minutes. A devastating thought struck him. *What if Ron can't grab the dog?*

Outside, Middlekauff kept calling to Rodeo. He looked into the dog's eyes. *Just give me a little help, boy.* Rodeo lifted his neck almost imperceptibly. Middlekauff reacted, stretching to the limit and grabbing a handful of collar, hair, and skin. With one yank, he pulled the 45-pound dog across his body and through the doorway.

Kidd felt the helicopter jerk and then heard Middlekauff back inside yelling, "I've got him!" As he applied power and lifted off, he turned and looked at Middlekauff, who was laughing as Rodeo licked his face.

"All right!" Kidd yelled over the cameraman's whoops. Middlekauff hooked up a small camera and held it at arm's length, pointing it toward himself and the dog, who had squirmed partway onto his lap.

Kidd grinned and keyed his microphone. "Take us live!" he radioed to the station.

Jim and Janice Thompson had spent the day driving through the foothills after being evacuated a second time.

Exhausted, they ended up in a Sacramento motel at about 5:30 p.m. They trudged into their room and turned on the TV.

The first thing to appear on the screen was a fisheye view of a black-and-white dog peering at the camera from inside a helicopter. Jim blinked and sat on the bed. "Look!" he said. "They've got Rody!" Janice sank down beside him, and they both stared in amazement.

"Janice and Jim Thompson," said the anchorman, "if you're watching, please contact the station. We have your dog!"

Later that night, Janice and Jim stepped hesitantly into the newsroom. Rodeo uttered a short whine and padded across the floor to them.

Janice knelt, and Rodeo nestled his head in her arms before turning toward Jim, eyes raised as if asking for orders. Jim reached down and scratched Rodeo's chest. Emotion clogged Jim's throat. *There's nothing left for you to herd,* he thought, *but it's sure good to see you.*

Originally published in the August 1997 issue of *Reader's Digest* magazine.

There Is Joy in Mudville

The year was 1965. Mickey Mantle, a New York Yankee, hit
the first indoor home run at Houston's new Astrodome. The
Giants' Willie Mays won his second MVP award. But one of
the most enduring baseball moments of the year featured
an Angel: Rev. Capistran Ferrito, a friar from Our Lady Queen
of Angels church in New York City. Exactly why the friar was
out playing ball in his habit—and church shoes!—on this day
is lost to history. Fortunately, this award-winning
photograph preserved the boyish joy on his face for
generations to come.
Photograph by John Duprey

PORK CHOPS AND POP-TARTS

The morning after my father stole me away from my mother in the middle of the night, I had leftover pork chops and strawberry Pop-Tarts for breakfast. It was all he had around, but it was oh so good. Mom's boyfriend had been molesting me, and I had been rescued. I was confused. I was happy to be with Daddy. I was sad to be without Momma. I was scared. I was a lot of things. But most of all, I was safe. Twenty-three years later, home from college for the summer, Mom's new boyfriend assaulted and tried to rape me. I fought back and escaped. Life has taught me to fight. And that includes fighting for a relationship with the woman who gave me life. Loving her, like living, is just like that breakfast I had so long ago…a strange medley of the salty and the sweet.

—Jannie Holland *Chicago, Illinois*

SAILOR'S SUNRISE

On my twenty-fourth birthday, I was standing a communications watch on the bridge of the U.S.S. *George Washington*. The captain was feared by the enlisted men and never spoke to anyone below an officer status. It was early and the sun was just appearing over the Mediterranean Sea. "Shipmate. Get over here!" the captain bellowed. "Yes, sir!" I ran from my alcove into view. "Look at that." He pointed to the red, glowing sun cutting through the fog over the still black sea. It was the most beautiful thing I had ever seen. I'll never forget his inadvertent birthday gift.

—Michael Sutch *Sellersville, Pennsylvania*

Lame Excuses

by Andy Simmons

Our humorist offers a handful of excuses for when "the dog ate my homework" just doesn't cut it.

Well, that's just great. Not only does some governor in South Carolina have a tryst in Argentina, his staff uses my excuse. Now I can never again trot out the old hiking-the-Appalachian-Trail-so-I-couldn't-be-reached defense. I don't even like to hike, but I do like a good Argentinean tryst, and I really love a good excuse. We all do—that's why we reach for one whenever we're trapped. "Any excuse is better than none," says John Rooney, a professor emeritus in psychology at La Salle University, "because if you tell a good story and entertain, that's sometimes more important than the truth."

I'm all for that, as is the woman in Ohio who was arrested for torching a bar's bathroom. When asked by a cop why she did it, she stated unequivocally, "I felt stressed because of the death of Michael Jackson." That's certainly more entertaining than "I was blotto." And what about the Polish woman who insisted that her teenage daughter came down with a bad case of pregnancy after swimming in a hotel pool? Were you entertained, or did you think, *That sounds plausible?* If the latter, then you'll believe these excuses.

* * *

Peter Ivan Dunne was awaiting trial in Ireland, charged with a sex

179

crime. Before the trial ended, he fled to England and was convicted in absentia. About to be extradited, he explained to a British court that he should not be sent back, because his experience with the Irish penal system had led him to believe that his right to life, as spelled out by article 2 of the European Convention on Human Rights, would be violated.

The lame excuse: They'd serve him red onions. Dunne's allergic to them, and he was sure the prison would make him eat the "potentially life-threatening" vegetable.

Did anyone buy it? The court decided that it was doubtful that the prison would have such a "cavalier attitude" toward his allergy and shipped Dunne back to Ireland.

When in doubt, blame booze! Unless, of course, the drunk excuse only makes matters worse. Last year, then–New York congressman Vito Fossella was pulled over in Alexandria, Virginia, by a cop and blew a 0.17 on the Breathalyzer—more than twice the legal limit. After the hangover, Fossella knew he'd better start thinking fast.

The lame excuse: His high blood alcohol level was a result of the alcohol-based hand sanitizer he'd used.

Did anyone buy it? After several "What do you take us for?" looks from the cops, DAs, the press—pretty much everyone—Fossella changed his plea from DUIHS (driving under the influence of hand sanitizer) to good old-fashioned DUI.

Marco Fella of England admitted attacking his girlfriend with a dog toy and, another time, biting her finger. But it wasn't his fault.

The lame excuse: "My client's temper snapped because he felt his partner was not making enough effort in the relationship," said his lawyer.

The lamer excuse: She wore baggy pants instead of the sexy thong he preferred.

The lamerer excuse: Biting and assault with a pet toy aside, Fella is not really violent—he just hadn't had his fill of Mars bars. See, Fella is a sugar addict and has a ten-Mars-bars-a-day habit. And if he's jonesing for one, well, he's not responsible for his actions.

Did anyone buy it? Possibly the Mars, Inc., marketing division, but that's about it. Fella enrolled in an anger management course.

Charles J. O'Byrne, the top aide to New York governor David Paterson, neglected to file tax returns for five years. "Neglected" is really the wrong word, says his lawyer: O'Byrne couldn't pay his taxes.

The lame excuse: He suffers from a medical condition called late-filing syndrome, which is caused by depression. And even though this depression did not stop him from being a highly functional professional or enjoying an active social life, it did seem to affect his ability to pay taxes—five years in a row.

Did anyone buy it? Not the American Psychiatric Association. An APA representative told the *New York Times* that it doesn't recognize late-filing syndrome as a psychiatric condition.

A $1,772.50 bank deposit showed up in Randy and Melissa Pratt's bank account as $177,250. No problem, said the Bloomsburg, Pennsylvania, couple. We'll just quit our jobs, close up the house, and move to sunny Florida. Bye! Of course, banks hate to lose that much money, so they sicced the cops on the Pratts. But the couple swore they weren't thieves and that it had all been just an honest mistake.

The lame excuse: Her husband was a roofing installer, said Melissa Pratt, so they often got large checks. And, well, all large checks look alike, so they didn't pay such close attention, because, after all, who pays attention to a check for $177,250?

Did anyone buy it? Would you? Melissa Pratt pleaded guilty to theft, and Randy Pratt was awaiting trial at press time.

* * *

Is it possible that Ralph Reese was fired from a Manhattan Whole

Foods as part of a cost-cutting program? The high-end supermarket isn't talking, except it claimed that Reese was shown the door after he was caught taking food.

Lame excuse: Was it fresh Chilean sea bass? A case of rice milk? A shipment of silken tofu? No, Whole Foods canned Reese for taking a tuna fish sandwich that was being thrown out.

Did anyone buy it? Reese's attorney, Elizabeth Shollenberger, didn't. She suspects the company wanted to trim payroll and unemployment insurance costs. She grants that Whole Foods has a policy against employees taking food without paying for it. But still, a tuna fish sandwich? Destined for tuna fish sandwich heaven?

"You wouldn't think a reasonable person would fire anyone over that," she says. Indeed, a study by the Urban Institute found that in these economically tough times, more and more companies are charging employees with misconduct so that they can avoid paying unemployment insurance, even to someone like Reese, who's never been accused of stealing food before. Either way, Reese successfully appealed to get his unemployment benefits.

Originally published in the October 2009 issue of *Reader's Digest* magazine.

Humor Hall of Fame

While taking stock of our products, I read aloud the final numbers to my boss. As he entered each one into a calculator, I deleted it off my mobile device. Only after I'd finished did we realize that he had entered the numbers on his desk phone's keypad.

—DAVID MARLAND ON QUORA.COM

As my two sons were climbing into the back seat of our car, Eric, five, yelled, "I call the left side!"

That didn't sit well with Ron, four. "No, I want the left side!"

"I want the left side!"

"No, I want the left side!"

Intervening I said, "Since Eric is older, he can have the left side."

"Thanks, Dad!" said Eric. "Which side is left?"

—JOSH WESTON MONTCLAIR, NEW JERSEY

We've Been Hit!

By Lynn Rosellini

Lightning had killed one climber. Rescuers had just a few hours to save the other 12.

Clinton Summers has sifted the questions in his mind a thousand times. Was there something he could have done? Clues he overlooked? Should he have listened when Erica complained of being cold and tired and wanted to turn back?

The night before, it had all seemed so joyful: Clinton, 27, and Erica crawled into sleeping bags in a tent pitched on a rocky moraine 10,800 feet up in Wyoming's Grand Tetons. The July 2003 trip marked their fifth wedding anniversary—how they'd laughed about it! "Some people go to a nice, cushy hotel," Erica, 25, joked, burying her blond hair in the folds of nylon and down. "Not us—we're sleeping on rock!"

No matter. It was a pleasure to drift off to sleep that night and not worry about being awakened by two-year-old Daxton, a chronic night visitor to their bed. Nope, Dax and his big sister, Adison, were back home in Idaho Falls with their grandparents. As for Mom and Dad, they were camping with friends in preparation for the adventure of a lifetime. In the morning, they planned to celebrate their anniversary with an ascent of the majestic 13,770-foot Grand Teton, one of the most challenging of America's alpine peaks. That night, on the rocks, Clinton and Erica Summers got the best night's sleep they'd had in years.

Shortly before 6 a.m., Rob Thomas poked his head out of the tent next door, careful not to wake his wife, Sherika. He inhaled the frigid morning air. Darkness still shrouded the peaks. The previous afternoon, the Summerses and Thomases had hiked the 6.2 miles from the Lupine Meadows trail head in the middle of Grand Teton National Park. Picking huckle-

At the moraine camp before the ascent, from left: Dave Jordan, Sherika Thomas, Steve Oler, Reese Jackson, Clinton Summers, Rob Thomas, and in orange jacket hidden behind him, Erica Summers.

berries and chatting as they went, they had pitched tents just 3,000 feet beneath the summit to get an early start on the ascent.

Rob and Clinton, friends since their college days at Idaho State, seemed a particularly unlikely pair. At six foot two, Rob wore a Marine buzz cut and an air of authority. Clinton, slightly built, five foot eight, had fine features and a soft-spoken style. What bonded them most was the outdoors: Both loved snowboarding, mountain biking, and, above all, climbing. One day the previous summer, the two men had summited "the Grand"—and phoned their wives from the top. Afterward, Summers arrived home practically bursting. "Erica," he told his wife, "we gotta do this!"

Now, almost a year later, the two couples huddled around a camp stove, waiting for glacier water to boil. As they sipped hot chocolate and nibbled oatmeal, other members of the climbing party emerged from tents on the moraine and in the meadow below. There were 11 men and 2 women on the climb, including Rob's brother, Justin, his father, Bob, Sherika's father, and friends and co-workers from the IT department of Melaleuca, a natural products company based in Idaho Falls, where Rob and Clinton worked.

Stretching, yawning, they began to pile on fleece and stuff gear into backpacks: shiny black fiberglass helmets, harnesses, and 200-foot lengths of red, yellow, and blue nylon rope. By 8 a.m., they'd all assembled at the Lower Saddle, the scenic 11,600-foot ridge between Grand and Middle Teton. High above, sunlight gilded the granite spires. Thousands of feet below, azure lakes shimmered in the Jackson Hole valley. Was there ever a more glorious day for climbing?

Above them, the rugged Grand was dappled with snowfields and etched with granite ledge. Rob and Clinton had chosen the Upper Exum Ridge

Sherika Thomas, Clinton and Erica Summers near Spaulding Falls, the day before the accident.

route, a popular but difficult ascent up the craggy south side of the peak. The Yosemite Decimal System, a rating method that measures a climb's difficulty, put the Exum Ridge route at 5.5 on a scale of 6. That means climbers have to work with ropes and rock anchors, and someone has to help belay them to prevent a fall. The route required climbers like Thomas and Summers who knew every ledge and handhold. On today's ascent, the first-timers would climb in four teams, each led by an experienced climber who had previously summited the Grand.

Erica Summers looked up at the peak, silhouetted against the hard blue sky. From the start, she'd had misgivings, which she'd confided to Sherika and others. Just the month before, a woman climber had plummeted 800 feet off a ridge on nearby Middle Teton. "People actually die in the Tetons," she had told Sherika on the day they took their families to lunch at Godfather's Pizza, a popular Idaho Falls restaurant. "Aren't you scared?"

It was atypical of Erica to be nervous about any outdoor adventure. She loved skiing and hiking; on her first date with Clinton, they'd gone snowboarding. And though no expert, she was a climber, too. After the birth of her two children, she had worked hard to shed pounds and get back in shape. Now, she was in good enough condition to do the climb, she'd decided—she wasn't going to disappoint Clinton.

Unlike her shy and more reticent husband, Erica was outgoing and gregarious, known for her big heart. Friends told the story of how she'd met a homeless woman with kids in the park, invited them home to

**Grand Teton summit
13,770 feet**

**Friction Pitch
100-foot,
5.5-rated crux
of the Upper
Exum Ridge**

**Lower Saddle
Starting point of climb
at 11,600 feet. Also site of
emergency helicopter pad.**

The route Summers and Thomas planned. Lightning struck the group while they were on Friction Pitch, the crux, or most difficult part, of the climb.

shower and do laundry, and sent them off with a pile of extra clothes. Her greatest delight was romping with Daxton and his four-year-old sister on the playground or at the zoo. Full of energy, she was also taking nursing classes at Idaho State. No, brightly dressed in orange and green hiking clothes, Erica was going up that mountain—even if she had to swallow an occasional twinge of fear.

The four teams picked their way past clumps of moss campion and alpine forget-me-nots. By 10:30 a.m., they had scrambled up talus to reach the base of a wide, flat ridge at 12,000 feet known as Wall Street—and came to a thudding halt. "Whoa, there's a lot of people!" exclaimed Justin Thomas, Rob's younger brother, squinting at climbers strung out along the rocky ledge. Ahead of them, a dozen or more figures waited their turn to rope up and cross Exum's legendary Gap. The 20-foot chasm is the route's first technical challenge, with 1,000 feet of open air below for those who misstep.

We've Been Hit!

At first, Rob Thomas wasn't worried about the wait. The group's unofficial leader, he studied the wispy clouds that had begun to trail across the azure sky. The summer had been a scorcher, temperatures topping 90 degrees on the sagebrush plains. All day, warm air rose from the valleys, colliding with cool air above to produce heavy clouds charged with electricity. Late afternoon thunderstorms were frequent.

Still, Thomas figured, it was early. They'd summit by 1 p.m. and be off the mountain by the time a storm hit.

*　　*　　*

But the wait in the chill shadows at the bottom of Wall Street turned into two hours, and the climbers' mood turned solemn. Erica was cold and tired. "I'm ready to turn back," she said, slumping onto a rock. But her friends wouldn't have it. "You're doing so well!" someone said. "We're at the most exciting part—just 1,500 feet from the summit!" Sherika Thomas advised her friend: "Eat something. You'll feel better." Getting down off the mountain was always harder than making it up, and it would be dangerous for Erica to head down alone with no one to rope her in.

Dark thunderheads were building in the northwest by the time the climbers reached the sheer rock face called Friction Pitch. At around 2:30 p.m., an icy rain pelted the group, and the bone-chilling cold seemed to go right through their layers of fleece. The brilliant, sunny day that had begun with such exuberance now seemed grim and soggy as they waited, once again, for a slower group of climbers ahead of them.

But Justin Thomas, who was also an experienced climber, shared a sense of foreboding as well. *Man, we shouldn't be waiting so long,* Justin thought. Nervously, he studied the clouds. *We gotta get off here.* Justin knew how quickly weather could turn in the mountains. The previous summer, he had narrowly escaped when a sudden electrical storm overtook his climbing group at the summit of 12,804-foot Middle Teton. With lightning flashing, thunder cracking, and static electricity so thick it raised the hairs on their arms, Justin and his friends had to practically run back down the mountain to safety. Now, he removed his cell phone from his pack and dialed his wife, Michelle. When her voice came on the line, he was surprised to find himself so tense he was choking back tears. "I love you," Justin said. "I'll see you later tonight."

Rob Thomas had been studying the clouds, too. Above him, another experienced climber had already ascended the wet, slippery granite of Friction Pitch and now stood at the top. As the two men conferred by radio, they decided that weather conditions made it too dangerous to continue.

Rob clicked off the two-way and sighed. He hoped that the first-timers wouldn't be too disappointed. "We're not going to summit," he told them. The safest way down was not to backtrack the 6-mile route they had come, but to continue up and over Friction Pitch. Then they could traverse the east ridge below, rappel 150 feet down a cliff, and do a quick scramble down a scree slope, and they'd be back at Upper Saddle in 90 minutes.

With slick, smooth granite and few holds, the 100-foot Friction Pitch—so named because a climber must depend on the friction of his feet against the wall—was the most difficult part of the climb. Thomas went up first and set three camming devices, spring-loaded metal anchors, into a crack in the rock at the top of the pitch. They would secure the rope. One after another, he began belaying climbers—his group first, then Clinton and Erica.

Nervous but steady, Erica came up, hoisting herself with a final push onto the ledge. Flush with relief, she settled into a sitting position next to a large puddle of water. When she'd heard they were not going to summit, she was happy. But now sitting at the top of the pitch, shoulder to shoulder with her husband, she understood his exhilaration. "It was worth it," she sighed, gazing at the view of Jenny Lake, Garnet Canyon, and a fairyland of peaks and glaciers that stretched to the Idaho border and beyond. The two savored the moment, feeling like they could see forever. Then the talk quickly turned to logistics. Erica would need to unrope, Clinton said. "When everyone's up, we'll work our way around the side of the ridge to the rappel." Already nervous about the steep descent, Erica was silent. Clinton watched his Melaleuca co-worker, Rod Liberal, coming up the rope from below. "You need to move so that Rod can sit there."

Rob Thomas, meanwhile, had climbed ahead, working toward the rappel route. Suddenly, he heard an odd, oscillating hum, like the drone of a hive of bees. "Honey, did you hear that?" he asked Sherika, below on a ledge. Before she could answer, a tremendous boom sounded all around them. A massive electric charge slammed Rob, causing every muscle to clutch. It was as if he'd been crushed between a speeding freight and a brick wall. He passed out.

When lightning strikes the body directly, it kills by stopping the heart. A partial strike often renders victims temporarily unconscious and paralyzed.

Knocked out, Thomas started to slide down the cliff headfirst. "Rob, don't you dare fall!" his wife yelled, planting both hands in his chest to keep him from careering off the ledge. Waking, he stared at her, uncomprehending. Then, gradually, he became aware of screaming.

He waited for the lashes to flutter, for her blue eyes to smile back at him. But she didn't stir.

On the other side of a granite outcropping, Clinton Summers had also been knocked unconscious. He awoke screaming, unable to move his legs or left arm. Smoke filled the air. The puddle of water next to him had evaporated. He turned to look at Erica, who was leaning, motionless, against his left shoulder. Her eyes were closed. Lips and throat black. The lightning strike had shredded her orange windbreaker and green zip-off pants. The right side of her body was bright pink. The smell of burnt hair was all around him.

I need to wake her up, he thought. He touched his wife's face. *Open your eyes, dear. Please, please, open your eyes!* He waited for her lashes to flutter, her blue eyes to smile back at him. But she didn't stir.

"Erica!" he roared. Then, holding her in his right arm. "Erica!"

Rob appeared next to him; bending over Erica's limp form, he checked for a pulse. There was none. He unclasped her black helmet. Her hair was matted with blood. Fluid leaked from her ears. The two men performed CPR—Clinton frantically forcing air into Erica's blackened throat, Rob compressing her chest.

"It's not working!" Clinton cried. Anguish tore at him.

"We need to pray for her," Thomas told his friend. Sitting on the rocks, the two held Erica's lifeless form and closed their eyes.

Far below, another motionless body hung suspended by a rope. Rod Liberal had been blasted off Friction Pitch. Now he swung in his harness, jackknifed in a horrifying 45-degree belly-up position.

*   *   *

The ranger station in the nearby town of Moose received a call from one of the climbers at 3:46 p.m. Forty-five minutes later, a Bell 206L-4 helicopter was speeding toward the site. But with cloud cover and very high winds, the rangers weren't sure that a rescue was even possible.

*   *   *

"I chipped a tooth, I can't be dead," Rod Liberal thought. His tongue felt the jagged edge. He had fallen about 30 feet until his rope jolted him to a stop. He opened his eyes and saw sky and a rope going straight up. He was swinging in his harness, face up, hundreds of feet of open air below. His back felt like it was breaking, and he couldn't move his left arm or right leg at all.

Liberal had been awestruck by the day's sheer beauty. He had snapped picture after picture on his Fuji digital camera: a sunrise bathing the entire valley in pink, a view west from the Lower Saddle of the Idaho side of the park, a photo of himself and two friends perched at the base of Wall Street.

Now, on a two-way radio clipped to his shoulder strap, he listened as Rob called for help. "We were hit by lightning. We have one deceased. Maybe two." *No,* Liberal thought. "I'm okay!" he tried to scream. But it was hard to get sound out. Hard to breathe. To ease the pain, he unclipped his backpack and let it slip off his shoulders. It plummeted hundreds of feet.

Liberal swam in and out of consciousness. An hour went by, then two. He lost track of time, but before long, darkness would close in, and the temperature would drop into the 30s. In his state, he wouldn't survive. "Please, not yet," he prayed, seeing visions of his three-month-old son, Kai. Liberal's parents were divorced, and he had rarely seen his dad while he was growing up. "Not yet," he said again.

What was taking so long? Rob Thomas, normally a take-charge guy, stood on the ledge, looking down at his two friends, one crippled, one dead. He had never felt so helpless. Where were the others? His father? His brother? How many were dead? Just then Rob's dad, Bob, appeared from behind a rock outcropping. They began yelling for Justin, and hearing no response, both began to weep.

The ledge above Friction Pitch was crowded now. Sherika Thomas, her father-in-law, and her own dad, Steve, kept doing CPR in the vain hope that Erica might revive. Deep down, they knew it was useless.

Rob Thomas was worried that Clinton Summers was becoming hypothermic. The ledge was shrouded in clouds and now a sharp wind had come up. Temperatures were dropping toward freezing. Clinton's shorts had been torn apart, and Rob could see that his left leg was badly burned. He removed Clinton's harness and helped him limp away from the edge of Friction Pitch—away from the spot where his wife's body lay. Then Rob dug through his own backpack and pulled out an extra windbreaker and long underwear. He gave them to Clinton and helped him pull them on.

In the next few hours, a helicopter twice hovered within 100 yards of their perch—and then disappeared. The rangers said by cell phone that clouds at 13,000 feet had wrapped around the Exum Ridge, impeding the rescue. The climbers might have to spend the night on the ledge.

Clinton will die, Thomas thought, *and maybe Rod and Justin, too.* Sherika's dad began piling rocks to construct a low wall that would shield the hikers from the wind, in the event they had to spend the night.

At 6:09 p.m., the clouds abruptly parted, and a ranger, suspended from the chopper on a 100-foot rope, touched down on the ledge. Leo Larson bent over Erica Summers where she lay on the rocks, eyes closed, face swollen and bruised. He checked her vital signs, and then he quietly pronounced her dead. He pointed at Liberal, hanging limply from the rope—"Is he dead?"

"No!" the climbers cried in unison. They screamed at Rod, urging

Rangers Craig Holm and George Montopoli prepare to attach a litter containing critically injured Rod Liberal to the chopper's rope for lift out.

him to move his arms or legs. All Liberal could do was gesture feebly.

An hour later, Clinton Summers was fitted into an evacuation suit—a sling-like harness attached to the helicopter by a rope—and flown off the ledge. Thomas and the other climbers who were still ambulatory started toward the fixed rappel route down.

Below, Justin Thomas and two others who had been blasted off the mountain by the lightning strike were rescued, too. Flung head over heels a hundred feet down the rocky cliffside, they had lain tossed upon rocks and ledges like so many crumpled tissues. The three were bleeding and partially paralyzed. Now a second Bell helicopter shuttled them off the mountain. The last one lifted off at 8:20 p.m.

With less than a half hour of daylight left, the rescue team worked quickly to save Rod. Earlier they had anchored ropes and rappelled down the cliff. They checked his signs, slipping an oxygen mask over his face. At about 8:00, they lowered a 100-pound litter down the rock face and transferred him into it, slowly hauling it back up the cliff with pulleys. Finally, at 8:57, they flew him off the mountain.

The helicopter then returned to hover over the ledge above Friction Pitch one last time. Ten minutes later, as golden light lit the cold, jagged peaks, the body of Erica Summers was lifted off the Grand.

About 1,000 people are injured every year by lightning in the United

States; 10 percent die. Erica Summers is the only person to be killed by lightning in the Grand Tetons in 100 years. Many more deaths occur in Florida, especially along Lightning Alley, between Tampa Bay and Titusville, than in the western mountains. But, ironically, lightning killed a 25-year-old woman hiking in the Colorado Rockies the day after the Teton climbers were struck.

Erica's funeral was held on her fifth wedding anniversary. Clinton was seated in a wheelchair, his children nearby. He had told them that their mommy was with Jesus. Now, he watched, wet-eyed, as speaker after speaker extolled his lovely, generous wife.

Rod Liberal spent 43 days in the hospital, with burns over 12 percent of his body, kidney damage, and a host of other complications. Justin Thomas and the two climbers with him suffered broken bones, muscle tears, gouges, and burns. Miraculously, 6 of the 13 climbers were unhurt.

For the friends who set out that July day, the tragedy on Grand Teton made them reassess their lives. "Do you just get up and breathe in and out after something like that happens?" says Rob Thomas. "Or do you strive for something great?" Rod Liberal often finds himself staring trancelike at his son, Kai, as he crawls about the floor. "I can't believe I'm still around and seeing him grow!" Summers is raising his kids alone now and cherishes every second. On Valentine's Day, the children went to their mother's grave site with cards they had colored themselves and taped them to a white balloon. Releasing it, they watched the balloon rise into the sky "so Mom can catch it."

Last September, Rob Thomas went back to Grand Teton. He set a cairn at the top of Friction Pitch where lightning took Erica Summers, and brought back a five-pound piece of granite to be engraved in her memory.

This summer a few of the friends who made that fateful climb will gather to tackle the unforgiving peak one more time. They will scale Friction Pitch and place a monument to Erica on the rock ledge where she died, where she felt like she was sitting on top of the world.

Originally published in the June 2004 issue of *Reader's Digest* magazine.

On the Move

While this image seems to be just another nature shot, it actually captures a silverback gorilla running through the green mountains of Rwanda, charging a younger male who had shown interest in one of the females.
Photograph by Thomas D. Mangelsen/mangelsen.com

Humor Hall of Fame

"Sometimes I like to sit my dog down for a performance review, just to remind him who's boss."

— @RMFNORD

Two dog owners are arguing about whose pet is smarter.

"My dog is so smart," says the first owner, "that every morning he goes to the store and buys me a sesame-seed bagel with chive cream cheese, stops off at Starbucks and picks me up a mocha latte, and then comes home and turns on ESPN, all before I get out of bed."

"I know," says the second owner.

"How do you know?" the first demands.

"My dog told me."

—FROM THE BOOK, *Laughter the Best Medicine*

The Bold Bus Driver

by Alyssa Jung

*Tim Watson's quick thinking saves
a little boy from danger.*

On a warm morning last summer, California bus driver Tim Watson was about halfway through his daily 15-mile express route from Milpitas to Fremont when an alert from the Valley Transportation Authority (VTA) flashed across his dashboard screen. A toddler had been kidnapped in Milpitas, the message read, and it asked that drivers be on the lookout for the boy.

The victim was described as a three-year-old child in plaid shorts and red shoes; the suspect, a man in his 20s wearing jeans and a black hooded sweatshirt and carrying a tan backpack. Tim felt his stomach drop when he realized that a man with a toddler on his hip had boarded the bus just ten minutes earlier. Tim distinctly remembered the boy's plaid shorts.

Tim glanced in one of his mirrors and saw the pair sitting in the last seat at the back of the nearly empty bus. Before alerting authorities, he wanted to confirm their identities. Pulling into a McDonald's parking lot, he announced that he needed to look for a lost bag. He moved slowly down the aisle, peering under each seat, until he approached the last row. As he bent down, Tim avoided eye contact with the man. "I saw the boy's red shoes," says Tim. "But I knew I had to keep cool."

Back behind the wheel, Tim apologized for the delay and pulled the bus onto the highway. Not wanting to arouse suspicion, he waited a few minutes, then radioed the bus dispatcher. "I believe I have the kidnapping suspect on my bus," he told the operator, keeping his voice low.

The dispatcher directed Tim to continue to his final stop at the Fremont BART subway station, where police officers would be waiting. "As I'm driving, all I can think about is what I'm going to do if I get there before the police," he says. So he slowed down, rolling along at 35 mph in a 65-mph zone.

As Tim was about to make the last turn into the BART parking lot, he saw from the side mirrors police cruisers pull up behind the bus silently but with red lights flashing. "The bus doesn't have a back window, so the guy had no idea they were there," says Tim.

He stopped the bus and opened the doors. In his right side mirror, Tim could see four cops waiting for the suspect with their hands on their holsters. As the man got off the bus with the boy, a police officer grabbed the child out of his arms, threw the suspect to the ground, and handcuffed him behind his back.

The police officers told Tim that about an hour earlier, the man, Alfonso David Edington, 23, had snatched the boy from the Milpitas library after he wandered away from his mother.

Tim thought about his own sons, ages 17 and 21. "I went back in the bus alone and broke down," he says. Then he climbed out again to check that the boy was OK. Tim found him sitting calmly in the front seat of a squad car, without a tear in sight. "I just smiled at him," Tim says. "I knew he was safe."

Edington was charged with felony kidnapping and faces up to 11 years in prison.

A few weeks after the incident, Tim received a certificate of recognition from the VTA Board of Directors, the Santa Clara Board of Supervisors, and the city of Milpitas, as well as a congressional resolution from Congressman Eric Swalwell. Still, Tim is humble about his actions.

"I try to teach my kids to look out for people who can't defend themselves," he says. "And that's what I did."

Originally published in the March 2016 issue of *Reader's Digest* magazine.

Friends Interrupted

by Jacquelyn Mitchard

If you have that one friend, you're rich.
That one friend is different from all the
others, dear as they may be.

I met Jeanine on my first day of high school, more than 35 years ago, at the age of 13. Painfully shy, I had signed up for student council because I thought it might save me from wandering around a huge high school shamefully alone. It was still early in the day. I'd already lost my new green trench coat and couldn't remember which building my locker was in. Standing there in the office, miserable, I wanted to vanish into the paneling.

I heard a girl's voice: "Do you have a lot of friends?"

When I saw her—tiny, delicate, with beautiful eyelashes—I smiled and answered, "Are you kidding? I'm the girl nobody knows."

"Well, I'm nobody," Jeanine said.

That was it. The two of us were instant friends. For the next six years, Jeanine and I spent hours on the phone each weekday and virtually every weekend night together. As boys came and went, we drowned our sorrows in tomato soup. In my mother's old Chevy, we cruised the West Side of Chicago. We sat on Al Capone's grave one Halloween night. Lying on blankets under the stars, we'd talk of our dreams, pouring our hearts out.

Jeanine wanted to sing on the Broadway stage. I wanted to write a novel. "Why not two? Why not five?" she pressed me.

As high school progressed, I became a student council officer and made friends by the score. Jeanine? She preferred the sidelines. She was like the angel in my pocket. I never forsook her, never excluded her. Other friends could not understand our devotion, because we seemed like such opposites. But we weren't.

Neither of us got much attention at home. Jeanine's parents worked long hours. Mine had other fish to fry, and those fish swam at the bottom of a highball glass. I don't think my parents ever attended a single high school event of mine, though my mother made sure I dressed well—she wanted me to be the prettiest girl (and the thinnest).

I didn't get home often enough to see Jeanine through the terror of her father's cancer.

Jeanine and I remained a sorority of two, and even college didn't intervene. Neither did Jeanine's early unplanned motherhood during our freshman year. After her daughter, Gemma, was born, Jeanine moved back home. My mother, I'm proud to say, offered them both love and support.

Unfortunately, Mama didn't get to play grandma for real. After she was diagnosed with brain cancer and given just a few months to live, I married a boy who was only a pal so she could see me in a wedding gown. When my marriage was quietly annulled, I came home for good, finishing school and working as a waitress to help my younger brother get through high school.

Jeanine and I were together again, this time with a baby seat in the back of the car. We picked up where we left off, the Beach Boys on the radio as we cruised familiar routes.

* * *

Then, in my early 20s, I took a coveted job on a Wisconsin newspaper and had to start work every day at 5 a.m. Spent and challenged, I didn't get home often enough to see Jeanine through the terror she felt when her beloved father learned that he, too, had cancer. And when he

Bestselling author Jacquelyn Mitchard (above left) with her longtime best pal.

died, I was too new at my job to take time off for his funeral. The last words Jeanine spoke to me, for four years, were "You betrayed me."

I said thousands of words, through the crack under her apartment door, in letters, in cards, pleading with Jeanine to understand. But she was stubborn and wouldn't forgive me.

When I married for real, Jeanine was not there. When my beloved firstborn son arrived, she wasn't there to be his godmother, as I was to Gemma. And when my second and third sons were born after my struggles with infertility, Jeanine wasn't there either.

But when cancer came to the door again, this time to claim my husband, Dan, Jeanine came, too, unbidden. We didn't talk about the lapse in our friendship until much later. Suffering through hellish grief, I was simply staggered by gratitude.

I kept thinking, *If Jeanine is with me, I can live through this. I can be okay. If Jeanine is holding me, helping me, I am home.*

I would never let her go again.

We resumed our marathon phone sessions, dissecting jobs, life, her dates, my lack of them. When others called me foolish, she told me to go ahead, to write my first novel during the two years after Dan died instead of taking a real job. You can do this, she said. All I wanted was to show my sons that no matter the size of the hole life drove through you, you still had permission to live large.

In the end, my novel, *The Deep End of the Ocean,* became the first book ever chosen by Oprah's Book Club. Jeanine cheered—as she did two years later when I married my husband, Chris. And after Jeanine graduated from college with a degree in theater, I cheered for her as she became a sought-after voice and acting teacher, winning roles onstage and in commercials.

* * *

Before Jeanine even turned 40, her legs began to hurt. Deep into my aerobics period, I teased her: "It's because you're such a weenie."

She wouldn't work out, but she did stretch, try massage therapy, and take vitamins. Then an e-mail from a friend broke the news that Jeanine had been too devastated to speak: She had multiple sclerosis.

MS eats away at the myelin coating surrounding the nerves and can disturb balance, vision, and cognitive ability. People may end up using a wheelchair or remain mobile into their 90s. Although it affects more women than men, it typically affects women less seriously, so we didn't think it would be so bad. It was, though. Jeanine was diagnosed with primary progressive MS, a rare form characterized by an almost continuous worsening of the disease, without relapses or remissions.

Four years ago, I realized that my fierce, beloved friend, dedicated actress that she was, had never seen a Broadway show. Together we went—Jeanine pushing her walker, the two of us wearing our fanciest sequined skirts—to see her favorite musical, *Man of La Mancha*. When Brian Stokes Mitchell sang of the impossible dream, the unbeatable foe, I had a brainstorm: I could use my small measure of new celebrity to raise money for something, and for someone. Jeanine had helped me craft the heroine of my sixth novel, *The Breakdown Lane,* a dancer who in one harrowing year loses her husband and develops MS. I would donate a portion of the book's sales and go from there.

Last spring, at an MS fundraiser in Washington, D.C., I was about to sign books when I heard the old Bill Withers song "Lean on Me." I looked up. There on the screen, larger than life, was a photo of me with my head leaning on Jeanine's shoulder. The coordinator read a letter Jeanine had written: "Jackie was popular; I was the little caboose. But she chose me, included me, and when she learned I had MS, she jumped in to help me beat this disease. She's more than a friend. She's my heart."

That goes for me, too. Jeanine has to lean on my arm when we walk. But I have to lean on her a hundred times a year, when I turn to her with problems no one else understands, problems no one else can see me through. As she describes them, they're like locational humor: To get it, you had to be there.

She always was.

Originally published in the October 2007 issue of *Reader's Digest* magazine.

Jacquelyn Mitchard reports that she and Jeanine are as close as ever:

"While the physical symptoms of MS continue to worsen, Jeanine never stops fighting for every inch of mobility. We remain the closest of friends, each other's confidante, sharing an unshakeable bond that has lasted more than fifty years," she said.

A FOSTER MOM'S LIFE

I remember the smell of her hair when she snuggled close, trying to crawl back into the womb from which she did not come. I can feel her fragile arms wrapped around mine, her soft cheek on my chest as she held on for life. I mean I can feel her. I hear her beautiful broken voice soar with glee because she was simple, and the most basic things brought her such peace. I feel her sweet breath against my face when she whispered in my ear that she loved me. Her desperate hands clutching my shoulders like it was a pivotal moment in time that we both needed to remember. And I do. I remember every moment of the two years she was with us. I remember the way my soul felt the day I had to give her back. And how it aches still.

—Keri Riley *Ninilchik, Alaska*

RED RIBBON SURPRISE

When I was in fourth grade, there was a flower show at school. Any student could enter. I left my house with a flower in a vase, but I dropped the vase on the way and ruined the flower. Then I saw a beautiful purple flower ahead of me. I took it and continued to school. I walked home later with a red ribbon attached to my purple flower—I won second prize. I was so happy. When I arrived home, I proudly showed my mother, who started laughing. I won with a purple thistle—a purple thistle is a weed.

—Donna Kelly *Winter Garden, Florida*

Mama and the Garfield Boys

by Lewis Grizzard, from the book
Don't Forget To Call Your Mama ... I Wish I Could Call Mine

For three years, I'd avoided the class bullies, but now my time had come.

W hat I recall most vividly about my first day at the school in More-
land, Georgia, where my mama taught was that, as my teacher, Mrs.
Bowers, welcomed us to second grade, the brothers Garfield set off a
small bomb on a window ledge.

The bomb blew out several windows, sent Mrs. Bowers screaming
to the principal's office, and I, along with several other students, wet my
pants. Mr. Killingsworth suspended the Garfields for a week, which is
what they wanted and why they set off the bomb. Frankie Garfield was
ten and David nine, and both had failed first grade several times.

Having your mother as a member of your school's faculty had its
advantages. I could go by her room on my way home and ask for a few
coins to spend on treats at Cureton and Cole's store. My friends and I
would sit outside and eat our candy and hope we could finish before the
Garfield brothers showed up and took it away.

I managed to stay unmarked by the Garfield brothers, other than a few punches to my arms and the day Frankie got me in a headlock and rammed my head into a pole. But Frankie had just been kidding around. When he was serious about hurting someone, he didn't let him go until he was bleeding and groveling for mercy.

In the fifth grade, I finally got mine. I was biking my way to Cureton and Cole's. At the end of the narrow path was a deep ditch that forced a hard left turn. The problem arose when Frankie Garfield ran up behind me. "Get that bike out of the way. I'm in a hurry," Frankie demanded.

The moment I slowed to make the turn, Frankie lifted the back of my bike and flipped it, with me astride, into the ditch.

I landed head first, and my bike landed on top of me. After seeing my nose bloodied, my face scratched, and a giant knot on my forehead, Frankie figured the job was done and proceeded to the store to detach other kids from their candy bars.

I rode my bike home as fast as I could. I looked like I'd been in an ax fight and finished fourth. I tried to wash away as much mud and blood as I could and even tried to press the knot on my head flat. That didn't work.

My fear was this: Mama would see me in this condition and force the truth out of me that I had fallen victim to a Garfield. She would tell the principal, who would suspend Frankie. That would delight him, but he would also be angry that I had ratted on him. He would pummel me. On top of that, he'd probably tell his brother, David, who would also take his turn at bruising my person.

I avoided Mama until dinner time. "What happened to your face?" she asked. "How did you get that knot on your head?"

"Bicycle accident," I said. "I was riding down the path and fell into the ditch."

"It was one of those Garfields, wasn't it?" Mama said. How did she always know those things? Still, I stuck to my story.

"Did one of those boys hit you?" she asked.

"No, ma'am," I said. Well, he didn't hit me.

"You've been down that path hundreds of times. Now you tell me what really happened."

I told her.

"I'll see Frankie Garfield in the principal's office in the morning," she said. "I'm tired of those boys bullying you children around."

Just as I thought.

"Mama," I started, "please don't tell Mr. Killingsworth. He'll call Frankie in and then Frankie will beat me up again, this time worse."

She looked thoughtful. "Okay, but I'm going to have a talk with Frankie myself."

I spent the next morning daydreaming about my funeral. There would be lots of crying, of course, and they'd probably sing "Precious Memories." It was a terrible thing to think about dying. I wondered if there would be baseball in heaven. I was certain that's where I'd go. The only Commandment I'd breached, besides killing that bird with my air rifle, was that I had coveted Bobby Entrekin's electric train. It blew real smoke. Mine didn't.

When school was over, I took another route home and hid under my bed. Forty-five minutes later, I heard Mama come in the house and call me. "I'm under the bed, Mama," I said.

"Well, come out from under there," she said. "Frankie Garfield isn't going to hurt you."

Mama had called the sheriff. That's what had to have happened. Frankie and his brother had been taken to jail.

"Come into the living room and sit down," Mama said. She had something to tell me.

"Before I talked to Frankie," she said, "I pulled his records. Do you know his daddy is dead, and they don't know where his mama is? His aunt is raising those boys alone. I talked to the other teachers, and they said his mama used to beat Frankie and his brother. They simply haven't known much love, and they don't have spending money like you. All they know is that they have to fight for everything they get. I really feel sorry for them."

This wasn't exactly what I had expected.

"Do you know what I did?" Mama asked.

I had the feeling that whatever it was she did, it hadn't involved the sheriff.

"I had Frankie come down to my room during recess and asked if he would help me put up the blocks and crayons from the morning. I told him if he did, I'd give him a quarter, and he and his brother could spend it however they wanted. He was as nice and cooperative as could be. So I told him if he would come back and help me tomorrow, I'd take him and his brother and you to the picture show Saturday."

Obviously, the ditch incident of the previous day had damaged my hearing. Me going to the picture show with the Garfields? Me, alone with them, in a darkened theater?

"I'm not going," I said.

"Yes, you are," Mama said. "The Bible tells us, 'Love thine enemies.'"

"The Bible also says, 'Thou shalt not kill.'"

"Those boys just need some love and attention," Mama replied.

Saturday morning, we drove to where the Garfield brothers lived. A woman appeared on the front porch in a tattered housecoat. Mama got out of the car. I stayed put. I heard the Garfields' Aunt Pearl say to Mama, "I shore do appreciate you doin' this for the boys. I ain't got no car to take 'em nowhere."

Mama said, "Frankie worked hard for me last week at school, and I know David is going to help me, too."

Frankie and David got into the back seat. They were wearing old clothes, but clean and fairly wrinkle-free. Both had their hair combed. I'd never seen a Garfield look anything like that before.

As we drove away, Mama said, "Son, Frankie's got something he wants to say to you." I sensed a certain embarrassment on his part, almost a shyness. Was this the same Frankie Garfield? He mumbled something I couldn't understand.

"Speak up," Mama said to him. Still unable to meet my eyes, he said, "I'm sorry I threw you and your bicycle in the ditch."

I couldn't believe what I was hearing. Frankie Garfield apologizing to me?

"And what else, Frankie?" Mama asked.

"I promise not to hurt anybody at school again," he said.

My God! A miracle. Dillinger goes straight. Attila the Hun agrees to stop raping and pillaging.

"What do you say?" she asked me. I was too stunned to say anything.

Mama finally said, "Tell Frankie you appreciate his apology."

"I appreciate your apology," I said to the front window. We rode to town in silence.

When Mama pulled up in front of the Alamo Theater, my eyes said to her, "Please don't make me get out of this car."

"Go ahead," she said. "Everything will be okay."

What the Garfields did was ignore me. They were so mesmerized by the picture show that they were not interested in killing or maiming anyone. Flash Gordon ray-gunned half the universe in the serial. There was a Woody Woodpecker cartoon. Randolph Scott saved the ranch again in the feature.

When Mama picked us up, Frankie and David began to recount the adventures they had seen on the screen.

After we pulled into their driveway, Frankie came to Mama's side of the car and said, "Miss Christine, do you need me to help you Monday?"

"I'll see you at school and let you know," she said. "Now, go tell your aunt Pearl about the show." Mama smiled as we drove away.

The Garfields never bothered anybody very much after that. And the three of us went back to the pictures a few more times. We never became good buddies or anything like that. But Mama's kindness toward them obviously had a profound effect.

They were always at her beck and call. They cleaned her blackboard and took the erasers out and dusted them. They watered the plants and found a special pleasure in feeding the fish Mama had in a small aquarium.

Mama had that thing some teachers develop, the idea that the students were her children, too.

She taught me a lot, my mama.

Originally published in the January 1992 issue of *Reader's Digest* magazine.

Humor Hall of Fame

I was driving when I saw the flash of a traffic camera. I figured that my picture had been taken for speeding, even though I knew I wasn't. Just to be sure, I went around the block and passed the same spot, driving even more slowly. But again the camera flashed. Thinking this was pretty funny, I drove past even slower three more times, laughing as the camera snapped away each time while I drove by it at a snail's pace. Two weeks later, I got five tickets in the mail for driving without a seat belt.

—ADAM J. SMARGON
NEWARK, DELAWARE

I was prosecuting a case involving a man charged with driving under the influence. The defense counsel was beginning to lose his cool with the police witnesses and implied that they had gotten their facts wrong.

"People do make mistakes, don't they, Officer Lock?" he demanded of one witness.

"Yes, sir," came the reply. "I'm Officer Webster."

The defense lost.

—ROGER GRAY ST. ALBANS, GREAT BRITAIN

"My Babies Are in That Car!"

by William M. Hendryx

She had left the children for only a minute. Now her driverless car was hurtling toward the fast-flowing river.

February winds were gusting outside the coin laundry as Joy Warren carried her basket to the car. The 37-year-old mother of seven had less than 20 minutes to pick up two of her older children from school in Fort Worth. "Let's go," she said to the younger ones. Faith, age five, jumped into the back seat of the 1978 Buick station wagon, and Stephen, three, followed. Joy strapped four-month-old Esther into the rear-facing car seat beside her.

Months earlier, thieves had broken into the car and damaged the mechanism that prevents the gear shift from slipping out of park when the key isn't in the ignition. Repairs, however, simply weren't in the budget. Joy and her husband, Bill, a computer programmer, had sacrificed to educate their children at Calvary Academy, a private school.

"We're going to be late," Joy told the kids 20 minutes later as the aging car began climbing the steep drive to Calvary Academy. Pulling into the far edge of the crowded parking lot, Joy could see bustling North Forest Park

Boulevard 150 yards below and, just beyond it, the Trinity River.

"Y'all stay put. I'll be back in a second," she said, turning to Faith and Stephen. "And keep an eye on Esther for me, okay?" She didn't like leaving the children alone, but the baby was sleeping soundly. And it would only be a moment or two.

Dashing the 40 yards to the school entrance, Joy had to wait for Adam and Lori. *They're taking too long,* she thought She had to get back.

As she raced down the incline, she glimpsed the five-year-old in the front seat, trying to stop the car.

As she finally hurried out the door, trailed by Adam and Lori, she spotted the Buick's chrome luggage rack moving in the distance. Oh, my God! The car had drifted off the lot and was coasting toward the grassy, tree-lined field below. This can't be happening!

Her heart in her throat, Joy raced after the vehicle. But the wagon gained momentum, and the gap between Joy and her three youngest children widened. As she raced down the steep incline, she glimpsed the five-year-old, now in the front seat, apparently trying to stop the car.

Joy kept up her pursuit, watching in despair as the car miraculously avoided one tree after another. Within seconds, the car swept through the school's seldom-used lower parking lot, missing every light pole, then turning sharply toward the four-lane, divided North Forest Park Boulevard. Like a runaway train, the vehicle plunged over a shallow culvert and, with a grinding thud, landed crossways to rush-hour traffic.

*   *   *

Seret Gomez, a petite 17-year-old, and classmate Daniel Whitehead, an athletic 16, were standing beside Daniel's car when suddenly they spotted the lumbering station wagon 200 feet below, with Joy running more than 100 feet behind. *It's heading for the highway!* Daniel thought. "Come on!" he called to Seret.

Summoning his athlete's speed, Daniel caught up with Joy as she hesitated near the highway. "Is anyone in there?" he called as he ran past, Seret only a few steps behind.

"My babies!" Joy gasped. "My babies are in that car!"

As the rampaging wagon entered the street, traffic in both directions screeched and swerved. Hurtling across the first two lanes, the Buick slipped through an opening in the tree-dotted median, then shot across the two southbound lanes without receiving a scratch.

Thank God! Joy thought. But her relief was quickly dashed. The car, moving at a speed of up to 30 m.p.h., now faced a greater peril. *It's heading for the river!*

Unable to swim, Joy felt helpless as the Buick careened down the bank and launched itself from a four-foot dropoff. Its wheels still spinning, the wagon sailed 20 feet before landing with a thunderous splash in the cold, muddy water.

Lord, help them! Joy screamed inside. *Who will save them now?*

Daniel saw the car tilting nose-down at a perilous 45-degree angle. Inside, he spotted Faith and Stephen, wide-eyed with fright, climbing into the back seat to reach a higher point.

Without thinking, Daniel dived headfirst into the river. Though a competitive water-skier, he was shocked by the icy chill and the strength of the current. He reached the vehicle in a few strokes and grabbed the front passenger door handle. But the water was only four inches beneath the window, and the door wouldn't budge. Not a good idea anyway, he realized. The car would instantly fill and sink.

Daniel was suddenly aware of a bearded stranger next to him. The man was trying to open the rear passenger door. Inside, Stephen and Faith were staring at the stranger through the foggy windows.

The car was settling deeper and deeper into the current. "We've got to break the window!" Daniel called to the man.

* * *

Two minutes earlier, Charles "Skip" Womack, 35, a bearded trucker from Alvarado, Texas, had steered his 18-wheeler around a bend on North Forest Park Boulevard just as a beige Buick wagon darted across the pavement in front of him. He flicked on his emergency flashers and pulled the flatbed to a stop just as the car splashed into the water.

Skip jumped from his cab and saw a young man darting into the roadway several yards to his left. Skip ran abreast of him toward the river. From behind, he heard a woman's urgent cries: "My babies! Someone help my babies!"

There're kids in there! he realized. Skip jumped feet-first, his plunge almost simultaneous with Daniel's. The numbing water swamped his high-top boots, and his jeans felt like lead. But when he spotted Stephen and Faith huddled in the back seat, he had just one thought: *If I don't get them out, they'll drown.*

Only vaguely aware that Daniel was next to him, Skip yanked on the door beside the back seat, but it was locked. Noticing a half-inch gap in the window, he painfully wedged his thick, workman's fingers through the slot and tugged at the glass. It wouldn't give.

Suddenly, another hand appeared at the window, as Daniel laced his smaller fingers farther into the opening. With one powerful snap, the two men shattered the safety glass into hundreds of pieces.

"C'mon," Skip called to Faith and Stephen. "We gotta get you out of here!" The Buick was sinking fast. Their faces filled with fear, the children scurried toward the open window. Holding onto the car with one hand, Daniel reached inside, hooked Faith beneath her left arm, and lifted her out. *She looks like she's in shock,* he thought, as he tried with all his strength to hold her out of the water. Daniel pushed away from the car to make room for the next rescuer. It was then that he spotted Seret next to the front door. She had followed him into the water.

*　　*　　*

Racing only a few steps behind Daniel, Seret had dived in, almost clipping Daniel's heels, and swallowed a giant gulp of muddy water. Her mind raced. *Keep us all safe. It's going to be okay. We can do this!*

She reached the wagon just as Daniel and Skip were removing Faith. Inside, she saw Stephen's wide eyes staring at her. *Good, he knows I'm coming to get him.*

Daniel hoisted Faith onto his back, wrapped her tiny arms around his neck, and set out for shore. But the current was too strong, and he was tiring fast. He changed course, swimming with the current, and finally made it to shore downstream. He passed the preschooler to the arms of her anxious mother. Joy Warren removed her jacket and wrapped it snugly around Faith, while a bystander helped Daniel from the water.

Meanwhile, Seret had inched along the car toward Stephen. She placed her foot against the door and yanked at the boy's arm, dragging him out the window. She tucked him under her arm and pushed slowly away from the car. But the 28-pound load was more than she had anticipated. Seret fought to hold him up, while straining to keep her own head above water. *I have to make it,* she thought. Then out of nowhere, another person appeared.

Alone now in the water, Skip Womack said a silent prayer: Lord, be with me!

Allan McGinnis, a 43-year-old telephone installer, had been driving along North Forest Park when he noticed a crowd at the river. As he slowed, he saw a car in the water and a teenage girl beside it. Jumping from his van, the six-foot three-inch Vietnam veteran plunged into the water.

Grateful for his water-jump training as a paratrooper with the 18th Airborne Corps, Allan quickly reached Seret and Stephen. Taking the boy from her and holding him straight out to the side, Allan fought his way to shore, using only his legs and left arm. After passing Stephen to a stranger, he climbed onto the bank and collapsed.

Alone now in the water, Skip Womack said a silent prayer: *Lord, be with me!* Through the windshield, he could see the baby strapped in the front car seat, the water already touching her legs. Skip pounded his fist on the frontdoor window again and again, but it was no use. If he was to save the infant, he'd have to get at her through the back window.

He'd have to crawl inside the sinking Buick.

* * *

Driving his old pickup toward his office at Southwest Roofing Company, Rodger Brownlee, 46, had just rounded a curve on North Forest

Park when he saw a throng of people and a Buick protruding from the water. A bearded man was banging on the passenger window with his fist.

Rodger hesitated. *There're so many people here already.* But he pulled over and trotted toward the river. By now, the man who had been pounding on the car window had crawled inside.

If the car sinks, that guy's in big trouble! Rodger thought. He yanked off his boots and charged across the bank, jumping in. He was at the car in moments but didn't dare grab hold. The least touch, he feared, might make it sink. All he could see of Skip Womack were his legs and feet. *Whatever you're doing in there, fella, hurry up!* he thought.

Skip had managed to squeeze through the window. Inside, he grabbed the front passenger headrest and pulled himself onto it.

There, within arm's length, was Esther—not making a sound as she stared up at him with bright round eyes.

Give me strength, Lord! Skip prayed as he felt the car settle deeper into the water. With the headrest pressed painfully against his chest, his heart pounding, Skip wrestled with the car seat's unfamiliar latch, but it refused to release. He tried to break the strap with brute force. Something snapped, but there was still no slack. Giving up, he forced the strap away from Esther just enough to squeeze her tiny shoulder from beneath it. The baby was free.

With his left hand, Skip took a fistful of the child's yellow jumpsuit, lifted her into the air over the seat, and began working his upper body back through the window inch by inch. When he was out of the car far enough, he twisted around and held the child over the water. His energy spent, he could only hope someone would be there to take her.

Just outside the window, a blond man was treading water. "Take the baby!" Skip called to Rodger Brownlee. Gripping the jumpsuit, Rodger tucked the infant face up under his right arm and kicked away from the car.

When Rodger finally felt his feet touch bottom, he was gasping. Swimming across the current with one arm, while keeping the baby's head out of the water, had left him completely drained. Struggling for a foothold, he passed the child to a waiting stranger, then found another extended hand to help him out. The stranger worked his way through the growing crowd to deliver the infant to her grateful mother. Joy held her baby tight, muttering a silent prayer of thanks.

As Rodger Brownlee got his footing, he turned to see Skip Womack only a few feet behind. With the aid of three others, Rodger assisted him up the bank.

Trying to catch their breath, the two men looked back in time to see the old Buick suddenly spin 180 degrees and disappear beneath the water.

At that moment, Engine No. 2 of the Fort Worth Fire Department screeched to a stop behind them. The time was 3:38 p.m.—only six minutes had passed since the car began its deadly descent.

*   *   *

Though Faith was visibly shaken, neither she nor Stephen was injured. Esther—held tightly in her mother's arms—was taken by ambulance to Cook-Fort Worth Children's Medical Center, where she was treated for a mild abrasion to the scalp and released. A short time later, Bill Warren, Joy's husband, arrived to take them home.

After brief talks with police and fire officials, Skip, Rodger and Allan all went their separate ways. Halfway through town, Skip began shaking so badly he had to pull his rig to the side of the road. He thought of his wife and their three children—how close he'd just come to leaving them behind. He thought of the miracle he'd lived through and how three innocent children were still alive because five strangers happened to be in the right place at the right time.

"The Lord gave us the strength to get them out and not to worry about our own lives while doing it," Skip says today. "We never would have made it otherwise."

The following Sunday, Calvary Cathedral, sponsors of Calvary Academy, honored the five rescuers at the morning service with a sermon about the good Samaritan. Three months later, last May 12, the grateful Fort Worth Fire Department—in a presentation before the city council—publicly acknowledged their selfless acts.

"The Lord has a reason for these kids being here," Joy Warren says, her eyes tearing as she glances over at Faith, Stephen, and Esther. "If he gives you a child, he has something in store for that child—especially for those three."

Originally published in the August 1992 issue of *Reader's Digest* magazine.

Swamp Buggy Queen

"A swamp buggy race is an event that started in 1949 with a bunch of old woodsmen and has evolved into this high-speed, crazy, world-famous race with lots of mud flying," says Jillian Sanchez. "The queen gets tossed into a big mudhole." When asked what she'd like to be besides Swamp Buggy Queen, she answers, "A cardiothoracic surgeon."

Photograph by Glenn Glasser

Heavy Metal MD

"I'll be a third-year resident in neurosurgery at Mount Sinai," says Jonathan Rasouli, MD. "I also play guitar— heavy metal. My number one hero [is] my dad. He came here from Iran right before the revolution and pulled himself up by his bootstraps. Number two: President Obama. I appreciate someone who is able to overcome a lot of odds without losing touch. Number three: Arnold Schwarzenegger. I love his movies!"

Photograph by Glenn Glasser

Pilot Down: The Rescue of Scott O'Grady

by Malcolm McConnell

Shot down over hostile territory, a young pilot struggles to get home while his family anxiously awaits news of his fate.

Air Force Capt. Scott O'Grady eased his F-16C fighter close beside the one piloted by his flight leader, Capt. Bob Wright. Through breaks in the clouds, they saw the green mountains of Bosnia far below.

Their mission that afternoon of June 2, 1995, was a routine combat air patrol policing a NATO "No Fly Zone." For months, no Bosnian Serb plane had challenged NATO fighters in this sector, and intelligence had reported the zone free of surface-to-air missiles (SAMs).

Suddenly O'Grady and Wright were jarred by the buzz and amber flash of their cockpit missile-warning instruments. "Missile in the air!" Wright called urgently.

Two supersonic SA-6 SAMs, hidden by the overcast, were streaking toward the F-16s. Seconds later, the missiles ripped through the clouds, exhaust plumes trailing. Wright and O'Grady threw their aircraft into evasive maneuvers. One missile slashed harmlessly past Wright's plane. The other scored a direct hit on the belly of O'Grady's fighter. Horrified, Wright watched the wings crumple and an orange fireball blossom around the cockpit. Then O'Grady's jet, canopy intact, disappeared into the clouds.

"Basher 52 took a direct hit—he's down," Wright radioed.

"Any parachute?"

"Negative."

Flames seared O'Grady's neck and licked under his helmet visor, singeing his eyebrows, as his F-16 tore through the cloud bank. The 29-year-old pilot could smell his hair burning. *Eject!*

Air Force Captain Scott O'Grady

O'Grady's left hand groped for the yellow ejection-seat handle between his knees. *Let it work,* he prayed.

The jet's Plexiglas canopy detached, and the seat's rocket charge fired. Seconds later, O'Grady heard the reassuring twang of his opening chute. He felt his heart pounding as he floated into clear sky. *I can't believe I'm alive.* Hanging beneath him on a tether, his survival pack whipped in the wind.

> *O'Grady jumped up, unsnapped his parachute, and shucked off his helmet. He needed a hiding place now.*

O'Grady was relieved to see that the winds were pushing him toward a brushy field and away from the orange-tiled roofs of the town of Bosanski Petrovac, a Bosnian Serb stronghold. He noticed hills rising to a green plateau about two miles to the southeast.

Then his stomach wrenched as he saw men in uniform pointing at him from a military truck parked along a highway. When he hit a clearing near the road, O'Grady jumped up, unsnapped his parachute, and shucked off his helmet. He needed a hiding place now.

Snatching his survival pack, O'Grady stumbled through the brush and, like a rabbit, burrowed into thick foliage, forcing himself deeper with his knees and elbows until he was completely covered.

He heard men calling to each other. *They know I'm here.* On his stomach, face thrust into the dirt, O'Grady tried to conceal his neck and ears with his green flight gloves. He heard boots thumping close by. O'Grady lay absolutely still, breathing shallowly. *At least they don't have dogs*, he thought. *At least Wright saw me eject.*

More than five thousand miles away in Skokie, Illinois, Stacy O'Grady stood on a ladder, helping decorate the gym of the school where she taught eighth grade. "Ms. O'Grady," a student interrupted, "your mother's on the phone."

Why would Mom call from Seattle? she wondered. *Scott!* Stacy scrambled down the ladder and raced to the teacher's lounge. Her mother confirmed her fears: Scott's plane had been hit by a missile; no one knew where Stacy's brother was, and no further contact had been made since the incident.

Stacy left school immediately and packed a bag to join her father, Dr. Bill O'Grady, a radiologist, at his home in Alexandria, Virginia. All she could think of was the time she and her mother had proudly pinned gold lieutenant bars on Scott. He had been so happy that day. It capped a youth devoted to adventure: skydiving, gliding, bobsledding. Stacy couldn't believe that Scott had not survived.

Aboard the amphibious-helicopter ship USS *Kearsarge,* 20 miles off the Balkan coast in the northern Adriatic, Col. Martin Berndt assembled members of the 24th Marine Expeditionary Unit, who were specially trained in combat search and rescue. Intelligence reports now confirmed that the ambush of the two F-16s had been a clever deception. The Bosnian Serbs knew that if the SA-6 mobile missiles had tried to track O'Grady and Wright directly, the cockpit instruments in the F-16s would have detected the radar immediately.

Instead, they had relied on civilian radars across the border in the

Serb Republic. The data were processed at an air-defense center in Belgrade, then transmitted by landline to three mobile SA-6 missile vehicles in the mountains near Bihać. Only at the last instant did SA-6 operators launch the missiles and then turn on their radar—giving the young pilots virtually no warning.

Berndt tapped the large tactical wall map of northern Bosnia. Normally, helicopter rescues were conducted under cover of darkness, with the pilots wearing night-vision goggles. But goggles couldn't detect power lines that snaked across the valleys. To avoid the SAMs, the rescue team might have to risk flying in daylight, threading their way along valleys, but that would expose them to antiaircraft guns and shoulder-fired missiles.

Berndt looked at Major Bill Tarbutton, 43, who would command the rescue aircraft, and Lieutenant Colonel Chris Gunther, also 43, who would lead the rescue team on the ground. "Right now," he told them, "the big questions are: Is O'Grady alive, and if so, where is he?"

Rifle fire cracked near O'Grady's hiding place, and bullets whipped through nearby brush. Instinctively, he thrust his face deeper into the dirt. They were shooting to kill. O'Grady prayed, trying to focus all of his concentration on the familiar words *Our Father, who art in heaven*....

Out of the corner of his eye, O'Grady could see shadows six feet away. Weapons rattled against branches as the soldiers made their way through the brush, using their rifle muzzles as probes. The men with the guns seemed to be circling him, toying with him. *Holy Mary, Mother of God, pray for us sinners*.... Soon the voices faded, and the rifles cracked from farther away.

Finally the sun passed below the western mountains. O'Grady heard the irritating, high-pitched whine of gnats and mosquitoes as they hovered about him. But he forced himself to continue lying motionless, his mouth dry from terror and thirst. When darkness fell, he could risk moving. He was determined to reach that plateau away from the highway and the town—the best place for pickup by a rescue helicopter.

For two days, the Marines aboard the *Kearsarge* had been on one-hour alert—but there was still no word on O'Grady's fate. Bosnian Serb TV had shown the wreckage of O'Grady's plane and announced that he had been captured. Major Tarbutton was skeptical. "If the Serbs had O'Grady," he said, "they'd show him on TV."

Colonel Berndt agreed. Later, an intelligence intercept reached him: Bosnian Serb soldiers had found a parachute but not the pilot.

O'Grady estimated that he had covered less than a mile in three nights.

But he'd worked by the book, moving only at night and finding secure hiding places well before dawn.

He thought about his survival equipment. In his

Hunger hadn't been a problem— but thirst was.

vest, the evasion map, radio, and smoke and signal flares were vital, and so was the Global Positioning System (GPS) receiver. This palm-size set processed signals from navigation satellites, giving him an accurate ground position and providing exact coordinates for rescue forces.

A separate survival pack contained a spare radio and batteries, a first-aid kit, and more flares. He also had a green foil thermal blanket, camouflage netting, face paint to help conceal him, and plastic bags and a sponge to catch and store rain for drinking water.

So far, hunger hadn't been a problem—but thirst was. That afternoon, O'Grady had drunk the last of his eight four-ounce pouches of water.

His evasion map showed the nearest stream was on the other side of Bosanski Petrovac, in the other direction from where he was headed.

Now, as dawn approached, O'Grady found another secure hiding place, spread his map as a ground sheet, pulled his thermal blanket across his shoulders, and draped a camouflage net over his body. He then turned on his survival radio and sent a brief coded signal. As sunrise filled the valley, he tried to get some sleep. *They're not going to capture me,* he vowed.

* * *

Television sets in Bill O'Grady's home were left on around the clock. Sitting on a living-room couch, Stacy O'Grady slipped into a shell of emotional numbness, mindlessly clicking the television remote, flipping through the channels, searching in vain for any sign of hope. Stacy, Scott, and their younger brother, Paul, had grown up in Spokane, Washington. From childhood experiences, Stacy knew that beneath his easy smile and soft-spoken charm, Scott had a tough core.

Stacy chuckled involuntarily, remembering the day when she was in sixth grade and a bully on the school bus was twisting her coat collar, choking her. Scott was smaller and lighter, but he seized the larger kid with a ferocious grip and glared so fiercely that the bully fled in panic.

Stacy was three years younger, but she and Scott shared the same birthday in October; they had always been close. She could picture the delicate silver crucifix she had given Scott before he left to fly fighters overseas. The thought that he was wearing it gave her comfort as she nodded off to sleep.

*   *   *

It was the afternoon of June 6, four days into his ordeal. Half dozing, he felt the snout of a cow nuzzling between his boots. After the animal left, O'Grady snatched a handful of grass to gnaw. If cows can live on it so can I. But by now his mouth was almost swollen shut from thirst, and he could swallow only a few blades. His eyes hurt, and his skin was badly wrinkled. He knew his dehydration was severe.

> *He shivered, his soaked flight suit a chilling weight on his body.*

Later that night, thunder cracked, followed by a downpour. He opened two plastic bags to catch the water. He also took the sponge from his survival kit to soak up the water pooling in his plastic survival pack. O'Grady drank greedily.

After the rain, the night grew colder. He shivered, his soaked flight suit a chilling weight on his body. When it started raining again, he packed his survival equipment. Since there was not much chance anyone would be out on a night like this, he'd risk moving faster toward the high ground.

O'Grady reached the plateau before dawn. A stone fence separated the pastures of the valley from the scrub brush to the south. He found a secure holding point, then set out to locate a landing zone for a rescue helicopter. The only open spot nearby was rocky, narrow, and sloping, with a crude fence blocking the far end. He read the display of his GPS set and noted his position on the map.

O'Grady hid again when daylight came but managed to sleep only fitfully. Hunger was nagging him. He noticed brown ants moving through the weeds near his elbow. He tried to scoop a handful but snagged only a few. They crunched in his mouth with a lemony tang—not much nourishment, but they moistened his tongue.

After sunset, his thirst returned with a vengeance. O'Grady had finished the rainwater, so he pulled off his wet boots and squeezed a few drops of water from his wool socks into a plastic bag. It was rancid but drinkable. He dozed off in the hours of early darkness.

He was awakened after midnight on June 8 by the blast of heavy antiaircraft firing nearby. O'Grady took a compass bearing on the sound. Seconds later, he heard a low-flying jet. It had to be a NATO reconnaissance plane looking for him. O'Grady stood cautiously, switched his survival radio to beeper, and pressed the transmit button. *This'll light up the world,* he mused. Both the NATO search planes and the Bosnian Serbs would hear the transmission. He had to wait to see who would find him first.

Just after 1:30 a.m. on June 8, Captain T. O. Hanford and his wingman, Captain Vaughn Littlejohn, were flying high above the dark mountains. After a report of a "possible beeper," Hanford was trying to contact O'Grady. For the next 40 minutes he called on the rescue channel. But there was no reply. At 2:07 a.m., with fuel low, Hanford tried O'Grady one last time. "Basher 52, this is Basher 11."

O'Grady's heart raced as he heard Hanford's voice. "Basher 11," he called. "Help!"

Hanford had to verify that the weak voice was O'Grady's. "Basher 52, what was your squadron in Korea?" Hanford asked.

"Juvats," O'Grady replied.

"Copy that," Hanford said, trying to keep his emotions in check. "You're alive. Good to hear your voice." For the next 10 minutes, Hanford circled as O'Grady used a voice code to reveal his GPS coordinates.

Then Hanford told O'Grady he'd be picked up "mañana."

"No," O'Grady replied. "I have to get out tonight."

Hanford reported back to his controllers, then to O'Grady. "You will be rescued, but you have to be prepared to signal in visual range." He added: "If you have an emergency, Basher 52, I will always be monitoring this channel."

In Virginia, the phone rang at 12:48 a.m. "Another reporter," Bill O'Grady said, groaning, as he pulled himself awake. It was Scott's wing commander, Colonel Charles F. Wald. "Dr. O'Grady, we've contacted him," Wald said. "He's alive. And we're going to go get him."

Overcome with emotion, the doctor raced to tell Stacy and Paul.

In the pastel dawn, the flight deck of the *Kearsarge* throbbed with the beat of the big helicopters' rotors. From a cockpit jump seat in Dash Two, one of two Super Stallion helicopters, Berndt's headphones crackled. "Pulling power," he heard Tarbutton call from the lead helicopter, Dash One, and then Berndt watched it rise.

There were now four choppers in a trail formation: Dash One and Dash Two, and two smaller Cobra gunships to guard the flanks. Far above them were two Harrier jets, launched from the *Kearsarge*. Across the northern Adriatic, NATO warplanes were assembling a protective umbrella for the Marine rescue effort.

At 5:43 a.m., they received the command to cross the Balkan coast.

They flew fast and low—no higher than 500 feet—to evade radar. Ahead, the mountains rose in a dark wall, silhouetted by the sunrise. In Dash One, Tarbutton saw that the valleys were choked with ground fog. This would shield them from visual detection but make navigating tricky.

"Twenty," announced an unseen airborne controller, code-named Magic, in a radar plane far above. They were 20 miles from O'Grady.

"Ten," Magic called. Now Tarbutton ordered the Cobras to press ahead, positively identify O'Grady, and check the landing zone.

Marine Major Scott Mykleby, lead Cobra pilot, flew his gunship toward the coordinates of O'Grady's position.

"I can see you," O'Grady radioed.

"Talk me on to you, Basher," Mykleby replied. A moment later, he heard O'Grady's excited shout. "You're overhead!"

"Pop smoke," Mykleby directed.

O'Grady pulled the tab on an orange smoke flare. Slowing to a hover, Mykleby searched the slope for the clearing that O'Grady said was nearby. O'Grady's little smoke flare was almost lost in the fog. Then Mykleby threw out a yellow smoke grenade to better mark O'Grady's position.

Captain O'Grady shares a hug with his sister, Stacy.

O'Grady warned Mykleby of the heavy firing he had heard the night before, then pulled on the bright orange knit cap from his survival kit. "I'm wearing an orange hat," he told Mykleby.

"Buster," Mykleby radioed Tarbutton— code for proceed ahead at maximum speed.

Tarbutton throttled up his engines and pulled the control stick into a hard climb. The two Super Stallions slashed across the fog bank and climbed the steep ridge.

The clearing was just large enough for the two Super Stallions to land with minimum clearance between the rotor tips. Marines piled out to form a security perimeter as Mykleby radioed O'Grady: "Run to the helicopter." O'Grady pounded through the thicket, his boots slipping on the wet rocks.

Berndt saw movement in the fog to the left. O'Grady's orange hat was bright in the mist. Sergeant Scott Pfister, crew chief on Dash Two, jumped from the hatch. O'Grady was wobbling, obviously exhausted. "Over here, sir," Pfister shouted. Throwing his arm under the young pilot's shoulder, he pushed O'Grady inside.

A Marine wrapped the pilot in a thermal blanket. O'Grady's hands were cold, wrinkled claws, his bearded face waxy. "Thank you, thank you," he kept saying.

Tarbutton ordered the formation to move up and out at maximum speed, flying only 50 feet above the rolling hillsides, so fast that obstacles rushed by in a blur. They were coming up to the final mountain range when the cockpit warning instruments gave a sharp beep.

Tarbutton caught a glimpse of movement to his left and heard Mykleby's warning: "SAMs in the air!"

Mykleby saw a chalk-white smoke trail corkscrew toward the helicopters from the left. As another missile sailed toward them, Mykleby popped a string of glaring magnesium flares to decoy the shoulder-fired SA-7s' infrared homing warheads. But even as he countered the missiles fired from the left, glowing orange baseballs sailed toward the helicopters from the right, incandescent red tracers of an automatic antiaircraft gun on the ground. The pilots threw their aircraft into violent zigzags. Sergeant Scott Pfister returned fire with a short, rattling burst from his .50-caliber machine gun.

As O'Grady hunched beneath a blanket, warmth slowly seeping into his chilled limbs, an assault-rifle bullet pierced the Super Stallion's tail ramp and ricocheted wildly around the troop bay. Two feet from O'Grady, Sergeant Major Angel Castro felt a blow on his side. He pulled out the empty canteen from his hip pouch. The green plastic was deeply gouged from the impact of the bullet.

The Cobra pilots wanted to engage the antiaircraft gun but if Tarbutton broke the gunships from formation, he'd have no protection crossing the coastal towns ahead. They had to hold course and take fire.

An amber warning light flashed, signaling one of Tarbutton's main rotor blades had been hit. Then Mykleby radioed that he also had a warning light.

Moments later, they flashed across the coastline, and the *Kearsarge* task force came into view on the horizon. "Mother in sight," Tarbutton informed the team.

O'Grady blinked at the dazzling surface of the Adriatic Sea, his face twisted with emotion. Colonel Berndt looked back from the jump seat, and O'Grady flashed a warm grin.

Just after 1:30 a.m. in Alexandria, Bill O'Grady received another call from Colonel Wald. "Scott is aboard the *Kearsarge*," Wald said. "He's dehydrated but otherwise fine." Scott's father rushed to tell Stacy and Paul the news. The family rejoiced. Stacy began counting down the hours when she would see her brother again.

On June 10, Scott O'Grady addressed reporters at Aviano Air Base in Italy. "If it wasn't for God's love for me," he said, "and my love for God, I wouldn't have gotten through it." But he also reserved special thanks for the "people at the pointy end of the spear"—the Marines who had risked their lives to save him. "If you want to find heroes," he said, "that's where you should look."

Originally published in the November 1995 issue of *Reader's Digest* magazine.

In the 25 years since this dramatic event, Scott O'Grady has written several books, including the bestselling Return with Honor *and* Basher Five-Two. *Several documentaries and movies were made based on his experiences.*

O'Grady completed a master's degree in biblical studies at the Dallas Theological Seminary in Texas. He lives in Texas, where he has been active in politics.

LET HIM GO, OLIVIA

There I was. Upside down inside the swimming pool.
Drowned. My parents were screaming. It must have been the
summer of '63. It was a gloomy day. Every Sunday we went
to my grandparents' house. My cousins and I were playing
alongside the pool. I must have slipped. At three years old, I
did not know how to swim. My mother was giving me CPR.
More than 20 or 25 minutes had gone by. The ambulance
had arrived. Everybody was staring at my mother. "Let him
go, Olivia. It's over." Even my father had some feelings of
resignation. Yet, she never gave up.

I write this story as a tribute to my mother, who, only four
years later, passed away. And also in recognition of editors
who made it possible for my mother to have read in *Reader's
Digest* the miracle made by another woman utilizing then
recently discovered CPR.

—Alejandro Arbide *San Antonio, Texas*

RANDOM RECIPE

Recently I was reminded of 60 years ago. We had been
married a little over a year, and I didn't know much about
cooking. Bill wanted chicken and dumplings. I had no idea at
19 years old how to fix that. We were new to Tulsa and didn't
know anybody. So I just randomly dialed a phone number in
our area and explained my situation. The lady didn't miss a
beat. She explained in detail. I must have listened well. Bill
thought it was great!

—Carmelita Pile *Los Angeles, California*

The Doctor Is In(sane!)

by Simon Rich, from the book *Hits and Misses*

*Getting medical treatment is never fun,
except on April Fools' Day.*

Dr. #1: You wanted to see me, sir?

Dr. #2: Yes, Dr. Metzger. I'm afraid I've got some bad news. I've been receiving complaints from your patients, and I've decided I can't allow you to make April Fools' jokes this year.

Oh my God.

I know you're disappointed, but my mind is made up.

What about the one where I tell the patient I'm out of anesthetic?

No.

What about the one where I put on a janitor's outfit, grab a scalpel, and walk into the operating room just as my patient loses consciousness? So he thinks he's about to be operated on by a janitor?

No.

What about the one where the patient wakes up after his operation and I start shouting, "Where's my stethoscope? Where did I leave my stethoscope?" And then I stare at the patient's torso with a look of horror, like I maybe left it inside his body?

No.

You can't do this to me! April Fools' Day is the highlight of my year. It's the only reason I finished medical school—to experience the holiday as a doctor.

I'm sorry, Sam, but my hands are tied.

What about the one where the patient wakes up and I'm wearing a robot costume, so he thinks he's been in a coma for 80 years? And I'm like, "Welcome to the future, Mr. Greenbaum. The world you remember is gone." You know, in a robot voice. So he thinks I'm a robot.

I get it. The answer is still no.

How can you be so cruel? I mean, for God's sake, what happened to the Hippocratic oath?

"First do no harm"?

That's how it goes?

Yes.

You sure it wasn't something about April Fools'?

Yes.

What about the one where I tell the patient his kidney operation was a grand success, but then, while I'm talking to him, I have an intern come in and say, "Dr. Metzger, you've got some dirt on your left shoulder"? And I start to brush my right shoulder. And the intern's like, "No, your left shoulder." And I'm like, "This is my left shoulder." And he's like, "No, it's your right shoulder. What's the matter with you, Dr. Metzger? Don't you know your left from your right?" And then we both look at the patient's torso with a look of horror, to imply, like ...

I know where you're going with this.

... to imply, like, maybe I operated on the wrong kidney? Like, maybe I did the left one instead of the right one because I don't know the difference between my—

No.

At least let me workshop it!

I'm sorry, Sam, but my decision is final.

(Pause)

April fool!

The Doctor Is In(sane!)

No way!
I can't believe you bought that!
Man, you got me good! Guess that's why you're the head of surgery.
Pass me my robot mask. It's time to make the rounds.

Originally published in the April 2019 issue of *Reader's Digest* magazine.

The Dream Horse and the Dining-Room Table

by Billy Porterfield, from the book *Diddy Waw Diddy*

*Making the promise to God was easy.
Keeping it was another matter.*

Since he was a kid on the Oklahoma prairie, Daddy loved the sweet, nutty smell of horses and mules. He had grown up working them in the fields. On Saturday afternoons, he had raced horses in the country fairs. He liked being in the saddle so much that he used his for a pillow in bed. It took some doing for Mother to get used to that.

If horses were Daddy's passion, working on oil rigs was his job. He was an experienced roughneck on a drilling crew. The money was good while the rig was running. But when a well was finished, the drilling crew had to move on. So our family drifted from job to job through the oil fields of Oklahoma and East Texas.

Daddy staggered drilling work with roustabouting: looking after existing wells and tank farms. The hourly wage was lower than on a rig, but the work was steady, the check came every week, and the company provided a house. These were never fancy, but our family made them home, however short our stay.

It was at one of these lease houses in Texas that Daddy bought War Cloud—a white-eyed, dapple-gray stallion. War Cloud was Daddy's dream horse. Every dawn before work, he spent an hour in the stable, feeding the stallion crimped oats and brushing his coat. Evenings, he rode until sunset.

He outfitted War Cloud's stall with every amenity: running water, a salt block, a tack box, blankets for every kind of weather, and a cabinet with all the ointments and pills an ailing horse could need. There was even a fan to keep the flies off.

Mother claimed the stable was furnished better than our company house. She tried to pretty things up for us, making oval throw rugs for the living room and bedrooms. Our floors were so clean you could eat off them. But she still wasn't satisfied. We ate at a table a neighbor gave us. It was rough and unpainted and she kept it hidden under oilcloth. Mother wanted a real dining-room suite.

One day she spotted a varnished walnut table and six chairs in the nearby town of Benavides. She could see it at home, covered with a lacy white tablecloth. But the set cost $100. At that price Daddy wouldn't even look at it. Had the woman lost her mind?

So our tiny mother put her dream aside and went on with her days—kneeling down, scrubbing the linoleum, standing out back at the roller washing machine, or bending over the ironing board, pressing jeans with a heavy steam iron. She smelled of soap and scorched cotton. We used to say Daddy wore the only starched, ironed underwear in the oil patch.

Mother had such a passion for spit and polish and the rightness of work that she was in perpetual motion. But all along, we sensed she was strangely fragile. In the fall of the year Daddy bought War Cloud, she finally pushed her body beyond endurance and came down sick. She ran a fever, had chills, and vomited all over the place.

An old Mexican doctor came out from Benavides, bent over the bed, and realized that Mother, already run-down and anemic, had eaten something spoiled. "She has ptomaine poisoning," he said. "It'll be touch and go because her fever is so high and she's terribly dehydrated."

Mother lapsed into a coma. We thought she was going to die. She came out of it, but then she kissed us all and settled into a strange calm.

Fay Talbot, a neighbor, moved in to keep Mother full of aspirin and liquids. Every morning, she bathed her in bed and changed her gown and sheets. Each day, the doc drove the 15 miles from Benavides. He said there was nothing to do but wait and pray.

Daddy slept on the living-room divan. One morning, he went out to the stable, where he thought we couldn't see him, and bawled. This rough man babbled to God, promising anything if his wife would get well. "I'll sell War Cloud, I'll buy that new dining-room suite, if only you'll bring her around."

We were never quite sure if it was Daddy's prayer, the old doctor's medicine, Fay Talbot's nursing, or her own drive, but Mother did recover. The day she thought she'd get out of bed and try her legs, Daddy slipped out and hauled War Cloud to the stock auctioneer in Benavides. He sold his pride to the highest bidder for $150.

Why he then went out and got drunk has always been a matter of family debate. I lean to the side that has him drowning in self-pity for losing his head and making such a promise to God. When it came down to death's door, he chose his wife over his horse. But now death had been set back, and his wife was on the mend. He might have figured he could have got by without losing either.

Anyway, after stupefying himself, my father staggered to the furniture store and bought the dining-room suite and a lacy white tablecloth. When he got back to the house, we kids—laughing and whispering—helped him set it up. Then we helped Mother out of bed and walked her to the dining room for the surprise.

"Well," Daddy asked, "what do you think?"

Mother's heart rose. Daddy had done a wonderful thing.

Then her heart fell: It was the wrong suite. This tacky furniture was not walnut; it was plain oak, painted blond.

She looked at her husband. She looked at her children. Tears came into her eyes.

"Why, Daddy—my darlings," she said, leaning on her husband, "it's perfectly beautiful. I love it."

Mother used that suite for 37 years, moving it wherever we went. One day, she stripped the painted finish and discovered a lovely natural grain in the wood. Then she stained it the deep walnut she'd always wanted. After Mother died, my sister took the table for her dining room.

We knew Mother was right. Painted or not, Daddy's table was perfectly beautiful.

Originally published in the December 1994 issue of *Reader's Digest* magazine.

Who Killed Sue Snow?

by Donald Dale Jackson

*The answer was surprising,
the motive . . . chilling.*

It was just after 6 a.m. on June 11, 1986, when Sue Snow, a 40-ycar-old bank manager in the Seattle suburb of Auburn, pulled herself out of bed. She went into the kitchen and took two Extra-Strength Excedrin capsules to help fight a throbbing headache. Then, after greeting her daughter, Hayley, she went into the bathroom and plugged in her curling iron.

At 6:40, Hayley, 15, noticed her mother was taking a long time. "Mom?" she called out. There was no answer—only the sound of running water. Entering the bathroom, she found her mother sprawled unconscious on the floor, her eyes open but unresponsive, her fingers splayed across her chest, her breathing labored. Rushed to a hospital, Sue Snow died hours later without regaining consciousness.

Doctors suspected an aneurysm in the brain but found no evidence of internal bleeding. The symptoms also suggested an overdose, but Hayley insisted her mother didn't drink or smoke, much less take drugs. Since the cause of death could not be determined, an autopsy was ordered.

During the examination, one of the pathologist's assistants detected a faint odor of bitter almonds emanating from the body—a telltale sign of cyanide. Could Snow have been poisoned? A lab test came back positive.

Police questioned the distraught family. Would Sue Snow have tried to poison herself? Certainly not, they said. But thinking back to that horrible morning, they wondered: Could the capsules have been tainted? Another lab test confirmed it: The capsules contained cyanide.

When ingested, cyanide prevents cells from using oxygen. It looks like table salt, and a small dose can kill rapidly. It's the perfect poison for murderers.

On June 16, the Food and Drug Administration published the lot number of the tainted capsules. The manufacturer, Bristol-Myers, cabled stores across the country to take the capsules off their shelves. Meanwhile, police found two other bottles of contaminated painkillers in Auburn and in Kent, a Seattle suburb adjoining Auburn.

Hysteria spread through Washington. Police stripped all nonprescription capsules from pharmacy shelves. The King County Medical Examiner's office began checking recent unexplained deaths to see if any were cyanide-caused, and a state of emergency was declared in the county.

*   *   *

The investigation was turned over to the FBI. Product tampering had been made a federal crime after seven Chicago-area people died from cyanide-spiked Extra-Strength Tylenol capsules in 1982—a case that remains unsolved.

Sixty agents were assigned to the Snow case. One of the agents who was to play a major role was Jack Cusack. At 43, the streetsmart, prematurely gray 16-year veteran knew how to read a killer's mind. His offhanded charm and casual style lured suspects and witnesses into giving him crucial information.

At first Cusack thought the killer might be a political terrorist or a disgruntled co-worker, but no one called to take credit or make demands.

Then on June 17, a 42-year-old woman named Stella Nickell telephoned the police. She reported that 12 days earlier, her husband, Bruce,

52, had died suddenly ater taking Extra-Strength Excedrin capsules.

Bruce Nickell had already been buried, and his autopsy reported the cause of death as emphysema. However, because he had volunteered to be an organ donor, a sample of his blood scrum had been preserved. A test of the scrum on June 19 showed cyanide present. By that time, the police had discovered two bottles of contaminated capsules in the home.

Someone must have mixed the cyanide in a container used earlier for crushing algicide pellets.

To an increasingly jittery public, it now looked as if a random killer was loose. A policeman in Auburn voiced the dread that many felt: "We've got a maniac out there."

Cusack searched for some connection between Bruce Nickell, a heavy-equipment operator for the state, and banker Sue Snow, but none became apparent.

Then an alert young chemist at the FBI crime lab in Washinton, D.C., discovered something peculiar about the cyanide in the five contaminated bottles—each contained tiny crystal-like specks of green. Breaking the particles down chemically, he identified the substance as an algae killer used in home fish tanks. He even came up with the brand name: Algae Destroyer.

Someone must have mixed the cyanide in a container used earlier for crushing algicide pellets.

Daily, the file on the killer grew thicker. An agent was needed who could cut through the ponderous material. Ron Nichols, an Annapolis-educated detective with a head for details, was chosen.

As Nichols read through the file, one thing kept bothering him. The FDA had examined more than 740,000 over-the-counter capsules in Washington, Oregon, Idaho, and Alaska. Only the capsules in five bottles had turned out to be laced with cyanide, and two of those were found in Stella Nickell's home.

If Stella had bought the two bottles at the same time, it would seem a simple case of bad luck. The problem was, Stella had said she bought them at different times in different stores. The odds that it was a coincidence were infinitesimal.

* * *

Stella Nickell seemed an unlikely suspect. A grandmother, she had two daughters and worked as a security guard at the Seattle-Tacoma airport. To all appearances she and Bruce had been happy together. They lived in a trailer on a large woody lot. Neighbors described her as cheerful and hard-working. She seemed genuinely shocked and despondent when Bruce died.

Then one of the agents remembered something seemingly insignificant from her investigation. "Stella Nickell has a fish tank in her trailer," the agent told Cusack, who by now had become the case supervisor.

By late summer, the agents began digging into the Nickells' life-insurance records.

Agents canvassed pet stores, asking if anyone recalled selling Algae Destroyer to Nickell. On August 25, they hit pay dirt. A clerk at a store in Kent identified Stella from a photo montage. He remembered her because she had a little bell attached to her purse. He called her "the woman who jingled."

The clerk's recollection, though tantalizing, was neither enough to support an indictment nor enough to convince Cusack this grandmother was a killer.

Yet, gradually, another side of Stella Nickell began to emerge. An FBI background check turned up convictions in California for check fraud, forgery, and child abuse between 1968 and 1971. The Nickells were chronically short of money. They barely survived a brush with bankruptcy, and before Bruce died, the bank was moving to foreclose on their trailer.

By late summer, the agents began digging into the Nickells' life-insurance records. Bruce's policy from the state paid Stella $31,000. But if his death was "accidental," she would collect an extra $105,000. Further, Stella had taken out two additional $20,000 policies on his life in the year before he died.

In all, she stood to receive $176,000 if Bruce's death were judged accidental. (For insurance purposes, death by cyanide poisoning is considered an accident.) But the doctor who examined Bruce's body had failed to detect cyanide. Curiously, Stella had called the doctor several times to question his findings that her husband had died a natural death from emphysema.

A chilling thought now crept into Cusack's mind. He tried to dismiss it. It persisted. There was the appalling possibility that Sue Snow was murdered—and many others could well have been—so Stella could make her husband's death look like an accident.

* * *

On November 18, Cusack and Nichols met Stella Nickell for the first time in an interview at FBI headquarters in Seattle. Cusack watched as a dark-haired, middle-aged woman in a buckskin coat came in. As she sat down, a bell on her purse jingled lightly.

Cusack wanted Stella to believe this was a routine interview, so he tossed out questions in a flow of easy conversation. He went over the details of her husband's death, where and when she had bought the tainted bottles. Had she ever bought Algae Destroyer? She told him no. Had she ever bought extra insurance on her husband? Again, she said no. That lie nudged Stella one rung higher as a suspect.

Finally Cusack asked if she would take a polygraph test. She refused, sobbing that she couldn't go through any more questions.

For several days, Cusack bided his time, hoping her doubts would wear her down. It was, he explained, his pebbles-on-the-roof technique. "The suspect gets the impression we're interviewing everyone they know. They begin to think we know about every mistake they make. It's like they're almost asleep at night, and there it is again—ping, ping, ping on the roof." Four days later, Stella called him and agreed to take the test.

During the subsequent polygraph, Cusack and Nichols watched Stella closely. When Cusack asked if she put cyanide in Excedrin capsules, she calmly denied it, but her jump in pulse rate and breathing convinced the agents otherwise.

Of course, believing she did it and proving it were two different things.

The agents knew polygraph data are normally inadmissible in court. They needed to corner their quarry and pressure her into a confession.

Cusack switched the machine off. "Stella, listen to me," he said softly. "Based on your physiological responses, I am positive you caused Bruce's death."

Stella went white. Then she looked coldly at Cusack and said, "I want to see my attorney."

*　　*　　*

Cusack realized that if he was going to crack this case, it would have to be without Stella's confession. He began phoning witnesses again, asking if there was anything more they could add.

Six weeks later, friends of Cindy Hamilton, Stella's 27-year-old daughter, called Cusack. Cindy had defended her mother when Cusack had questioned her months earlier. Now, after the polygraph, she had begun to have second thoughts. And when Cusack questioned her this time, a grisly tale unfolded. Her mother, she said, had talked about killing her stepfather for years. Stella was bored, but she didn't want a divorce because she'd lose half the property.

Stella had even talked about hiring a "hit man" to shoot Bruce or run his car off the road. Once, she tried to poison him with toxic seeds, but they only made him drowsy. A few months before his death, Cindy said, Stella began talking about cyanide.

When her mother told her about Bruce's death, Cindy said, Stella had looked hard at her and said, "I know what you're thinking, and the answer is no." So Cindy had stifled her suspicions until the polygraph results revived them.

Cindy talked for nine hours straight. Cusack tried to remain calm, but his mind was racing. This could bring a conviction, but Cindy hadn't seen her mother pack cyanide in capsules or place bottles in stores. There was no smoking gun.

Cindy agreed to testify so long as her mother was not executed. Cusack assured her that the most severe penalty in a federal product-tampering conviction was life imprisonment. But a warning light was blinking in his brain. What if this were only a mother-daughter feud? Will she flip-flop and deny everything in court?

One part of Cindy's conversation haunted Cusack. "I knew my mother was capable of doing this," she had tearfully confided. "I just didn't want to believe it." Cusack now realized the enormity of what Stella had done. She had killed an unsuspecting victim to make the murder of her husband seem accidental so she could collect more insurance money. She had even filed a wrongful-death suit against Bristol-Myers for "contributing to" her husband's death!

What they needed was that last link in the chain of evidence against Stella Nickell.

Cusack wondered: What if Sue Snow's daughter, Hayley, also had taken the capsules that morning? What if the other two bottles had found their way into people's homes? How many people would Stella Nickell willingly have killed for an extra $105,000?

By February 1987, with the grand jury now hearing testimony, the FBI team had shrunk to Cusack the interviewer, Nichols the analyzer, and an energetic rookie named Marshall Stone. What they needed was that last link in the chain of evidence against Stella Nickell. But most of the leads they checked out went nowhere.

Learning that Stella was interested in tarot cards and fortune-telling, they visited dozens of occult shops, searching for a connection to cyanide. They found nothing.

Then Cusack remembered something Cindy had told him. In the months before her stepfather's death, her mother had researched cyanide at libraries. Stone volunteered to canvass the local libraries. One of the first he visited was in Stella's hometown of Auburn.

"Do you have a library-card holder by the name of Stella Nickell?" Stone asked the librarian. The woman searched the library's files and returned with a piece of paper, which she handed to Stone. It was an overdue notice for a book Stella had borrowed and never returned. Its title: *Human Poisoning.*

Armed with Stella's card number, Stone combed the aisles for all the other books Stella had borrowed. When he opened a volume on toxic plants called *Deadly Harvest,* he found her number stamped twice on the checkout slip—both dates before Bruce's death.

He packed the book and the volumes that covered cyanide from three encyclopedias and sent them to the FBI crime lab. Fingerprint analysis revealed 84 of Stella's prints in *Deadly Harvest*—the biggest concentration on the pages discussing cyanide.

* * *

Stella Nickell pleaded not guilty in a federal court trial that began in April 1988. It took 31 witnesses to stitch together a portrait of a woman in an unhappy marriage who felt financially desperate and saw murder as a solution. The prosecutor called her an "icy human being without social or moral conscience."

The jury found her guilty on May 9. Judge William Dwyer, citing "crimes of exceptional callousness; and cruelty," sentenced Stella to 90 years, with no parole consideration for 30 years.

As a result of the case, the FDA tightened its regulations, requiring more antitampering protection for over-the-counter medicines. Bristol-Myers, the maker of Excedrin, joined the manufacturers of Tylenol and other drugs in abandoning two-piece nonprescription capsules, replacing them with one-piece "caplets," thus effectively ending the threat of capsule tampering by crazed killers.

When he thinks about the case now, Cusack wonders about the "what ifs." For instance, what if the curious FBI chemist hadn't detected the tiny specks of algae? Stella Nickell might have committed the perfect crime. But she didn't. Plain, dogged persistence nailed her.

"It's the old lesson," says Cusack. "You turn every stone, leave nothing to chance. This time, it worked."

Originally published in the February 1991 issue of *Reader's Digest* magazine.

House of Cards

by John Colapinto, from *Vanity Fair*

*It was the greatest scam
in the history of professional bridge—
and one player put a stop to it.*

On August 22, 2015, Boye Brogeland posted a provocative comment to the website Bridgewinners.com. "Very soon there will come out mind-boggling stuff," wrote the Norwegian bridge player, then age 43 and ranked 64th in the world. "It will give us a tremendous momentum to clean the game up."

A few days later, Brogeland launched his own website, Bridgecheaters.com. The home page featured a huge photo of Lotan Fisher and Ron Schwartz, a young Israeli duo who, since breaking into the international ranks in 2011, had snapped up the game's top trophies. They appeared under the tagline "The greatest scam in the history of bridge!"

Brogeland posted examples of what he claimed to be suspiciously illogical hands played by the pair. He also laid out a pattern of alleged cheating and bad sportsmanship going as far back as 2003, when Fisher and Schwartz were in their mid-teens.

For the game of contract bridge, it was an earthquake equal to the jolt that shook international cycling when Lance Armstrong was banned from competition for doping. Fisher and Schwartz denied all wrongdoing and hired lawyers who dispatched a letter

Norwegian whistle-blower Boye Brogeland

to Brogeland threatening a lawsuit and offering to settle if he paid them US$1 million. In a message he denies was intended for Brogeland, Ron Fisher posted to his Facebook page: "Jealousy made you sick. Get ready for a meeting with the devil."

*   *   *

Brogeland lives in Flekkefjord, Norway, with his wife, Tonje, and their two young children. Having learned bridge at the age of eight from his grandparents, he fell in love with the game and turned pro at 28. In 2013, he was recruited by his current sponsor, Richie Schwartz (no relation to Ron), a Bronx-born bridge addict who made a fortune at the racetrack in the 1970s. Brogeland says Richie Schwartz pays him travel expenses and a base yearly salary of US$50,000—with big bonuses for strong showings in tournaments.

Not long after Brogeland joined Richie Schwartz's team, he learned that his employer was also hiring Fisher and Ron Schwartz, about whom he had heard misgivings from other players. Over the next two years, Brogeland and his five teammates won a string of championships.

Nevertheless, Brogeland says he was relieved when, in the summer of 2015, Fisher and Ron Schwartz were lured away by Jimmy Cayne, former CEO of the defunct investment house Bear Stearns. "When they changed teams," Brogeland says, "I didn't have to be faced with this kind of environment where you feel something is strange but you can't really tell."

Fisher, meanwhile, was enjoying his position at the top of the game, where the lives of many successful young pros resemble those of globe-hopping rock musicians. Convening nightly at a hotel bar in whatever city is holding the competition—Biarritz, Chennai,

Chicago—they drink until the small hours. Charismatic and darkly handsome, Fisher posted Instagram photos of himself in well-cut suits, behind the wheel of luxury cars, or partying with an array of people.

There was only one problem: the persistent rumors that he was a cheater. "But it's an unwritten rule that you do not publicly accuse anyone—even if you're sure," says Steve Weinstein, a top American player. It was a Catch-22 that Fisher seemed to delight in flaunting, shrugging off questions about his suspicious play. "He had the Nietzschean superman personality," says Fred Gitelman, a professional player who has won championships worldwide. "He just thought he was in a different league."

Contract bridge is built on the rules of the 18th-century British card game whist. Four people play in two-person partnerships. The player to the dealer's left leads with a card of any suit, and each player in succession plays a card of the suit led; the highest card wins the trick.

It's a simple game, slightly complicated by the existence of the trump: a card in a suit that overrules all others. In whist, trump is determined randomly. In auction bridge, a game popularized in England in 1904, each hand has an opening "auction," where the teams, communicating solely by way of *spoken* bids, establish which (if any) suit will be trump and how many tricks they think they can take. Pairs who take more tricks than contracted for are awarded extra points.

Contract bridge emerged from refinements American railroad magnate Harold S. Vanderbilt introduced in 1925. He sought to spice up auction bridge by awarding escalating bonus points to pairs who took the greatest risk in the opening auction, and imposed steep point deductions on those who failed to make the tricks contracted for. Thus did a polite British parlor game take on some of the sweaty-palmed excitement of the big-money trading of Wall Street.

The American Contract Bridge League (ACBL), the game's governing body in North America, lists only 168,000 members, with a median age (despite the hotel-bar set) of 71.

Yet the professional tournament game is a serious pursuit, with

Ron Schwartz (left) and Lotan Fisher

wealthy enthusiasts assembling stables of top players, paying them retainers and bonuses—all for the privilege of playing hands with the pros in important tournaments. With six world championships under her belt, Gail Greenberg, one of the game's greatest female champions, says that such paydays have fueled cheating by players hoping to be recruited by deep-pocketed sponsors or to hang on to the one they've got.

Pairs are forbidden to say what high cards they hold or in what suit they might be strong—except by way of the koan-like bids ("Two no trump"). Any other communication is outlawed. In one of the game's biggest scandals, British champion J. Terence Reese and his partner, Boris Schapiro, were discovered in 1965 using finger signals to communicate the number of hearts they held.

Tournament organizers would eventually respond by erecting screens to block partners' view of each other. When players were discovered communicating via footsie, barriers were installed under tables. Pairs can come under suspicion even when no signalling is detected.

"In bridge at the highest level," says Chris Willenken, a leading American professional, "the best players play in a relentlessly logical fashion, so when something illogical happens, other good players notice it. And if that illogical thing is consistently winning, suspicions can be aroused."

*   *   *

Less than a month after Lotan Fisher and Ron Schwartz had left Richie Schwartz's team, Brogeland met the pair as opponents, in the quarter-final of the 2015 Spingold at the Hilton hotel in Chicago. Brogeland's team was the clear underdog, but it won by the slimmest margin possible: a single point.

Or it seemed to. Fisher immediately contested the result on a technicality. After an arbitration that stretched until 1:30 a.m., the win was overturned: Brogeland's team had now lost by one point and been knocked out of the tournament.

That night, a crushed Brogeland could not sleep. He rose at 7 a.m. and opened Bridge Base Online (BBO), a website that archives tournament hands, to see exactly how he had lost. He immediately noticed something odd. Ron Schwartz had opened a hand by playing a club lead. Yet, Schwartz's hand indicated that a heart lead was the obvious play.

Then, he says, he saw something even stranger. In one of the hands, Fisher had claimed 11 tricks. Except Fisher, as BBO showed, held the cards for just 10 tricks. Brogeland thought it was a mistake and immediately contacted his sponsor. In any event, challenges must be raised within a half-hour of a match. The loss would stand.

When he gave suspect hands to the ACBL, he was told to supply more.

* * *

Brogeland spent the next two days at the tournament scouring BBO and comparing notes with other players. By the time he flew back to Norway, he was convinced Fisher and Schwartz were signaling to each other, but he had no idea how. Still, he believed that if he amassed enough illogical hands, he could make a convincing case, however circumstantial.

Brogeland contacted governing bodies on both sides of the Atlantic. When he gave suspect hands to the ACBL, he was told to supply more. "They had plenty of hands," he says. "Fifty, 60. I said, 'How many do you need? One hundred? Two hundred? Please do something!'"

Robert Hartman, the CEO of ACBL, declines to discuss the specifics of ongoing investigations but admits that the process for reviewing cheating can take a year or longer to play out.

Fisher and Schwartz aren't the only pair suspected of cheating in recent history, either. Fulvio Fantoni and Claudio Nunes of Italy—ranked first and second in the world in the 2014 European Championships—have also been reported to the ACBL by a colleague, and an investigation into allegations against the pair is still pending.

For his part, Brogeland had no intention of waiting. Despite the risks to his career and reputation—not to mention the fact that he would be challenging rich and powerful interests—he decided to bypass the official channels and go public. And so, on August 28, 2015, he went live with Bridge Cheaters, where he laid out his evidence.

Experienced cheating investigators were underwhelmed. Kit Woolsey, a mathematician who has previously done statistical analyses for the ACBL

Cullin was convinced the board's placement signaled what suit the partner should lead with.

to help implicate cheaters, wrote on Bridge Winners, "His example hands are an indication of possible wrongdoing, but I do not believe that by themselves they are proof of anything."

Barry Goren, a U.S. professional, excoriated Brogeland for publicly accusing the pair without due process. "Personally," Goren wrote on Bridge Winners, "I think Boye should be thrown out of bridge for the way this was handled."

As if in tacit acknowledgment of how his failure to uncover actual signalling by Fisher and Schwartz weakened his case, Brogeland had included links to three YouTube videos of the pair in match play. On August 30, Brogeland's friend Per-Ola Cullin, a semiprofessional bridge player, watched one of the videos. In it, Fisher makes a suspicious heart lead.

Cullin noticed that Schwartz set down the small slotted board that holds the cards. This was normal. But he didn't place the board in the center of the table, its usual spot. Instead, he slid it a few inches to the right, to one side of the opening in the trap door of the anticheating screen. Cullin decided to watch the previous hand. The board had been positioned in the same peculiar spot—but this time by Fisher. As with the succeeding hand, the team led hearts. "My adrenalin started pumping," Cullin says. "I started watching all the matches from the European championships."

After several hours, Cullin was convinced the board's placement signaled what suit the partner should lead with. At a little after 3 a.m., he texted Brogeland, who forwarded the information to Woolsey.

Three days later, Woolsey posted to Bridge Winners an essay entitled "The Videos Speak," confirming Cullin's hypothesis. Fisher and Schwartz were suspended by the ACBL and placed under investigation by that body and the European Bridge League (EBL). It was an extraordinary exoneration for Brogeland. But he wasn't done yet.

*　　*　　*

Maaijke Mevius, a 45-year-old living in the Netherlands, is a physicist and an avid recreational bridge player. Galvanized by the evidence against Fisher and Schwartz, she wondered if she could spot any illegal signalling in YouTube videos. While watching Fantoni and Nunes, she grew convinced she had decoded how they were using card placement to signal to their partner whether they held any high honor cards (ace, king, or queen). Mevius emailed the information to Brogeland.

On September 13, 2015, Bridge Winners published "The Videos Speak: Fantoni-Nunes," a damning analysis by Woolsey. In a statement from that month, the pair said, "We will not comment on allegations at this time."

On Bridge Winners, the first reader comment in response to this news said it all: "Is this the end? Speechless now..."

It wasn't quite the end. Brogeland soon received an anonymous email tip from someone identifying himself as "No Matter." The tipster advised looking at videos of Germany's Alex Smirnov and Josef Piekarek, as well as the Polish pair Cezary Balicki and Adam Zmudzinski. In subsequent emails, No Matter pointed out what to watch for: signalling based on where the pair put the special bidding cards in the bidding tray that is passed between the players during the auction.

Smirnov and Piekarek, told of the discovery, admitted to the violation in a statement. Balicki and Zmudzinski denied the charges.

Still more astonishing, however, is the fact that Brogeland believes the person behind the mask of No Matter is the disgraced Lotan Fisher.

Brogeland cannot explain why Fisher would assist in the quest to root out cheaters—unless, by helping to expose others, he hoped to take the focus off himself. Fisher, in an email to this writer, claims that he only aided No

Matter and that his motivation was the same as Brogeland's—to clean up the game. "I love [bridge] more than Boye or anyone else," he wrote, adding, "My next step is to prove that me and Ron Schwartz didn't cheat. NEVER."

* * *

In May, Bridge Winners announced that the EBL had issued Fisher and Schwartz a five-year ban from its events and a lifetime ban on playing as partners. The other pairs have also faced repercussions from various leagues and events.

Brogeland's actions have also had a more permanent effect on the game. In December 2015, the ACBL held one of bridge's biggest annual tournaments, the American nationals. For the first time, the ACBL had installed small video cameras and microphones at the tables to record all matches from the quarter-finals through to the finals—since no one imagines that every dishonest pair has been rooted out.

Before the end of the tournament, ACBL CEO Hartman convened the first meeting of a new anticheating task force—including Willenken, Woolsey, and Cullin—who discussed means for streamlining the process of submitting complaints and investigating them.

Meanwhile, the International Bridge Press Association named Brogeland the Bridge Personality of the Year for 2015. When he arrived for his first match at the Denver nationals last autumn, he had to fight his way through the crowd that had collected outside the tournament room. "Thank you for your service," said a bearded man who had stopped Brogeland at the door of the game room.

"Well, I had to do it," Brogeland said, shaking the man's hand and trying to move off.

"You really put yourself on the line," the man persisted.

Brogeland smiled. "Bridge deserves it," he said, then headed for his table.

Originally published in the 2017 *Reader's Digest* international Edition.

SURF SOLDIERS

We're just kids, 20-somethings sitting around a beach
bonfire, drinking beer, and telling stories. It's been a long
day, but our faces glow with more than firelight. Daniel
and I love traveling, and we talk about where he traveled
before Afghanistan. They all cringe as they recall the smell
of the poop lakes in Iraq, and Dorian laughs loudly. We're
just kids at the beach, but I realize what an outsider must
see. I'm surrounded by young soldiers, young vets, single/
double amputees in wheelchairs, burn victims relaxing in
the shadows, glass eyes twinkling from the flames. They're
wounded soldiers I'm helping rehabilitate with "surf therapy."
We surfed all day today and we'll surf all day tomorrow.
That's what an outsider would see, but in my mind, I'm just
a girl with a surfboard sitting among heroes, trying to make
them feel like a couple of kids at the beach.

—Caroline McCandless *San Diego, California*

ANIMAL INSTINCT

My stepdaughter Pamela, a veterinarian, was visiting her
aunt when they noticed a butterfly flying erratically around
the room. Cupping it gently in her hands, Pamela realized
a quarter of its wing was missing. While Auntie held the
wings still on a table with toothpicks, Pamela performed
surgery with scissors and contact cement. She fashioned a tiny
prosthesis from a napkin and gently attached it to the wing.
A minute later, the creature fluttered out a nearby window.
While the two women congratulated each other, the butterfly
reentered the room, flew around, and landed directly over
Pamela's heart.

—Robert McCormick *Kings Beach, California*

Sweet Dreams

This haunting photo of four sisters asleep in their bed is a testament to the privilege and trust that photographers earn. Our most intimate and vulnerable moments are when we sleep.

Photograph by Maggie Steber

Finding Gilbert

by Diane Covington

While stationed in France during World War II, an American soldier took a seven-year-old orphan under his wing. Decades later, his daughter made it her mission to locate that boy.

Gilbert Desclos sat in the tall grass on the cliff above Omaha Beach and shivered in the sea air. The sun rose over the trees as he hugged his bony knees tight to his chest and pulled his worn wool sweater around him.

Ever since the arrival of les Américains, his world had changed. Overnight, a military camp had sprung to life on the empty field just below his home in Normandy. For seven-year-old Gilbert, an orphan, it was a boy's dream. His caretaker, Mrs. Bisson, had to drag him in at night.

Now he watched, wide-eyed, as jeeps roared up the road and men in white caps scurried about, emptying trucks loaded with guns, ammunition, food, and giant duffel bags. He yawned as the smell of bacon, eggs, coffee, and toast wafted up from a massive tent. He tilted his small head back, breathing in the aromas. His stomach growled.

Donald K. Johnson, a lieutenant in the Seabees, the U.S. Navy's Construction Battalion, held a clipboard and checked off the morning's accomplishments. The infirmary tent was complete; now the medics and

The author, near her home in Nevada City, California. Insert: Gilbert Desclos (middle), 1944

doctors had a decent place to treat soldiers. The showers worked.

Johnson and his men had been busy since dawn, and it was now noon. He dismissed them, then took a moment and touched the breast pocket that held the photo of his wife and two young sons. It had been more than a year since he'd seen them.

When the lieutenant turned to go, he spied something in the tall grass on the hill. Was that a child? He waved. A small hand waved back. Johnson beckoned. There was a moment of hesitation, then the boy, barely taller than the grass, made his way down. Johnson knelt to look into the child's thin face.

He tried out his high school French: "Comment t'appelles-tu?"

The boy's sparkly blue eyes shone. "Gilbert," he said.

Johnson shook his hand. This little guy looked like he could use a good meal, and the camp had more than enough food. In his halting French, he invited Gilbert to have lunch. When the boy nodded, Johnson lifted him onto his hip, as he might've done with one of his own sons, and headed for the mess tent.

Inside, dozens of young soldiers ate, talked, and clanged their cutlery. Gilbert's eyes grew wide. Johnson piled two plates high with roast beef, potatoes, carrots and peas, freshly baked bread, and apple pie.

The men at the officers table smiled and made room for the two of them. Gilbert took small bites and, chewing slowly, ate everything on his plate. Johnson patted his head: "Très bien!" Gilbert smiled.

After lunch, Johnson held Gilbert's hand, and they walked into the June sunlight. He knelt beside the boy and explained that he had to go back to work. Gilbert nodded and ran back up the path to the tall grass, turning around to wave.

At 1800 hours, as Johnson was again heading for the mess tent, he saw Gilbert sitting in the same spot. He motioned, and Gilbert ran to him.

Johnson with daughters Sharon, five, and Diane, three, at their Escondido, California, home in 1952.

Dinner was fried chicken, mashed potatoes, corn, biscuits, and chocolate cake. Johnson again filled two plates, but Gilbert didn't eat as much as he had at lunch; it was clear that the boy wasn't used to so much food. But he sat close to Johnson and smiled his shy smile, taking big breaths between bites, as if willing himself to eat as much as he could.

After dinner, Johnson knelt close to Gilbert. "Bonsoir," he said. "A demain," till tomorrow. He watched the boy walk up the path and out of sight.

*   *   *

From that day on, Gilbert ate with Johnson, three meals a day, soon filling out from all the rich food. The other soldiers didn't mind; in fact, the boy helped ease their homesickness. Gilbert giggled when Johnson carried him around on his shoulders and soon began riding along in the jeep down to the beach, where Johnson supervised the unloading of ships. When Johnson oversaw construction projects in the camp, Gilbert tagged along. If Johnson left camp with his crew to rebuild a road or a blown-out bridge, Gilbert waited for his return.

As the summer of 1944 passed, Johnson's French improved, and Gilbert learned to say hello, goodbye, thank you, jeep, ship, and ice cream. He could also say Lieutenant Johnson.

In mid-October, when Johnson received orders to leave France, he drove to the local authorities in Caen to make some inquiries. He discovered that Gilbert had been abandoned at birth and had no living relatives. But when he asked if he could adopt him, the answer was firm: no.

Lieutenant Johnson was my father. Stories about the young boy and wartime France were an element of my childhood, as constant as the roar of Dad's motorcycle as he rolled in each evening at 5:45 after his commute from San Diego, where he worked as a civil engineer for the Navy.

At 6 p.m. sharp, my family gathered around the yellow Formica table that took up most of our small kitchen. Dad and Mom sat on each end, my sister across from me, our older brothers next to us.

Dad looked straitlaced in his short-sleeved white shirt, skinny tie, and plastic pocket liner holding a pen, a notebook, and sometimes a slide rule. But his eyes told you he was kind, funny, a bit mischievous. His stories made me laugh, and when he described his time in France, I could picture it all: the French countryside, the huge Navy ships, and Gilbert Desclos.

> *Gilbert had been abandoned and had no living relatives. But when Johnson asked if he could adopt him, the answer was firm: no.*

Dad always said Gilbert's name with a kind of reverence and the way the French would, with a soft g sound.

I knew he had tried to adopt Gilbert and bring him home. I thought about that sometimes, wondering what it would have been like to have another older brother at the dinner table.

As I grew up, Dad's stories seemed to belong more and more to my childhood, put away with my dolls and coloring books. After I married and had my own family, Dad visited Europe again, stopping in Paris. He told me how he tried to find Gilbert's name in the phone book but couldn't. I remember how his shoulders slumped and his head hung down as he told me about his failure.

In my father's old age, when he could no longer walk and had lost his eyesight, I would sit with him as he talked about his life. When he spoke about France, his eyes shone. They glistened with tears when he mentioned Gilbert, pronouncing his name with that special softness. I stroked his fragile hand, wishing there were something I could do.

*   *   *

After Dad died, in 1991, I wanted to learn more about World War II. I traveled to France in 1993 to tour the beaches and write about the 50th anniversary of the D-day invasion. I stood on the cliffs above Omaha Beach, now the site of the American cemetery where nearly 10,000 U.S. soldiers are buried. The air stung my face as I wiped away tears, remembering Dad, wishing I could ask him more questions.

In my article for my local California newspaper, I mentioned Gilbert Desclos. The press attaché at the French consulate in San Francisco read the story and contacted me. Learning that I was going back to Normandy to accept a medal in Dad's honor, she insisted I try to find Gilbert: "The French don't move around as Americans do. He's probably still nearby."

After the medal ceremony, I placed an ad in the local paper. Thinking it would take months, if not years, to find Gilbert, I listed my address in California, then left on a tour around France with Heather, my teenage daughter.

The next morning, Gilbert Desclos, reading his newspaper, wept when he saw my father's name. He called the paper and learned I'd left the area, so he wrote to my home address. My sister, collecting my mail, recognized the name, ran to a friend's, and faxed it back to France. I received it the night before Heather and I were to travel back to Paris and then home.

I called Gilbert and, stammering through my emotions, arranged a place to meet him that evening. As my daughter and I sat at a sidewalk café in Caen, waiting for Gilbert and his wife to arrive, I fidgeted in my metal chair, watching the passing faces. Could I possibly be meeting the boy from my childhood stories? And how would I know him?

Then a trim, well-dressed man walked up, smiled, and said my name. When I looked into his eyes, I saw the same expression of kindness that Dad always had; Gilbert actually resembled Dad somehow.

At his home, after dinner, Gilbert uncorked a dusty bottle of Calvados. As we sipped the apple brandy and talked, I realized that all the years of studying French vocabulary and irregular verbs had prepared me for this moment.

He asked questions about Dad, about our lives, about how Dad had died. He told me how he'd struggled after Dad left France, living in an orphanage, lonely and sad—but that in his teens, a sweet woman had brought him to live with her family. Nourished by those years of love and caring, he went on to join the military, find a good job, and marry his wife, Huguette. Together, they raised their daughter, Cathy.

> *I sat at a café and waited. Could I possibly be meeting the boy from my childhood stories?*

But he had never forgotten Dad. He had always insisted to Huguette, Cathy, and later his two grandsons that he had a family in America who would come and find him one day.

I told him that Dad had never forgotten him either—that he had talked about him for the rest of his life, even at the end. I could tell that meant everything to Gilbert.

He told me the same stories my father had told, but from a child's perspective: his fascination with the military camp, the delicious food, Dad's gentleness. Remembering the lieutenant's arms around him, he wept again. We sat together, silent and moved, missing the father who had loved us both.

* * *

Gilbert took a gulp of his Calvados and told me his version of the October day in 1944 when he and Dad said goodbye on Omaha Beach.

Dad held him close. Gilbert hung on tight, burying his head in Dad's thick, wool Navy coat. Cold October winds whipped the sand around them as men rushed by, carrying their heavy seabags on their shoulders, excited to be going home.

"Do you want to come with me to America?" Dad asked.

"Oui," Gilbert murmured.

They boarded the ship. The captain, who'd been watching, shook his head. "Johnson, off the record, if you're caught, I know nothing about this." Dad nodded, shifting Gilbert's weight on his hip.

But within the hour, a storm raged. Twenty-foot waves lashed the hull of the ship. There was no way the boat could cross the English Channel until the storm had subsided.

As the sun set, the wind slackened and sailors prepared for departure. Moments before the ship was to sail, French gendarmes pulled up on the beach, demanding to speak with the captain; a Mrs. Bisson had reported that her ward had not returned home, and they were looking for him.

As Gilbert remembers it, the captain called for Lieutenant Johnson. There was a long, strained pause. The lieutenant appeared at the top of the gangplank, holding Gilbert in his arms. Gilbert sobbed and clung to him. "Non!" he wailed. "Non!" The gendarmes had to pull him away. The ship sailed without the boy, whom Mrs. Bisson placed in an orphanage the same day.

Gilbert put the cork in the Calvados bottle. "Your father said he would come back for me. I have been waiting 50 years for some word from him."

We sat in awkward silence until Gilbert's daughter asked, "Why didn't he? Why didn't he come back?"

I couldn't think of what to say in English, let alone French. Then Cathy said softly, "Le destin." It was Gilbert's destiny to stay in France and have his family and his life there.

As we said goodnight, Gilbert took my hand. "I always knew that

Diane (seated, center), Gilbert (behind her), and their families—reunited at last.

I would hear from your father, that someone would come," he said. "Thank you."

I didn't sleep that night, picturing the goodbye on that desolate beach, imagining the police pulling a part of Dad's heart away. And how—why—had Dad carried that secret for the rest of his life? Was he ashamed that he hadn't fulfilled his promise? And why hadn't I helped Dad find Gilbert before he died?

As the clock ticked on the bedside table, I realized I would not find answers from the past. But we could go forward from here.

For the next two years, Gilbert and I wrote, phoned, and e-mailed. In 1996, my mother, my sister, Heather, and I traveled to France for a celebration that received coverage in the same newspaper I'd used to find Gilbert.

A year later, the Desclos family came to America, welcomed by 40 members of the Johnson clan, spanning four generations. At dinner one night, Gilbert read aloud a letter he'd written for the occasion, as I translated into English. He shared memories of my father and told us what it meant to finally come to America. It was a dream, he said, that he had thought would remain a dream.

Other relatives and I returned to France several times through the years. Then, a few months before my planned visit last January, Gilbert was diagnosed with liver cancer. He died four days before my arrival.

I made it in time for his funeral. In his tiny village in Normandy, bells tolled as relatives and friends braved the cold to fill the church. The tricolor French flag draped his coffin, carried by an honor guard of fellow veterans.

I sat with Gilbert's family in the front pew and listened to the tributes to his life. During the service, the priest asked me to place on the coffin a photo of my father and one of Gilbert from 1944 together in one frame.

As candlelight flickered on the faces in the photographs and music echoed off the walls of the old church, I realized that Cathy was right: It was le destin that the naval officer and the little boy had found each other and destiny that they'd gone their separate ways. But it was also destiny, I knew now, that had brought them back together.

Originally published in the June 2009 issue of *Reader's Digest* magazine.

Friendship in Black & White

by Martha Manning, from the book *A Place to Land*

Crossing all kinds of lines and boundaries, two women find friendship and strength.

Raina Graves and I first met in 1995 when I volunteered for a "Santa" program in my town of Arlington, Virginia. I was given Raina's wish list for herself and her three children. I had all the gifts wrapped and ready to deliver to the group that would distribute them. Then I was thrown a curve: The group's assistant said they were terribly backed up and asked me if I'd mind delivering the gifts myself.

My idea of a perfect charity was to help people without actually having anything to do with them. In every volunteer situation in which I was the helper coming face-to-face with the helpee, I felt shame for my relatively privileged position; then I was paralyzed by my paltry efforts.

At first, things with Raina were just as awkward as I'd feared. Not that she wasn't friendly and grateful when I brought my haul over to her apartment. But she was black, which made me feel uncomfortably like Lily White Lady Bountiful. My husband and I were by no means rich, but it was painfully clear that Raina had none of the supports that we took for granted, no safety net beneath the tightrope she'd been walking since she was in her late teens. Later I learned her story: Until the birth of her twins, she was either in school or working. Her mother, brothers, and sisters struggled financially. Her children's father left her with a broken heart and no child support.

So when things got tough for Raina, she wound up homeless, and when I met her, she had just moved from a temporary shelter to a partially subsidized two-bedroom apartment that she shared with her mother, her three young children, and a niece.

Another difference between the two of us was that she was younger, in her late 20s, and I was definitely middle-aged. Still, we were somehow drawn to each other. She called to thank me for my Christmas visit; then two weeks later I called her back, just to see how she was. In trading the day-to-day details of our lives on the phone, we ended up sharing some laughs. She had a great laugh. It sang. There's something so freeing about laughing with someone. It opens invisible doors.

Soon we were talking often. Then came the day when she took me up on my offer to baby-sit. When I arrived at Raina's apartment, I was reminded how involved and involving child care is. Three-year-old Jade was a real drama queen, and the twins, Darren and Deven, one year old, were adorable but high maintenance, like all babies. Nap time couldn't come soon enough, and when Raina got home, I flew out the door, relieved. But soon I was up for it again.

The kids started coming over to our house. After one visit, my husband, Brian, said to me, "You know what, I haven't heard you laugh like that in a couple of years! They bring something out in you that I haven't seen in a while." They brought something out in him, too. I could see my husband falling in love with the children—a guy who ended up with one child instead of the three or four he'd always expected. Still, it took Brian some time to let go of his protectiveness of me, the fear that I would be overwhelmed by becoming too involved.

One day I said to Raina, "I think it's time for a girls' outing." The kids were in day care, so we'd have no interruptions. But I immediately

Martha (left) and Raina saw each other through life's tough times.

felt self-conscious. We had known each other for five months now; maybe she wanted things to stay the way they were, with us relating to each other through the kids. But she responded with enthusiasm. We went to lunch at the Olive Garden. Everything was delicious, and we even ordered dessert. "Just what I need—more pounds," I said.

"I know," Raina commiserated. "I still have to take this weight off from my pregnancy."

"Yeah, me, too," I said.

"Guess you're taking it real slow," she said with a smile. My daughter, Keara, was 19 and away at college.

I was not sure I wanted to get into this, but if she was going to know me, she had to know it all. "Actually, I've had terrible trouble with depression. Bad enough for years of medicines that make you gain weight as a side effect, bad enough for me to go into the hospital and have ECT." When she looked puzzled, I explained, "Electroconvulsive therapy. Some people call it shock treatments."

Portrait of a family united by heart if not by blood. Baby Josiah was born after Deven's death—a new nephew for "Aunt Martha."

I sensed her wondering what I had to be depressed about. "Let's face it, I have a great life," I said. "But the kind of depression I get is often not connected to outside circumstances. It's a living hell."

"Why haven't you told me all this?" she asked.

"I don't know. I guess I was worried what you'd think of me. How comfortable you'd be leaving the kids with me." Tears stung my eyes. "I'm sorry."

"Martha, what are you sorry for?"

"For crying. You have so much to deal with."

"I've known you carry burdens you don't talk about. I'm sorry you've had such hard times." She grabbed my hand and squeezed it. I squeezed back. Something had shifted. I had needed her, and in spite of myself, had let her know it.

After that, the barriers fell away. Raina told me one time, "You're the only white person who's given me anything that I haven't felt 'less than' for taking." The children began calling us "Aunt Martha" and "Uncle Brian." Sleepovers for them at our house were a frequent pleasure and gave Raina a needed break. Months, and then years, flowed along happily in this way.

One day in September 1998, Raina called me, her voice sounding strained. "Martha," she said, "I have bad news." Deven, three now, had been diagnosed with neuroblastoma, a cancer of early childhood. The disease had spread to his bone marrow, stomach, and a kidney. The prognosis was poor.

Treatment was aggressive: chemo, two stem cell transplants. It was a long, tough process, and Deven was an absolute pain to the hospital staff. He raised holy hell even at something as innocuous as a thermometer or a blood pressure cuff. The only thing that calmed him was if his mother, or I, in a pinch, stayed with him. One day I went to the hospital to take over from Raina for a while. Deven insisted on being held the whole time, even when I had to go to the bathroom. There I was, sitting on the toilet with a boy on my lap hooked up to a pole with a bunch of flashing lights and tubes and beeping sounds. If it hadn't been so awful, it would have been funny.

As the treatments took effect, things began to look up for Deven, and then something else wonderful happened: Raina learned that Habitat for Humanity was planning to build some new houses in Arlington. If accepted into the program, Raina could contribute her own sweat equity and buy a house for a low down payment.

We worked together on the application, and to everyone's elation, the family was accepted as a Habitat partner family. Then came even better news: Deven's treatment had been successful. His little bald head started to fill out with downy black hair. He was in remission.

Remission is a beautiful word.

*   *   *

But this time of joy was destined to last less than a year. One day in March 2001, my phone rang at 11 p.m. It was Raina. Deven had relapsed.

He lost ground quickly. The living room of Raina's new duplex became a hospital room. Keara's bright blue futon from her first college apartment was spread out like an island where Deven could lie and people could sit around the edges for visits. It also had room to hold the amazing array of supplies needed for home care. A nurse named Maureen, from the local hospice, came in to help; she was capable, upbeat, and cheerful.

On a Sunday in August, we gathered in Raina's living room. Surrounded by family and friends, Raina prayed aloud as she held Deven, barely conscious, in her lap. She prayed and talked to him, touching him softly, lovingly. Deven's breathing became the focal point. There was a longer time between each breath. Raina rocked him and whispered to him, and I swear she walked with him as far as she could go, like a mother helping her little boy make the transition to school or to another place where she could not accompany him the whole way. Then his breathing stopped. I was so thankful that we weren't at the hospital, where beeps would announce his death.

Maureen, the nurse, listened to his heart with her stethoscope and used her fingers to register the rhythm in his wrist. "He's gone," she said solemnly. Raina rocked him and wept. She invited Darren and Jade to come close, to touch their brother and talk to him. There was no hurry to do anything else.

After the funeral home van had taken Deven away, we all formed a circle, full of sorrow and joy. Holding hands, standing shoulder to shoulder, we prayed aloud, giving thanks for Deven's life and for the love that bound us together.

* * *

Five months later, I found myself falling further and further behind, slowing down, withdrawing. I was afraid Raina and the kids were beginning to pick up on the way I was fading. I had been turning down invitations to see them, not stopping by as much. I let the machine pick up most of my calls. My doctor kept telling me not to automatically jump to conclusions about this depression being as bad as the last. I just had to hold on while the medicine kicked in.

Friendship in Black & White

One day while Brian and I were at the doctor's, Raina stopped by and left a card and flowers on the front steps. On the card she had written, "We love you so much. God bless you and keep you." I sat down on the steps and burst into tears.

After I pulled myself together, I called to thank her. At the sound of her voice, I started crying again. "Martha, what's the matter?" Raina asked.

"I am so scared." Then, with an effort, I shifted gears. "How are you?"

"Well," she answered hesitantly, "I just found out my electric got cut off."

"What do you have to do to get it turned back on?"

"Deliver $64.43 at the office before the end of the day. The thing is, I deposited my first check from the new job"—Raina had begun working at her kids' school as a lunchroom aide and office assistant—"but the bank said because it was a new account, it would take a few days to clear."

"Give me a few minutes, and I'll call you. You know the can I save quarters in? We may be able to make it."

I spilled everything out on the bed. I had it! It wasn't all rolled, but I had it. "Come on over," I told Raina. "We've got it." I piled it all into an old makeup bag. Breathless and relieved, she collected the money and ran out to pay the bill before the office closed. I put my flowers in a vase. And took a nap.

There's really never a question of whether we have enough to share with someone else. My friendship with Raina has shown me that if we have anything, anything at all, we have something. A card, a laugh, a makeup bag with change. Whatever. We can make it enough.

Originally published in the September 2003 issue of *Reader's Digest* magazine.

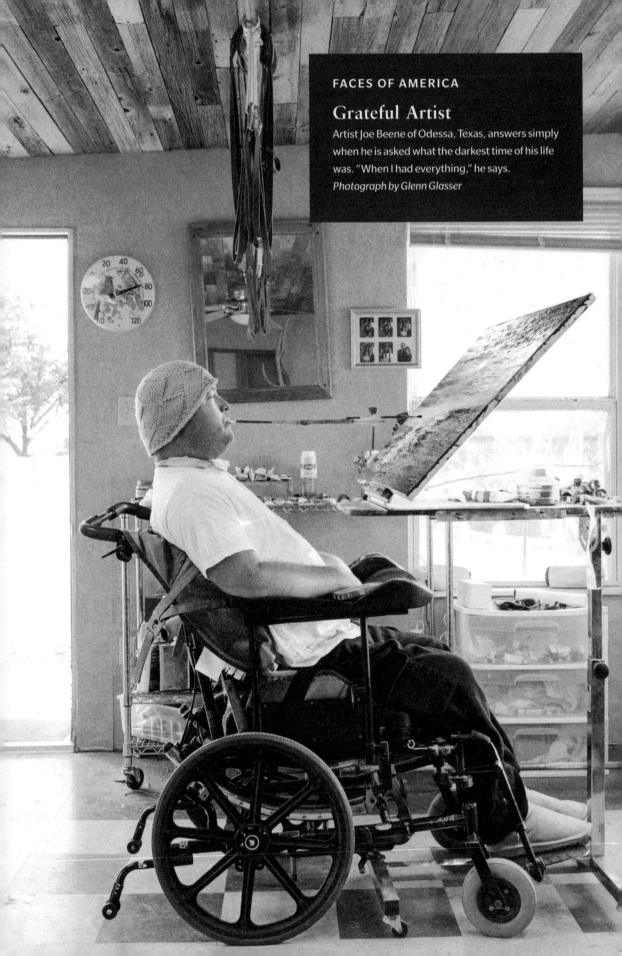

Beautiful Belly Dancer

Pat Marggraf of Berkeley Springs, West Virginia, describes how her difference led to her unique talent. "I was born without hip sockets. Growing up was rough," she says. "Children were cruel. But one of the reasons I can belly dance so easily is because my hip sockets are different."

Photograph by Glenn Glasser

Out of the Blue

by Bethany Hamilton with Sheryl Berk and Rick Bundschuh,
from the book *Soul Surfer*

*I had no warning at all, not even the
slightest hint of danger on the horizon.
The water was crystal clear and calm...*

It was more like swimming in a pool rather than the deep ocean waters
in Kauai, Hawaii. The waves were small and inconsistent, and I was just
kind of rolling along with them, relaxing on my surfboard with my left
arm dangling in the cool water. I remember thinking, *I hope the surf
picks up soon,* when suddenly there was a flash of gray.

That's all it took: a split second. I felt a lot of pressure and a couple
of fast tugs. I saw the jaws of a 15-foot tiger shark cover the top of my
board and my left arm. Then I watched in shock as the water around
me turned bright red. My left arm was gone almost to the armpit, along
with a huge, crescent-shaped chunk of my red, white, and blue surfboard.

Except for the fact that it was Halloween, it had been a morning like
any other. My mom, Cheri, and I set off before dawn looking for a good
surf spot. When we arrived at our destination, a place called Cannons,
the sun wasn't up yet. I got out of the car to take a look, but it was too
dark to see the water. I couldn't hear much either. If the surf is really big,
you can actually hear it cracking on the reef from a long way away. "It
doesn't seem like much is happening," I said.

"I guess we should head back," Mom said with a sigh. She was equally disappointed. "Maybe the surf will come up tomorrow." I knew that if I didn't surf, I would be home doing social studies, English or math. Because I was working to be a profes-

The Hamilton family (left to right): Cheri, Tom, Bethany, Timmy and Noah—with Ginger, their Shar-Pei.

sional surfer, I was homeschooled so I'd have the time to practice, but my parents piled on the homework.

I had started entering competitions while I was still in grade school. Traveling around the state of Hawaii isn't easy or cheap, and my parents aren't rich; Dad is a waiter, and Mom cleans rental condos. We had to come up with money for entry fees, airline tickets, car rentals, food, and hotel costs. And unlike with golf or some other sport, if you win, there is little or no money, especially in the kid and girl divisions. But my parents were willing to sacrifice for me. With their support, I entered my first major competition at age eight, the Rell Sunn contest at Makaha

The waves were big, and I could feel the adrenaline rush.

Beach on the island of Oahu. The waves were big, and I could feel the adrenaline rush. A lot of young kids get intimidated when the surf starts getting huge. Me? I live for it— the bigger the better! I ended up winning all my heats and the division championships.

After that, I entered more and more contests and did pretty well in most of them. It seemed possible that I could become a professional surfer like a couple of other girls from my island have done. At least my parents and my two older brothers thought so. It was what I wanted more than anything in the world.

As Mom and I were driving away from Cannons, I gave it one last shot: "Let's just check out Tunnels Beach." Tunnels is a short walk from Cannons; surfers like it because way out on the edge of the reef is a lightning-fast wave almost year-round.

"Sure, we can go take a look," Mom replied and started to park the car. About that time, a black pickup truck turned into the lot. It was Alana Blanchard, my best friend, her 15-year-old brother, Byron, and her dad, Holt. Okay, I thought, maybe this wouldn't be a total washout after all. Even though the waves were crummy, it was sunny, the water was warm, and my friends were here to hang with.

"Can I stay, Mom?" I asked.

"Just make sure Holt brings you home," she called, and with that, I raced down the trail with my friends to Tunnels Beach. I was happy that I was going surfing; I was happy to be with my friends. I felt the warm water slosh against my ankles, and just before I jumped in, I looked at my watch.

It was 6:40 on that beautiful Halloween morning in 2003.

Lying on my surfboard, watching my blood spread in the water around me, I said to my friends nearby in a loud yet not panicked voice, "I just got attacked by a shark."

Byron and Holt got to me in a flash. Holt's face was white, and his eyes were wide. "Oh, my God!" he said, but he didn't freak out. Instead, he took control of the situation: He pushed me by the tail of my board, and I caught a small wave that washed me over the reef. It's a miracle that it was high tide. If it had been low tide, we would have had to go all the way around the reef to get to shore. As it was, the beach was still a long quarter mile away.

My arm was bleeding badly but not spewing blood like it should with a major artery open. I know now that wounds like mine often cause the arteries to roll back and tighten. I was praying like crazy: "Please, God, help me, let me get to the beach," over and over again.

Holt took off his gray long-sleeve rashguard shirt. The reef was shallow now, only a couple of feet deep, so he stood up and tied the rashguard around the stub of my arm to act as a tourniquet. Then he had me grab onto the bottom of his swim trunks and hold on tight as he paddled both of us toward shore. Byron was already ahead of us, stroking like crazy to the beach to call 911. Holt kept having me answer questions like "Bethany, are you still with me? How ya doing?" I think he wanted to make sure that I didn't pass out in the middle of the ocean. So I was talking, just answering his questions and praying out loud and watching the beach get closer and closer.

Once we reached the shore, Holt lifted me off the surfboard and laid me on the sand. He then tied a surfboard leash around my arm to stop the bleeding. At that point, everything went black, and I'm not sure how long I was out of it. I kept coming in and out of consciousness. What happened after that is confusing, a mix of sights, sounds, and feelings. I remember being cold. I heard this happens when you lose a lot of blood. People brought beach towels and wrapped me up in them.

I remember starting to feel pain in my stump and thinking, *This hurts a lot.* And I know I said, "I want my mom!" I remember being very thirsty and asking Alana for water. So she ran up to a visitor, Fred Murray, who had heard cries for help and dashed to the beach while the rest of his group, here on Kauai for a family reunion, relaxed at a beachfront rental home.

"Come with me!" he yelled, and they both raced back to get one of his family members, a man named Paul Wheeler, who was a captain and a paramedic at a Hayward, California, fire station. Alana explained to him, as best she could in her state of shock, what had happened and that I needed water.

Paul didn't hesitate. He bolted out the door to be by my side. I remember his face and the compassion in his voice. I think everyone was relieved that there was a professional on the scene; I know it comforted me. Paul examined the wound. Alana came with water, but Paul advised against it. "I know you're thirsty," he told me, "but you're going to need surgery, and you want an empty stomach."

I remember starting to feel pain in my stump and thinking, **This hurts a lot.**

A neighbor brought a small first-aid kit, and Paul slipped on gloves so he could wrap my wound in gauze to keep it clean. I remember wincing as he covered it up, but I knew he had to do it. Paul felt my pulse. He shook his head. "She's lost a lot of blood," he said quietly.

I remember thinking, *Why is the ambulance taking so long to get here? Please, please hurry!* Holt decided we couldn't wait any longer. He, Paul, and Fred Murray lifted me onto Holt's board and carried me to the parking lot, where they put me in the back of the Blanchards' truck. Again, I kept passing out, only catching glimpses of what was going on and bits of frantic conversation.

Then, at some point, emergency vehicles arrived. I remember their sirens, high-pitched and shrill. I remember being stuck with needles and being slid onto a stretcher and into the back of the ambulance. I remember most clearly what the Kauai paramedic said to me. He spoke softly and held my hand as we were pulling out of the Tunnels parking lot. He whispered in my ear, "God will never leave you or forsake you."

My dad knew in his heart that the 13-year-old girl had to be either me or Alana.

*　*　*

My dad had been scheduled for knee surgery that morning and was already at the hospital on the operating table, anesthetized from the waist down. His orthopedic surgeon, Dr. David Rovinsky, was preparing to start the operation when an emergency room nurse burst into the room. "Just a heads-up, Dr. Rovinsky," she announced. "There's a 13-year-old girl coming, a shark attack victim. We're going to need this room right away."

My dad heard her and knew in his heart that the 13-year-old girl had to be either me or Alana. The doctor tried to calm him. "I'll go and try to find out what's happening." Within five minutes, Dr. Rovinsky returned. His face was pale, and there were tears in his eyes. "Tom, it's Bethany," he said softly. "She's in stable condition. That's all I know. I'm going to have to roll you out. Bethany's coming in here."

My dad later told me that his hour in the recovery room was torture. "I tried to will the feeling back into my legs so I could run in there and see you," he admitted. "I had no idea how bad you were—I prayed all you needed were just a few stitches." But just as his heart had told him that I was the one who had been attacked, it also told him it was much worse than a few stitches.

Mom had been informed only that I'd been attacked but given no details of my injury. As she rushed to the hospital, her longtime friend, Evelyn Cook, reached her on her cell phone. "Cheri, she's lost an arm." Mom dropped the phone, pulled the car over to the edge of the road, stared at her two hands on the steering wheel, and broke down weeping.

* * *

Dr. Rovinsky assured my parents that the odds were in my favor: I was young, in great physical shape, the cut had been direct rather than a ragged tear, and my calmness had kept my heartbeat slow enough to keep the severed artery from quickly draining my blood supply. Everyone's fast reactions had also been a big help. "Look," he told her, "a lot of things had to have gone right for her to make it to this point. She's got everything going for her."

Working tirelessly on that isolated farm, my grandfather taught me that we should accept and be grateful for what we have—whether it be much or little. We must bear the burdens and relish the joys. There is so much we cannot control, but we must try to make things better when we are able. We must depend upon ourselves to make our own way as best we can.

He also was optimistic that I would be able to compensate well with one arm in the future. In fact, he figured that even a prosthetic arm might have a 50/50 chance of being practical. "A lot of kids get used to making do without the missing limb," he told my mother. "And Bethany is a fighter."

It took two operations to treat my injury. Dr. Rovinsky first had to thoroughly clean the wound, since shark bites tend to have a high risk of infection. Then he isolated the nerves and cut them, causing them to retract and reducing the potential for "phantom pain"—the feeling of an ache in a portion of a limb that no longer exists in reality but still sends signals to the brain. Most of the wound was then left open but packed with gauze for several days to ensure that no infection took place.

Three days later, Dr. Rovinsky performed a second surgery that included closing the wound by using a flap of my skin.

At one point in the days that followed, I said to Dad, "I want to be the best surf photographer in the world." That was my way of saying, "I know my surfing days are over." He just nodded—"I'm sure you will be"—and tried to smile. He knew what I meant.

But a few days later, I started thinking about going surfing again. However, the doctor had said I had to stay out of the water for three to four weeks after the second surgery. In the meantime, there was plenty to occupy my time and thoughts. The main thing was getting used to the reality of my injury. When a nurse came to change the dressing on my arm a couple of days after I was released from the hospital, it was the first time that any of us had seen just how much of my arm was missing. My grandmother went out on the porch and cried. It shook my brother Timmy up so much that he went to his room and stayed in bed all afternoon.

I knew then that I was going to need help from someone much bigger than me if I was ever going to get back in the water.

My parents had a rough time, too. As for me, when I looked at that little stump of an arm held together with long black stitches, I almost fainted. It was a lot worse than I had imagined. I knew then that I was going to need help from someone much bigger than me if I was ever going to get back in the water.

In my first weeks at home, my family and I experienced an outpouring of aloha. For those who make Hawaii their home, aloha means much more than hello and goodbye. It goes back to the old Hawaiian traditions, and it means a mutual regard and affection of one person for another without any expectation of something in return. It means you do something from the pureness of your heart.

Take the folks from my church: When we got home from the hospital, we discovered they had come into our house and radically cleaned the place, putting flowers everywhere. For two weeks, every night, someone showed up with dinner. People kept stopping by and offering to help out in any way they could.

I was also really moved by the number of people who wanted to help raise money for my family. People didn't ask us; they just looked at the situation we were in and said, "I want to help this family. They're gonna need it."

On Saturday, November 15, only a few weeks after the attack, hundreds and hundreds of people descended on the main ballroom of the Kauai Marriott in Lihue for a silent auction that included more than 500 donated items. Because I was still trying to build up my strength, I couldn't attend, which was a bummer, because I'm the type of person who never likes to miss a fun party—especially one in my honor.

On a huge stage, some of the island's most sought-after names performed, like surf legend Titus Kinimaka and singer Malani Bilyeu. Even rock icon Graham Nash, formerly of the legendary Crosby, Stills, Nash, and Young, came to sing on my behalf. My dad was floored: He told me he hadn't seen the island come together like this for a cause since the aftermath of 1992's Hurricane Iniki, which devastated most of Kauai. Who would have ever thought I would be as important as a natural disaster!

The bidding was fast and furious, and when it was all over, donations from the night totaled about $75,000. It made us feel humble and loved.

That aloha spirit wasn't limited to Hawaii. My folks, checking their mailbox, were astounded to find thousands of letters awaiting them, from all over America and the world. In the envelopes were good wishes along with checks or cash, sometimes hundreds of dollars, sometimes a five-dollar bill. We really don't know why so many people wrote, prayed, or gave, but we are very, very grateful for each one of them.

One organization, Save Our Seas, learned what had happened to me and heard me say in an interview that if I couldn't surf again, maybe I would take surf pictures. So they offered to train me. It was an awesome offer that I still might take them up on. But first there was something I had to do.

The day before Thanksgiving, a small group of family and friends went with me to a beach off the beaten path. We arrived late in the afternoon, and when we came down the trail, we saw that the place was about as good as it ever gets. The surfing area was packed with local talent. This was the day that I would see whether I could surf again.

My brother Noah wanted to film my first ride on his video camera, so he put it in an underwater housing and swam out with it. My dad took off work and came in the water for a front-row view, just swimming along with me and shouting "Go, girl!" at the top of his lungs. Matt

"We both try hard to beat each other," says Bethany, *"and are happy for the other if she wins."*

George, a family friend and writer for *Surfer* magazine, was with us. And of course Alana and a bunch of my friends were there, too.

Alana and I walked into the surf together just like we did on that early Halloween morning. It felt so good to step into the liquid warmth and taste the salty water. It was like coming back home after a long, long trip. To think I had come so close to losing forever all these things that I loved so much: the ocean, my family, and my friends.

Alana paddled through the rolling white water (surfers call this soup) and headed farther out to the blue unbroken waves. I decided to make it easy on myself and ride some soup

It was like coming back home after a long, long trip.

to begin with. In some ways, it was like learning to surf all over again. I had to learn how to paddle evenly with one arm, and when I felt the wave pick me up, I had to put my hand flat on the center of the deck to get to my feet rather than grab the surfboard rail the way you would if you had two hands.

My first couple of tries didn't work: I couldn't get up. I thought it was going to be easier than it was. My dad kept shouting, "Bethany, try one more time. This one will be it!"

Then it happened. A wave rolled through, I caught it, put my hand on the deck to push up, and I was standing.

It's hard for me to describe the joy I felt after I stood up and rode the wave in for the first time after the attack. Even though I was all wet, I felt tears trickling down my face. Everyone was cheering.

That day I caught a whole bunch of waves, and getting up got easier and easier. One thing led to another, and soon I was back on the competition circuit, once again working toward a professional career.

Sometimes people ask me if I am ever scared of sharks now that I am surfing all the time again. The answer is yes; sometimes my heart pounds when I see a shadow under the water. Sometimes I have nightmares. And I am not ready to go out and surf Tunnels again; I'm not sure I will ever go back there.

Yet even when my nerves get the best of me, I do know this: God is watching out for me, and while I don't want to do something stupid like paddle out where someone has just seen a shark, in the end, I trust him to take care of me.

The other day I got an e-mail telling me about another kid who lost his arm. He is an eighth-grader from Raleigh, North Carolina, and he is very

"Maybe I look a little different, but that's okay. I'm cool being me."

athletic like me, only his big sport is wakeboarding. He even had taken up guitar like I had before the attack. The lady who wrote me knew that Logan was pretty down, and she hoped I might be able to cheer him up.

I grabbed the phone, called his house, and said, "Hey, Logan, this is Bethany Hamilton from Kauai, Hawaii. You probably heard that I lost my arm to a shark."

"Yeah," he said softly.

"I just want you to know that I'm surfing in the national finals with one arm."

"Yeah? Cool," he said.

"Look, I know you may not feel great right now. But I know that you can do a whole lot of stuff, too. You can and you will. Okay?"

We chatted some more, and I could feel his mood brightening. "Keep in touch, and let me know what you're up to," I added. He promised he would, and I know that Logan is on the road back.

Moments like this make me think I may be able to do more good having one arm than when I had two. I think this was God's plan for me all along. I am not saying that God made the shark bite me. I think he knew it would happen, and he made a way for my life to be happy and meaningful in spite of it happening. If I can help other people find hope in God, then that is worth whatever I've lost.

Originally published in the December 2004 issue of *Reader's Digest* magazine.

A documentary, Bethany Hamilton: Unstoppable, *was released in 2019, before the launch of Bethany's online inspirational program,* The Unstoppable Life. *Bethany is married to Adam Dirks, and they have two sons.*

Humor Hall of Fame

"After you acquire the power of speech, we need to talk."

As my wife and I prepared for our garage sale, I came across a painting. Looking at the back, I discovered that I had written "To my beautiful wife on our fifth anniversary. I love you . . . Keith." Feeling nostalgic about a gift I'd given her 25 years earlier, I showed it to her, thinking we should rehang the picture. After gazing at my message for a few seconds, she replied, "You know, I think a black marker would cover over all that so that we could sell it."

—**KEITH CHAMBERS** MAITLAND, FLORIDA

When I was a proofreader, I shared with my coworkers this example to illustrate how writing can skew based on gender: A professor wrote on the blackboard, "Woman without her man is nothing." The students were then instructed to insert the proper punctuation.

The men wrote, "Woman, without her man, is nothing." The women wrote, "Woman! Without her, man is nothing."

—**SUSAN ALLEN** PHOENIX, ARIZONA

On a business trip in California, I realized that I had forgotten my wife's birthday the day before. Assuming I was in big trouble, I went to the jewelry section of a San Francisco department store. After explaining to the saleswoman that I desperately needed a gift to make up for my forgetfulness, she quipped, "I'm sorry, but we don't have anything that expensive."

—**EDWIN L. RAY** TACOMA, WASHINGTON

"Looks like someone got lucky."

The Pig That Changed My Life

by Steve Jenkins, from the book *Esther the Wonder Pig*

Steve Jenkins had owned many pets.
But Esther the "mini pig" turned out to be
a class—and a size—of her own.

One night about five years ago, I was on my laptop in the living room when I received a Facebook message from a woman I knew from middle school, someone I hadn't spoken to in 15 years:

"Hey, Steve," she said. "I know you've always been a huge animal lover. I have a mini pig that is not getting along with my dogs. I've just had a baby, and I can't keep the pig."

It's true that I've always loved animals. My very first best friend was my childhood dog, Brandy, a shepherd mix, brown and black with floppy ears and a long, straight tail. So I was intrigued. A mini pig sounded adorable. In hindsight, of course, the whole situation was bizarre, but I've always been a trusting person.

I replied with a casual, "Let me do some research and I'll get back to you," but I knew I wanted the pig. I just had to figure out how to make it happen.

I lived in a three-bedroom single-level house in Georgetown, Ontario,

Always eager to help, Esther checks on what Steve's got cooking. (No, it isn't bacon.)

a small community approximately 30 miles west of Toronto. It's tricky enough bringing a pig back to the house you share with two dogs, two cats, your longtime partner, your two businesses, plus a roommate. But on top of that, only nine months earlier, I'd brought our cat, Delores, home without talking to Derek about it. He didn't react well.

So I had to plan this right, to make it look as if I wasn't doing something behind Derek's back, even though I was doing something behind Derek's back.

A few hours later, I got another message from the friend:

"Someone else is interested, so if you want her, great. If not, this other person will take her."

You're probably smart enough to recognize this as a manipulative tactic, and normally I'm smart enough, too. But I was not letting that pig go. So I told my former classmate that I'd take the animal. I gave her my address, and we agreed to meet in the morning.

I knew nothing about mini pigs. I didn't know what they ate; I had no idea how big they got. Once I started doing some Internet research, I found a few people claiming that "there's no such thing as a mini pig," but I was blinded by my sudden obsession and my faith in my onetime friend. She had said the pig was six months old and spayed and that she'd had her for a week, having gotten her from a breeder. It seemed this mini pig would grow to be about 70 pounds, maximum. That was pretty close to the size of Shelby, one of our dogs. That seemed reasonable.

When we met the next day, I watched the woman handle the pig, and I could tell there was zero attachment.

The pig was tiny, maybe eight inches from tip to tail. The poor thing had chipped pink nail polish on her little hooves and a tattered sequined cat collar around her neck. She looked pathetic yet lovable. I'd met the pig 12 minutes ago, and I already knew she needed me. Ready to drive home with the newest member of our family, I had only a few hours to figure out what to tell Derek.

The pig sat in the front passenger seat, skittish and disoriented. I talked to her and petted her while we took back roads to our house and I planned my "please forgive me for getting a pig" dinner for Derek. (The likely menu: bacon cheeseburgers and homemade garlic fries.)

Esther may outweigh the dogs by almost 600 pounds, but they're still great playmates.

Steve (left), Derek, and their menagerie try to pose for a family photo.

When we got home, the cats were their typical curious but uninterested selves when faced with the pig. The dogs are excitable around baby animals and children, so they whined and jumped. I held on to the pig securely and let them sniff her a little before I hid her in the office. I figured I'd better get Derek in a good mood before springing the new arrival on him.

When I led him to the office and revealed my surprise, Derek stood in the doorway like a statue. Every emotion other than happiness flashed across his face. It didn't take more than a half second for him to know what I had done and what I wished to do next.

He was furious. He ranted about how irresponsible I was. He insisted there was no more room in the house. The only positive thing I could say was, "She's a mini pig! She'll stay small!"

I knew that what I'd done was wrong, but I hoped I could smooth things over. Soon enough, the lovably adorable pig did the smoothing for me. One night we were having dinner, and Derek started talking about where the pig's litter and pen would go. You don't "build a pen" for someone you're getting rid of. Within two weeks, we christened her. We wanted to evoke a wise old soul. "Esther" felt right.

As soon as the veterinarian saw Esther, he shot me a bemused look.

"What do you know about this pig?" he asked. I gave him the story, or at least the one I'd been told.

"I already see a problem. Look at her tail. It's been docked," he said.

"Is that why it's a little nub?" I asked.

"Exactly," he said. "When you have a commercial pig—a full-size pig—the owners will generally have the pig's tail cut back. This minimizes tail biting, which occurs when pigs are kept deprived in factory farm environments. If Esther really is six months old, she could be a runt. If that's the case, when fully grown, she could be about 70 pounds."

"OK," I said. No news there.

"But if she's a commercial pig and not a runt— Well, I guess we'll cross that bridge when we get to it."

The vet explained that the only way to know anything for sure would be to weigh and measure Esther and start a chart. Pigs have a very specific rate of growth.

On our next vet visit, a few months after we'd adopted Esther, I had to admit that she'd been growing quickly. Over that short time, she'd started closing in on 80 pounds. It was becoming clear that I'd probably adopted a commercial pig—and she was going to be enormous.

I hadn't known I'd wanted a pig, but the joy I felt once I knew I would always be going home to her made me smile. Everything about Esther was precious: the way she shuffled around, the way her little hooves slid along the floor when she ran, the funny little clicking noise she made when she pranced. She'd also nuzzle our hands to soothe herself, licking our palms and rubbing her snout up and down on us as she fell asleep. And she stayed precious, even as she approached her full-grown weight of 650 pounds.

Now, I admit there's nothing all that peaceful about being startled awake at 3 a.m. by a 650-pound pig barreling down a hallway toward your bedroom. It's something you feel first: a vibration that rumbles through the mattress into your consciousness. You have only moments to realize what's happening as you hear the sound of hooves racing across the hardwood, getting louder by the second.

Within moments, our darling pig, Esther, comes crashing into the room, most likely spooked by a noise. She launches onto our bed much the same way she launched into our lives. And while it might be a mad scramble to make space for her—there are usually two humans, two dogs, and two cats asleep there—it's more than worth it for the excitement she has added to our world.

One thing I hadn't expected was just how many behaviors Esther would share with the dogs. She'd play with a Kong toy as they would, shaking it back and forth. She'd want to chase the cats and cuddle when she was tired, climbing into our laps to nuzzle—even as she outgrew the dogs by 10, 20, 30 pounds and more.

And just like the dogs, she often wanted our attention. She started playing and doing hilarious and clever things on her own. (She can open the refrigerator!) So we treated her like one of the dogs. And that struck us to our cores.

What made pigs different? Why were they bred for food and held in captivity while dogs and cats were welcomed into our homes and treated like family? Why were pigs the unlucky ones? Why hadn't we realized they had such engaging personalities and such intelligence? And where would Esther be now if she hadn't joined us?

And so a few weeks after getting Esther, we realized we had to stop eating bacon. Shortly after that, with some difficulty, we cut out meat entirely. And a few months after that, dairy and eggs followed. We were officially vegan—or "Esther-approved," as we like to call it.

In 2014, we moved a half-hour drive from Georgetown to Campbellville, Ontario. There, we founded a farm where we care for abandoned or abused farmed animals—so far, six rabbits, six goats, two sheep, ten pigs (not including Esther), one horse, one donkey, three cows, three chickens, and a peacock. Esther has changed our lives—that's obvious. And now it's our turn to try to change the world for other animals. The name of our farm? The Happily Ever Esther Sanctuary.

Originally published in the April 2017 issue of *Reader's Digest* magazine.

To My Daughter, on Acquiring Her First Car

by Paul Gallico

Words of wisdom on the power and privilege of car ownership.

My dear daughter,

Congratulations, and welcome to the Club! You are taking delivery of your first automobile, for which you have been saving for so long. The moment seems of sufficient importance for me to trot out the family soapbox and mount it for an oration. For not until you have a husband and start a family of your own will you be taking on as great a responsibility as you are this week.

When your glittering machine arrives, you will be the possessor of one of the most extraordinary objects of our modern civilization: slave, genie, seven-league boots, and magic carpet all rolled into one and at the same time an extension of your own person, your brain, your muscles, your reflexes. You have bought yourself independence from schedules and timetables, the freedom of the open road, to come and go when and where you please.

301

But never forget this: You cannot escape from having a fallible human being behind the wheel of your car, and now that human being will be you. The key word *fallible* covers every frailty to which mortals are prone. It is common to emphasize the dangers of driving and drinking—but one single moment's negligence, drowsiness, or wandering of attention while cold-sober can have the same effect. You need no longer place your life in the hands of another, and for that I am glad. But from now on, you will be taking it into your own.

Your driving teacher will have taught you all you should know about the control of your car, its operation, the rules and regulations of the highway code, and how to handle yourself and your machine on the road. But there are other things—ethical, philosophical, mechanical—which occur to me, and one of these is the nature of the beast.

For it is you who are solely the master of the machine that serves you. It is completely subject to your will. It cannot think for you or warn you. It can shout when you push the horn button, but it cannot see and it cannot hear; it cannot make decisions of any kind. It will carry you as directly and unfeelingly into catastrophe as it will carry you safely where you want to go. If you ask it to do something disastrous, like overtaking on a blind curve or at the crown of a hill, it will obey. If you command it to ignore road warnings, it will carry out those commands. This marvelous, magic servant depends upon you to help it around a bend or over an icy road. If you fail it or demand more than it is capable of, it will turn on you—and it can be as dangerous as a maddened elephant.

Now, too, you will be called upon to protect your passengers as well as yourself, and here again you will find that you must alter your thinking. Whenever you are driving a friend, your responsibility increases to the point where you must begin to regard yourself as a professional. The moment you have another in your car, you become akin to the engineer in the cab of his locomotive, to the pilot in his airplane cockpit, to the captain of the ship on his bridge. And you must accept the same obligations. Other humans have entrusted themselves to you; even though they have not paid for a ticket, you have entered a moral contract to deliver them safely to their destination.

And what about that poor, vulnerable creature who walks highways and byways with no protective shell of steel about him—the pedestrian? You were once one of these, subject to being bullied, threatened, ignored or cursed at by drivers who succumb to the delusion that ownership of an automobile gives them the right to lord it over those on foot.

Now, as the pilot of your own car, will you remember your frustrations as the stream of traffic refused to wait for you at a crossing, or your terror when some speeding motorist bore down upon you? Will you remember, now you are at the helm of a vehicle that can accelerate from zero to 60 miles an hour in seconds, that walkers have a rhythm of thinking and moving different from yours? They daydream, counting their worries or their blessings as they go; lost in thought, they step off the pavement without looking. Their reflexes vary. Because the slightest nudge from your fender can put them into a hospital, it devolves upon you to do their safety thinking for them.

As for children, the load put upon you is even greater, and you must be prepared to accept it. There will be toddlers who break away from their families suddenly and run out into the middle of the road; older ones who chase a ball that has gotten away; still others who ride wobbly bicycles. I have not given you any specific driving advice; I will give you only one rule that I have followed always: When passing children anywhere within range, take your foot off the gas and rest it on the brake. The split second gained in stopping may save a young life.

For we hold in our hands the power to work untold miseries upon the lives of strangers, killing or maiming them, robbing parents of children or children of parents, bearing the guilt of leaving people strewn by the roadside, dead or dying, in a disaster that no insurance money can make good. It need never happen to you. For all the warlike toll of dead and wounded listed in the newspapers following a holiday weekend, there are thousands upon thousands of motorists who chalk up a lifetime of mileage without so much as a scratched fender. They are those who know that the moment you exceed the speed limit or ignore the danger and warning signs, you are overruling the judgment of the engineers who built the road, traffic experts who have tested it for safety, and the police who have seen people die on it.

Your best guarantee of safety is to stay alert and concentrate every moment not only on what you yourself are doing but on what everybody else is doing at the same time, and where you are in relationship to the road and other vehicles. You will even develop a sixth sense that will tell you what another driver is going to do before he does it, and allow you to take precautions. Experience will enable you to recognize the elements of an accident building up ahead of you and to take the necessary steps to avoid it. It is a full-time job, isn't it?

Why drive, then? Why own a car? Because, as you will discover, it provides tremendous satisfaction, pleasure, and freedom. Indeed, I deeply envy you the thrill of taking off on your first trip—that marvelous anticipatory moment when you slide behind the wheel, turn the key, and feel the throb of the engine, ease into gear, and, your own mistress, move off into the unknown. And the most wonderful part of it all is that this thrill will never diminish; for me, it is still there after a quarter of a century. May it bring you, too, long years of the joy and happiness of freedom.

Your loving father

Originally published in the July 1970 issue of *Reader's Digest* magazine.

He Paints
Their Final Portraits

by Juliana LaBianca

*A World War II veteran
brings fallen heroes back to life.*

Alex Yawor leans in to study his nearly finished portrait of a man in uniform. He picks up a thin paintbrush and, resting an arm against a maulstick, carefully fills in a badge on the soldier's chest. As he does so, he quietly asks, "Why did you have to die?"

The old man thinks about this a lot. Almost every day for the past seven years, he has sat behind a wooden easel in his daughter's basement-turned-studio in Hopewell Township, Pennsylvania, and painted portraits of servicemen and -women who will never see the final product. He then frames, boxes, and ships the paintings to the families, free of charge.

On a certain level, Alex can relate to those he paints. A World War II Marine veteran himself, Alex fought in the brutal battles of Saipan, Tinian, the Marshall Islands, and Iwo Jima. But ask him about it and he'll demure. "I don't like to talk about my service," he says.

Alex's postwar transition was difficult. "I didn't leave the house for a year," he says. Itching to get his mind off the war, he took up painting.

Now, more than 30 years into his retirement from a local steel mill,

Alex Yawor forms a unique bond with each of the men and women he paints.

the 93-year-old uses his talent to paint portraits of fallen military heroes, most of whom were killed in Iraq or Afghanistan. To date, he has completed 111 of the 16-by-20-inch portraits based on photos parents have sent him. His hands aren't as steady as they used to be, and many of his subjects' uniforms have intricate details, so each painting takes about a week to finish.

It's an emotional pastime for Alex. "I cry a lot while I'm painting," he says. He also talks to the men and women, greeting fellow Marines with a rousing "Semper fi!"

Alex began the project in 2009, after reading a news clip about a woman who had done something similar. To find contact information for parents who might want portraits, he reached out to veterans' groups and the American Gold Star Mothers, an organization for mothers who have lost military sons and daughters.

"I hung up the phone with Alex thinking I had just received the best New Year's present since 1988," says Norma Luther, a former president of the American Gold Star Mothers. Norma's son, Army Captain Glen P. Adams Jr., was killed in 1988 in a helicopter accident in Germany. Glen, whom Norma remembers for his warm smile and laugh, "a soldier of soldiers," was 27. Alex painted a portrait of him for Norma.

Parents often write Alex heartfelt notes. One mother told him how, after she hung the portrait in her son's old bedroom, she would walk in and it would feel as though he was still there.

"When you first get the painting, you just want to sit and cry for about two hours," says Norma, who keeps the portrait of her son displayed as a focal point in her living room, above a sword and scabbard Glen gifted to her and his father upon his graduation from West Point. "I cannot put into words the comfort it has been to have his picture smiling at me every day."

Reactions like that make the work feel like a calling. "I believe certain people were put on this earth for a reason," Alex says. "If I live to be 100 and am able to paint, then I'll paint for the parents who want portraits."

For now, Alex will rinse his brushes and finish up for the day. "Good night," he'll say to the man on the canvas.

Once it's dry, he'll ship the portrait to another family. Or, as Alex says, "send him home."

Originally published in the October 2016 issue of *Reader's Digest* magazine.

SILENCE

Silence, how I miss you. You were a great companion in this busy world. You provided nourishment—my own private retreat—the ability to think through problems to a solution. You made a "to-do list" tangible. Where have you gone? You have deserted me. You have run so far from my life that my heart aches to feel your presence again. I wonder sometimes if you were ever in my life or if it was only my imagination. I have come to realize that you cannot be around my children. They are loud. They scream, they yell, they slap, bite, giggle, and sing! You cannot exist anywhere around them. I am sorry to see that you have gone. I hope to be with you again someday. Although it was an easy decision for you to leave, please know I am still adjusting to enduring without you.
— Michele Weisman *Brentwood, California*

MY FAVORITE BARISTA

One morning, I jokingly told my husband he dropped the ball because he didn't make me coffee, and I was having trouble getting motivated to start the day. My five-year-old son overheard me and asked me to explain what "dropped the ball" meant. A few minutes later, he came into our bedroom holding an overflowing coffee mug with a dishcloth underneath it to catch the drips. He said to my husband, "You dropped the ball, but I picked the ball up," and he handed me the worst tasting, most watered down, but sweetest cup of coffee ever.
— Jennifer Stockberger *Mount Vernon, Ohio*

Weed It and Reap

by Susan Sarver, from *Country Living*

*My father found plenty of good
in these pesky plants.*

To my eyes, my parents' vegetable garden was as big as a soccer field. I'd always imagined this was done to satisfy the perpetual appetites of five children. It wasn't until I married and had two children of my own that I figured out the real purpose of such a large garden. It wasn't the need for more vegetables; it was a need for more weeds.

All five of my parents' children were born "deep feelers." We worried over the most common things. My brothers worried about making the Little League all-star team. My sister wondered whether little Bobby had a crush on her or was just faking nice because she had a new puppy. I worried about whether I was up against the work of Sarah Jane or her mother at the 4-H fair.

My father grew up a farm boy and believed that the only way to flush a worry out into the open was by plenty of sweat. Only the juices of physical labor could lubricate the mind enough to separate life's dilemmas into manageable chunks.

Dad could read signs of trouble on our faces. "The garden needs weedin'," he'd say. "You go out and get started, and I'll be out in a little bit." Sure enough, he'd come and join us just about the time we'd weeded enough to begin talking about whatever was troubling us. As we talked, we'd yank up weeds as though they were conquered fragments of our concerns.

In fact, weeding could whittle away more than worries. A few of us children were prone to quick flares of temper. Pulling up weeds on a hot afternoon was one of the fastest ways to simmer down a streak of fury.

The weeds worked equally well for choking out the bickering and battling that increased immensely during summer months. Mom believed that vegetables eased tensions nearly as well. Picking and shelling a few rows of peas with the enemy was enough to prompt a truce.

Tomatoes were another story. Feuding siblings were never sent to the tomato patch. Put a couple of irascible children there, and they were bound to seek out the most rotten, bug-filled tomatoes-turned-weapons—and there was no better target for a mushy tomato than the upturned bottom of a fellow feudling. Mom made this mistake only once.

During the weedless winter, we might have succumbed to the weight of our worries had Dad not come up with able substitutes. In the back yard, for example, he kept a pile of bricks, which he claimed he'd one day form into lampposts. For some reason, that brick pile always seemed to be in the way of a growing bush or the basketball hoop.

Quite suspiciously, the mountain of firewood delivered every year faced the same fate. No matter where we stacked it, its placement called for a major shuffle. As we set out to relocate the woodpile, not only did we forget about what had ruffied us in the first place, but a solidarity developed inspired by the injustice of our common sentence.

Eventually, Dad grew concerned that our garden's prolific weeds might prove insufficient to match the mounting worries of my two high-school-age brothers, and he began to survey the fields of a nearby farmer, who had weeds so hardy that they threatened to choke his soybeans. He was looking for a couple of young weeders to work up and down the rows with machetes.

That conversation elevated the image of weeds, transforming them into the green gold on which my brothers grew rich. Although I begged for a chance to whack my fair share, Mom wouldn't hear of one of her daughters sweating over a machete. So I sat by and watched my brothers' bank accounts grow like the muscles in their arms. Though I envied them, I tried not to show it, as I knew where I'd be headed if my face bore evidence of my feelings.

These days, I watch my own children grow increasingly concerned over the dilemmas of childhood. It would help to have a weed patch in which to work their worries over. But as I look at my suburban lot with its too tidy, too mulched, too weedless patch of garden, I know they could barely break enough sweat over it to dilute even a small concern.

So every summer we pack up our worries and haul them 300 miles to my parents' garden. It's the one place in the world where we stand a chance of working out our worries before we run out of weeds.

Originally published in the September 1995 issue of *Reader's Digest* magazine.

CREDITS AND ACKNOWLEDGMENTS

"Lost in the Arctic" by Robert Gauchie, *Reader's Digest,* January 1970

"The Cellist of Sarajevo" by Paul Sullivan, *Hope* (November 1996), copyright © 1996 by Paul Sullivan; *Reader's Digest* November 1996
  Photograph on page 4 by azazello photo studio/ Shutterstock; page 6 by Paul Salmon

"A Shepherd's Healing Power" by Jo Coudert, *Reader's Digest,* December 1996
  Photograph by Ravell Call

"Exonerated!" by Kyle Swenson, *Cleveland Scene* (December 3, 2014), copyright © 2014 by *Cleveland Scene*; *Reader's Digest,* May 2015
  Photograph on page 18 by Lisa Ventre/University of Cincinnati; page 27 by Phil Long/AP Photo

"The Newlyweds" by Martha Weinman Lear, *Reader's Digest,* February 2005

"Speared Alive" by Chris Bohjalian, *Reader's Digest,* December 1993

"A Boy and His Dinosaur" by Dave Barry, *Reader's Digest,* November 1995

"Antonia's Mission" by Gail Cameron Wescott, *Reader's Digest,* June 2004
  Photograph on page 46 by Lenny Ignelzi/AP/ Shutterstock; page 48 Don Bartletti/*Los Angeles Times* via Getty Images

"Flight 93: What I Never Knew" by Lyz Glick and Dan Zegart, *Reader's Digest,* September 2004
  Photograph by Laura Pedrick

"Best Teacher I Ever Had" by David Owen, *LIFE* (October 1990), copyright © 1990 by David Owen; *Reader's Digest,* February 1991

"One Minute Left" by Sara Jameson, *Reader's Digest,* April 1997
  Photograph by Robert Sebree

"Uncle Jim's Wink at Life" by John L. Phillips, *Reader's Digest,* September 1993

"Green Eggs and Sam" by Penny Porter, *Reader's Digest,* May 1999

"Mercy for a Thief" by Jen McCaffrey, *Reader's Digest,* October 2018
  Photograph by Jillian Clark

"Sniper on the Loose" by Kathryn Wallace, *Reader's Digest,* October 2007
  Photograph on page 94 by Liza Gizara/Workbook Stock/Jupiter Images; page 103 (inset) courtesy Blasneck Family; page 104 by Matt York/AP Images

"And a Child Shall Lead Them" by Henry Hurt, *Reader's Digest,* January 1997
  Photographs by Henry Hurt

"Lucy, Me and the Chimps" by Janis Carter, *Smithsonian* (April 1981), copyright 1981 by Janis Carter; *Reader's Digest,* August 1992
  Photograph on page 116 by Abeselom Zerit / Shutterstock; photograph on page 118 by Gordon M. Burghardt

"The Prisoner of Mensa" by Rick Rosner, *Reader's Digest,* October 2016

"POW Poet" by Dawn Raffel, *Reader's Digest,* May 2013
  Photograph on page 127 courtesy John Borling; photographs pages 128 and 130 by Anna Knott

"The Man in the Cab" by Irving Stern, *New York Newsday* (August 8, 1991), copyright © 1991 by Irving Stern; *Reader's Digest,* July 2013
  Photograph on page 134 courtesy Irving Stern; page 135 by Rob Howard

"From Darkness to Light" by Christopher Carrier, *Reader's Digest,* May 2000

"Into the Wild" by Peter Michelmore, *Reader's Digest,* May 2003
  Photograph on page 145 by J. P. Fruchet/Getty Images; page 149 by Erik Butler and illustration by 5W Infographic

"A Simple Shortcut That Will Set You Free" by Elise Miller Davis, *Reader's Digest*, April 1970

"A Life Apart" by Cathy Free, *Reader's Digest*, September 2008
Photographs by Joanna B. Pinneo/Aurora

"The Dog in the Flood" by Barbara Sande Dimmitt, *Reader's Digest*, August 1997
Photograph by David Fukumoto

"Lame Excuses" by Andy Simmons, *Reader's Digest*, October 2009

"We've Been Hit" by Lynn Rosellini, *Reader's Digest*, June 2004
Photograph composite on page 281 Bob Thomas/Jim Reed (lightning); pages 282–283 by Bob Thomas; page 284 by Beth Wald/Aurora

"The Bold Bus Driver" by Alyssa Jung, *Reader's Digest*, March 2016

"Friends Interrupted" by Jacquelyn Mitchard, *Reader's Digest*, October 2007
Photograph by Phyllis Redman

"Mama and the Garfield Boys" by Lewis Grizzard from the book *Don't Forget to Call Your Mama. . . I Wish I Could Call Mine*, copyright © 1991 by Lewis Grizzard, published by Longstreet Press; *Reader's Digest*, January 1992

"My Babies Are in That Car!" by William M. Hendryx, *Reader's Digest*, August 1992

"Pilot Down: The Rescue of Scott O'Grady" by Malcolm McConnell, *Reader's Digest*, November 1995
Photograph on page 222 by Everett/Shutterstock; page 224 by T. Haley/SIPA; page 231 Robert Trippett/SIPA

"The Doctor Is In(sane!)" by Simon Rich from the book *Hits and Misses*, copyright © 2018 by Simon Rich, published by Little, Brown and Company; *Reader's Digest*, April 2019

"The Dream Horse and the Dining-Room Table" by Billy Porterfield from the book *Diddy Waw Diddy*, copyright © 1994 by Billy Porterfield, published by HarperCollins Publishers; *Reader's Digest*, December 1994
Photograph on page 238 MarkSpirit/Shutterstock

"Who Killed Sue Snow?" by Donald Dale Jackson, *Reader's Digest*, February 1991

"House of Cards" by John Colapinto, *Vanity Fair* (February 2016), copyright © 2016 by John Colapinto; *Reader's Digest International*, November 2017
Photograph on page 252 by Christian Arp-Hansen; page 254 by Boyer Bogeland

"Finding Gilbert" by Diane Covington, *Reader's Digest*, June 2009
Photograph on page 262–264 by Erik Butler; page 264 (inset), 265, and 269 courtesy Diane Covington

"Friendship in Black & White" by Martha Manning from the book *A Place to Land*, copyright © 2003 by Martha Manning, published by Ballantine Books; *Reader's Digest*, September 2003
Photographs by John Madere

"Out of the Blue" by Bethany Hamilton with Sheryl Berk and Rick Bundschuh from the book *Soul Surfer*, copyright © 2004 by Bethany Hamilton, published by MTV/Pocket Books; *Reader's Digest*, December 2004
Photograph on page 280 by Alex Viarnes; page 282, 289, and 290 courtesy Hamilton family

"The Pig That Changed My Life" by Steve Jenkins from the book *Esther the Wonder Pig*, copyright © 2016 by ETWP, Inc., published by Grand Central Publishing; *Reader's Digest*, April 2017
Photographs courtesy Steve Jenkins and Derek Walter

"To My Daughter, On Acquiring Her First Car" by Paul Gallico, *Reader's Digest*, July 1970

"He Paints Their Final Portaits" by Julia LaBianca, *Reader's Digest*, October 2016
Photograph on page 306 by Mike McGregor

"Weed It and Reap" by Susan Sarver, *Country Living* (August 1994), copyright © 1994 by Susan Sarver; *Reader's Digest*, September 1995